An Introduction to
Social Anthropology

LUCY MAIR

AN INTRODUCTION TO
Social Anthropology

SECOND EDITION

CLARENDON PRESS · OXFORD

Oxford University Press, Walton Street, Oxford OX2 6DP

OXFORD LONDON GLASGOW
NEW YORK TORONTO MELBOURNE WELLINGTON
IBADAN NAIROBI DAR ES SALAAM LUSAKA CAPE TOWN
KUALA LUMPUR SINGAPORE JAKARTA HONG KONG TOKYO
DELHI BOMBAY CALCUTTA MADRAS KARACHI

ISBN 0 19 874011 5

© OXFORD UNIVERSITY PRESS 1965, 1972

FIRST EDITION 1965
SECOND EDITION 1972
REPRINTED 1975 and 1977

PRINTED IN GREAT BRITAIN
BY RICHARD CLAY (THE CHAUCER PRESS) LTD
BUNGAY, SUFFOLK

Preface to the Second Edition

MY AIMS in revising this book have been two: to put more clearly some of the issues in matters of controversy, notably the relationship between our subject and sociology, and to extend the discussion of aspects of social anthropology which are receiving more attention today than they were five years ago. It has also been possible to take account of recent writing on old themes. Thus I have been able in the chapter on economics to revise the account of the *potlatch* in the light of Drucker and Heiser's reinterpretation of Boas's texts. I have added to the same section of the book some account of the economy of food-collectors, who until recently have been neglected by anthropologists; some discussion of the notion of surplus and its significance for the development of exchange; and some more recent views on the question of primitive money. The chapter on law contains a more extended discussion of the treatment of this subject by British and American anthropologists; I think it important to note in this context that the principle of reciprocity, now widely treated as a discovery of Lévi-Strauss, was first introduced to social anthropology in Malinowski's *Crime and Custom*. I have added to the section on land law an account of the rather unusual Tiv system described by Bohannan. I have also revised the chapter on the study of social change; in the course of doing so I was happy to read the argument of a distinguished historian that the most significant aspect of his subject today is the nature of the changes produced by industrialization, and I am grateful to Professor Plumb and the editors of *Encounter* for permission to quote his words.

LUCY MAIR

Contents

1. What Social Anthropology Is   1
2. How Social Anthropology Developed   17
3. Some Matters of Current Discussion   32
4. Social Differentiation   54
5. Kinship and Descent   69
6. Sex, Marriage, and Family   83
7. Politics without the State   109
8. Primitive States   124
9. Law   139
10. The Organization of Production   160
11. The Exchange of Goods   179
12. Money   195
13. What Is Religion?   210
14. Religion and Society   232
15. Related Subjects I: Social Change   262
16. Related Subjects II: Applied Anthropology   285
17. Related Subjects III: Race Relations   304
    Index   311

CHAPTER 1

What Social Anthropology Is

ANTHROPOLOGY means 'talking about man', as psychology means 'talking about mind'. The cliché 'I'm interested in people', and the exclamation 'Aren't foreigners extraordinary!' must have been current in some form or other since man learnt to use language. The greater part of all human discourse is concerned with what people do (sometimes the speaker, perhaps more often other people), and everyone who has the opportunity of travelling away from his own home is struck by the differences between the way of doing things that he is used to and what he finds elsewhere.

Anthropology is sometimes thought of as the study which tells us 'all about man'. To those who take this view, it comprises in fact the subjects that were flourishing about the middle of the nineteenth century, when the idea of a 'science of man' first began to take shape—physical anthropology, social (or cultural) anthropology, archaeology, and linguistics. An alternative view is that social anthropology is a branch of sociology, and its nearest neighbours are the other social sciences. That is the point of view taken in this book.

Differences between societies

Sociology, then, is the study of society, and social anthropology is a branch of this. Why should anyone be asked, or wish, to study society? We all live as members of society. It might be thought that we know all about it from our own experience. Most of us grow up learning how to behave towards our fellows, and by the time we are grown up we take it for granted that there *is* only one way to behave. Then perhaps we may go abroad, for a holiday or for longer, and we very soon find that the rules are different in other countries. Some of us just take this as proving the inferiority of other nations, and few of us ever learn that in the eyes of the other nations, who take different rules for granted, *we* are the inferiors. 'No Other Country,' said Dickens's Mr. Podsnap, 'is so favoured as This Country.' 'And other countries?' asked a foreign guest at his dinner table. 'They do how?' 'They do, sir,' replied Mr. Podsnap, 'they do—I am sorry to be obliged to say it— *as* they do.'

Social anthropology has been very largely concerned with peoples who 'do' very differently from 'This Country' or from any other of the industrialized nations that are commonly called (with a fine disregard of geography) 'western'. Its centre of interest has always been the peoples who are called 'primitive', or, when there is time to speak at greater length, 'peoples of simple technology'—peoples who have to get on without our array of gadgets, not only without radar and mechanical transport, but without money and without writing. Lacking these means of conducting their affairs, they have to organize their lives very differently from ourselves. But if we study the kind of societies that they live in, and compare them with those of the western world, we can see that certain fundamental principles of life in society are to be found both among 'them' and among 'us'. It is by comparing many different kinds of society that people find the common principles.

The 'primitive' or 'simple' societies differ very much from one another—perhaps more than the industrialized societies do. Can we account for these differences? Sometimes people think they are due to the character of the different peoples—to qualities that they have 'in their bones' or 'in their blood', that they all inherit from their parents. Or is there some determining influence in the environment, in the sources of their livelihood, for example, or in the climate?

The explanation of differences between peoples—and sometimes even between individuals—as manifestations of 'national character' is extremely popular. Most of us have a mental picture of a typical German, or Russian, or West Indian, and when we hear that the German government, or the Moscow Communist Party, or a coloured bus conductor, has done something that we don't think we would do in their place (or something that we don't like) we account for it by the peculiar character that we associate with this mental picture.

You will often hear people say, of outsiders whom they don't like, that characteristics such as 'cruelty' or 'laziness' are 'in their blood'; and if a man or woman is very good at something, you may hear it said that navigation, or music, was 'in his (or her) blood'. In fact, if you find that a musical genius is raised in a musical family, this is much more likely to be because he was set to practise at the age of three than because of anything he has inherited. The question of the relation between the capacities we were born with and the kind of people we become is a very complicated one, which will have to be dealt with fully in a later chapter. But every student of anthropology should be warned at the outset of two things. First, the physical qualities that we do inherit are *not* carried in our blood, although this has been assumed for so long that it is sometimes difficult to avoid using the popular phrase 'blood relatives'. Second, the question how individual persons behave and the question how different societies are organized are quite separate questions; you cannot explain differences between societies by saying they are made up of different kinds of people. Some differences between societies reflect differences of technology; there are broad contrasts between the industrialized societies which use mechanical power on a large scale and those that have to get on without machines. But within each of these two broad classes there are all kinds of differences, and these simply cannot be accounted for by differences in hereditary make-up.

What about the explanation in terms of geography? The people who live in countries where water is desperately short have to organize themselves so as to take advantage of what water there is—moving with their cattle in search of grazing, or building their houses near permanent water and sending their young men away with the cattle. People who live in countries infested with tsetse fly have to do without cattle. People who live on islands generally build sea-going craft and learn to sail by the stars; but there are people in the Nile basin who have never made canoes. People who grow their food on limited areas of land have to have rules saying who is entitled to use the land.

But we do not find that all cattle-keepers, or all islanders, have the same kind of society, by any means, and many of the differences between them cannot be correlated with environment at all. A very difficult environment limits what people can do. An extreme example of a people constrained by their environment are the Turkana of Northern Kenya. In their arid country they have to be constantly moving with their cattle in search of grazing and water. Half a dozen people or so move together. Even what we think of as the population of a small village—say a hundred people—could not find subsistence for themselves and their flocks at one time in the same place. So the Turkana have no villages, no village headmen, no village moots where people can discuss and settle their quarrels; they are as nearly without political organization as any people we could think of. But of all the peoples of the world only a small minority have to cope with such extreme difficulties. The majority are able to live in permanent villages or larger concentrations, where the generations succeed one another in the same place. They are by no means all alike, and where they differ one cannot account for this by rainfall or temperature, or the kind of vegetation that the soil will produce.

Perhaps at this point we should ask what kind of differences matter to the social anthropologist. The casual traveller notices that some people eat cheese for breakfast, and some would rather entertain you at a restaurant than invite you home; some seem to like talking all at once in loud voices, while others orate one after the other, nobody's remarks having any very close connection with those of the previous speaker. These are very superficial differences. Anyone who spends rather more than a holiday fortnight will probably become aware of more significant characteristics of the foreigners he is living among. He will notice that they have different rules about whom one may marry and what must be done to make a marriage legal; about who has claims on the property of a person who dies; about who is entitled to give orders that must be obeyed, and how such rulers are chosen; and different ideas about the nature of the world and of unseen beings who concern themselves with human affairs.

This is the kind of question that social anthropologists are interested in; not just the kind of things you can see people doing every day, but behind the everyday behaviour, the way they are *organized* so as to be a *society* and not just a lot of people who happen to be in the same part of the world.

The rules of behaviour in which this organization consists, the *social facts*, are the subject-matter of the student of society. Can they be explained by something behind and apart from the society whose rules they are—by the peculiar quality of some men's minds or the length of the rainy season in different parts of the world? Durkheim, the great French sociologist from whom British anthropologists have drawn much of their inspiration, said No. The social, he said, can be explained only by the social. In other words, one can see that certain kinds of arrangement are characteristic of peoples of simple technology, or that certain inheritance rules and certain marriage rules are often found together; but it is no good going outside society for explanations of what happens within it.

The scope of social anthropology

The earliest anthropologists would have said that what they were interested in was 'all about man'. They could not foresee that the range of studies that throw light on man's history, on his social behaviour, on his biological and physiological characteristics, would grow to be so vast that nobody could hope to master the whole field. Today there are different views about the best way to group these various subjects. Some believe in the 'integration of anthropological studies'. This means in practice the retention, with the addition of one more subject, of the group that were thought of as together making up the science of man at the time when the Royal Anthropological Institute was founded in 1843.[1] For adherents of this school social anthropology should be linked with physical anthropology, or the classification of humanity into races, with archaeology, or the study of the

[1] As the Ethnological Society of Great Britain.

buried relics of earlier societies, and with linguistics, the study of the principles of language. As all these studies have grown into separate specialisms, and a whole new family of social sciences has grown up, some have thought it preferable to link social anthropology with these latter, and physical anthropology with biological studies. In any case, the field of social anthropology is now so large that few people can hope to make themselves experts at the same time in it and in any of the other branches of anthropology in the wider sense. Every social anthropologist must speak the language of the people he works with, but few can make an intensive study of linguistics.

The new subject of *ethology*—the study of the behaviour of living animals—is clearly linked with social anthropology. Specialist studies in this field are generally made by zoologists. The interest of the subject for social anthropologists is that we can see in the behaviour of animal populations many parallels with our own, and so can expect to learn which of our tendencies are genetically 'built in'; for example, many animal species recognize a relationship of dominance and submission, an elementary form of that recognition of authority that is the basis of all political systems. At present ethologists differ on the rather important question whether animals are naturally 'aggressive'. Some of them tend to forget that humans have gone further than other animals in the capacity for checking their impulses, and try to interpret our behaviour as if we were more like apes than we are. But as the subject develops it is bound to throw more and more light on the springs of human behaviour.

The social science that is closest to social anthropology is sociology. Yet there are strong, and divided, views on the relation between them. Each claims to study 'society'; not a single aspect of it, such as economics or politics, but all of it. Sociology is much older than social anthropology; it began with Auguste Comte (1798–1857) in France, and Herbert Spencer (1820–1903) in England. The two men who are regarded as the founders of the British tradition in social anthropology, Malinowski and Radcliffe-Brown, the latter in particular, drew on the ideas of the French sociologists of the late nineteenth century; and Radcliffe-Brown, in a presidential address to the Royal Anthropological Institute, said he was 'quite willing to call the subject comparative sociology if anyone so wishes'. He himself certainly liked to frame his generalizations in terms of society as such, and not of particular kinds of society supposed to belong to the special province of the anthropologist. A contemporary sociologist, Donald MacRae (one of the few members of his profession to have followed a university course in social anthropology), has said categorically: 'I cannot see that there is—or can be—anything but an identity in our theory.'[2] Many of the newer British universities have combined departments in sociology and anthropology, and one of them proudly calls itself anthropology although it has two professors of each subject (all of them with degrees in social anthropology).

What is the division then? One basis of it is implicit in the last statement: universities give separate degrees in the two subjects. But there must be a reason for this. The reason is a simple one, but it is a matter of practice rather than theory: they deal with different subject-matter and to a large extent by different methods. It might be said that they are branches of the study of society, as botany and zoology are branches of biology. Sociologists expect to study the industrialized societies that have come into being in the last century and a half. They do not claim to take these vast organizations as wholes, but look at different aspects. They get their background from records, historical and statistical, and their contemporary material largely from questionnaires, which obtain information on a limited number of points from a large number of people. They do not have to begin every book with a description of the society they are dealing with, because it is the type of society in which their readers live.

Anthropologists work in alien societies—'other cultures', as they are called in the title of an introduction to the subject by the Oxford anthropologist John Beattie. These are, in the main, societies that have got on until recently with-

[2] D. G. MacRae, *Ideology and Society*, 1961, p. 48.

out the machine technology on which industrial societies rely, and often without such means of communication as writing and a generally accepted currency. Anthropologists in 'pre-literate' societies have little in the way of records to work on, and they have to produce a picture of the whole society before the reader can begin to understand the particular problem that the anthropologist has been examining. Although their fundamental interest is the *structure* of the society—the relationships of claim and obligation that knit the society together—they must also record the *culture*, or, as older writers would have put it, the customs or ways of behaving of the people who form it. Many of them are concerned with symbolism and with people's interpretation of the world they live in; neither of these matters is part of the normal concern of sociologists. The anthropologist's technique is what is called 'participant observation'; he lives in a village (or a neighbourhood in town), speaks the local language, watches and joins in activities, follows the process of quarrels or crises. This technique is appropriate only to work in small populations, and some of the most revealing anthropological work has been done in a village of a dozen huts.

Of course individual scholars cross the boundaries, and of course the boundaries are not always as clear in real life as I have made them. Japan is one of the leading industrialized nations of the world, but it is very exotic to Anglo-Saxons. A distinguished sociologist who worked in a city ward in Tokyo said, as anthropologists say when they want to demonstrate the value of their subject, that you do not know how to judge or interpret your own society until you have looked at something quite different. From the other direction, anthropologists have worked in such institutions as mental hospitals and factories, treating these as 'whole societies' for the purpose of their studies; others have sought to apply their experience in the analysis of kinship to London populations.

In British usage social anthropology is distinguished from *ethnology*, which is interested primarily in the past history of peoples without written records, and is therefore closely allied with archaeology. Another technical word, *ethnography*, refers to the process of collecting data by direct inquiry and observation, whatever the theoretical purpose of the inquiry, and also to books in which the emphasis is on the description of the society studied rather than on general theoretical problems.

Some key terms

A few anthropologists in Britain, and a great many in America, call themselves *cultural* anthropologists and maintain that their primary interest is in *culture*. These people are in the direct line of descent from Tylor and Boas. Those who call themselves students of *society* are the intellectual descendants of Durkheim and Radcliffe-Brown.[3]

Tylor, in a book published in 1871, defined culture as 'that complex whole which includes knowledge, belief, art, (techniques) morals, law, custom, and any other capabilities and habits acquired by man as a member of society'.[4] This definition— which is really an enumeration—has sometimes been compressed into the statement that culture comprises all kinds of learned behaviour; and in practice the distinguishing feature of the study of culture is often said to be that it is concerned with customs and 'ways'. By 'art' Tylor meant 'techniques', and because some leading students of culture, such as Boas in America, have been concerned with the collection of specimens for museums, the objects which the techniques create are often called 'material culture'. A culture is the common possession of a body of people who share the same traditions; in social terms such a body is a society. At the time when Malinowski's pupils were embarking on their first fieldwork, they chose the 'society' they would go to and prepared themselves to study 'its culture'.

They did not, however, suppose that all they had to do was to enumerate the traits that made up the culture. Such an approach can easily lead to absurdity, as when customs of such widely different significance as parliamentary government and eating with chopsticks are treated on the same level, as just 'ways' (a genuine example). Malinowski did

[3] See pp. 26–8.
[4] *Primitive Culture*, 5th edn., 1913, Vol. i, p. 1.

not let his pupils make that kind of mistake, for he insisted that culture was to be analysed not into traits but into institutions; for him parliamentary government would have been an important element of culture, but chopsticks would have been a small part of the complex of institutions meeting the needs of nutrition.

If people are thought of simply as bearers of culture, it may be dangerously easy to think of a culture as a set of rules and techniques with independent existence; this is what is sometimes called the *reification* of culture. But in America one school of anthropologists has pursued a line of study that brings people into the picture, the study of culture and personality. Very roughly, this implies the assumption that a culture both reflects and creates a typical personality in the people who share it. It has not found many adherents in Britain.

When British anthropologists say they are interested in social rather than in cultural facts, they mean that they are interested in the interactions of people living in society, and not in the personal characteristics of individuals, even when these are thought of as the product of their culture. We are still apt to say that a field study is concerned with *a* society, and it is worth asking what we mean by this.

Radcliffe-Brown said that an anthropologist's field of study could be 'any convenient locality of suitable size,'[5] and that, having selected his 'society' in this way, his task was to study its *structure*. This word is now the central concept in a large part of the work being done in social anthropology. It means that we think of the *society,* not the culture, as an orderly arrangement of parts, and that our business is to detect and explain this order. It consists in relationships between persons which are regulated by a common body of recognized rights and obligations.

In the discussion of social structure two concepts first made popular by Linton in America are very widely used: *status* and *role*. *Status* means a person's position relatively to that of others with whom he is in social relationships. Terms denoting status always imply a relationship with

[5] *Structure and Function in Primitive Society,* 1952, p. 193.

somebody else: for example, son, headmaster, husband, shop steward. One person may have many statuses, as these examples show. He can also be said to have a total status, which is relatively high or low in relation to other members of his society. But status as such is a neutral word: when it is used to describe something that people strive for, it is incorrectly used. Status may be *ascribed,* as by the rule that Queen Elizabeth II must be Queen of England because she is the elder daughter of King George VI; or *achieved,* as by the political career that brought John Kennedy to the position of President of the United States. For every status there is an appropriate role. People are expected to *behave as if* they loved their wives and respected their headmasters, whatever their actual sentiments may be; and while the psychologist may be interested in the reasons why some people find marriage or school intolerable, the social anthropologist is concerned with the way the roles are defined by society and what happens when they are not properly performed. Roles comprise duties of leadership, command, protection, obedience, co-operation, the making of gifts or payments on appropriate occasions, and so forth. In ordinary language a role means a part in a play, and this is just what makes it appropriate here. The lines are written for the actor, but he can play them well or badly, forget them or gag, present the audience with a new conception of the character he is playing or with one so far from what they think it should be that they reward him with catcalls instead of applause. In the same way we all do what we can to play our less spectacular roles, and it is largely when people get new ideas about how to play them that social change comes about. The rules defining the roles are called *role expectations. Social control* comprises the whole range of social pressures directed to make people play their roles in accordance with these expectations.

In one sense the actor has to stick fairly closely to his lines—in the sense that every society has its recognized ways of expressing the relationships in which the roles must be played. To take a very simple example, for Hindus the polite way of greeting is to put both hands together in the attitude that Christians associate with prayer; for Chinese it is to bow while concealing the hands in one's wide sleeves; for western Europeans it is to shake hands. These are cultural differences. Culture is the way in which social relationships are expressed and symbolized. It is what the anthropologist in the field sees first, and it must constitute a very large part of his description. As Nadel put it, culture and society are two dimensions of all social life. Nevertheless, Radcliffe-Brown said truly that the two definitions of anthropology, as concerned with culture and with society (or social structure) lead to two different kinds of study, between which it is hardly possible to obtain agreement in the formulation of problems.[6]

Something has been said already about the kind of society that anthropologists study. As long as they do consider their main subject-matter to be a particular kind of society, they will have to find words to indicate what this is. This is awkward, because the peoples to whom most of our research has been directed are coming to resent any description that seems to allot them an inferior status. A word that has been much used is *primitive*. Nineteenth-century writers meant by it to describe a condition of humanity that was in some sense childish in comparison with their own adulthood. No wonder the new nations resent the word. Durkheim used it to indicate the most rudimentary form of any institution that could be found; thus in his discussion of religion he gave reasons why ancestor-worship could not *really* be called primitive.

If we use the word today we are not thinking of mental or moral qualities, but of little-developed techniques. Some anthropologists write of *societies of simple technology*, but this is a clumsy phrase if it must be often repeated. But 'simple' can be used if it is understood that this is what it means. An adjective which has not yet given offence is *small-scale*, denoting the narrow range of social relationships to which societies of simple technology are confined. People sometimes speak of a *face-to-face* society, a term which implies that all members of the society are in constant contact, or at least known, to one another. This would

[6] op. cit., p. 189.

describe only the smallest of the social units that anthropologists are concerned with.[7]

It is obvious that the societies which have only recently begun to enter the machine age are not all at the same technological level. Nobody could apply the word primitive to the ancient civilizations of the Far East. But they have some of the characteristics of the small-scale society, and anyhow, anthropologists have found them an appropriate subject of study. Some writers therefore distinguish between *primitive* and *peasant* society. For them a primitive society is one which is almost wholly self-contained and in which people get their food and other necessities directly by their own work, and a peasant society one of cultivators who live in small communities, still largely self-sufficient, but having some relations with a wider society, in particular selling their surplus in a market and accepting an external political authority. Some make the same distinction between 'tribal' and 'peasant' societies. A good many so-called 'peasant' societies are rapidly changing into populations of rural wage-earners.

But the word 'tribal' has also been used to distinguish countrymen from town-dwellers, as in the title of a study by Philip Mayer, *Townsmen or Tribesmen* (1961), of a population of South African Bantu who go to work in urban employment but try hard while they are there to keep to their own customs. Again, the word 'detribalization', which implies the loss of characteristics described as 'tribal', is frequently used, sometimes by people who think they are talking about a good thing and sometimes by people who think they are talking about a bad thing; as generally used nowadays, however, 'detribalization' refers to the adoption of city ways of life in cities, and not to the rejection of traditional ways in the country.

But even if there is a general notion of what a *tribal society* is, there is no agreement at all about what a *tribe* is. This word has been used by two contemporary anthropologists with a definite meaning, but unfortunately not with

[7] Students contemplating examination questions should not be daunted by the use of these different words as alternatives: they all refer to the same kind of society.

the same meaning. Evans-Pritchard, writing of the Nuer of the southern Sudan, observes that this population of some 200,000 with a common name, a common language, and a common culture, is divided into distinct political units. He calls these divisions tribes. If one is using the word in this way it could be defined by saying that the tribe is a politically organized subdivision of a wider ethnic (or cultural) unit. This would be in accordance with the usage by which the Tswana of Botswana are said to be divided into eight tribes, each with its own chief. The word could be applied to the subdivisions of the six million Ibo in Nigeria and in many other cases.

But F. G. Bailey, writing of India, uses it in quite another sense. He too has to take account of current usage, which is to classify the population of India into tribal peoples and those who are organized according to the Hindu caste system. There is an official list of tribal peoples entitled to special protection of various kinds. But when one tries to say what are the characteristics that they all have in common and that caste people do not have, this turns out to be impossible. Bailey[8] argues that 'caste' and 'tribe' do not describe kinds of society which are wholly different, but ways of organizing people for certain sorts of co-operation. For the purpose of organizing economic life people in a subsistence or peasant society must have access to land. In a tribal organization everyone has a claim to land by virtue of his membership of a clan, and all clans are equal in status. This is just what Durkheim[9] meant by the 'mechanical solidarity' of a society all the divisions of which are alike. In a caste system the dominant caste owns the land, and economic life is organized through the rendering of services by other castes in return for rights to cultivate or a share of the harvest. This is what Durkheim called 'organic solidarity' based on the division of labour. Tribal societies are ideally egalitarian, caste societies ideally hierarchical. Actual societies combine both elements. But this very interesting exposition certainly does not, and was not

[8] ' "Tribe" and "Caste" in India', *Contributions to Indian Sociology*, October 1961, pp. 7–19.
[9] See p. 27.

intended to, give a universally applicable definition of the words 'tribe' and 'tribal'.

The word *group* has a special meaning in the language of social anthropologists. It does not mean, as it does in every-day speech, any collection of people. It means *a corporate body with a permanent existence*; a collection of people recruited on recognized principles, with common interests and rules (*norms*) fixing the rights and duties of the members in relation to one another and to these interests. The common interests can be called property interests, if property is very broadly defined. As Leach has put it, they may include 'not only material goods and rights in land but also rights in persons, in titles, in offices, in names, in rituals, in forms of magic, in techniques, in songs, in dances . . . and so on and so forth'.[10] In many simple societies the most important corporate groups consist of people linked by *descent*.[11]

It is not hard to recognize the corporateness of a descent group; this can easily be tested by the criteria just quoted from Leach. But there are aggregations of people who have something in common and yet not quite enough for us to assert that they are corporate groups. What is in question here is some kind of community of feeling or interest, something more than a common characteristic that is perceived by outsiders. People who have emigrated from the same country to the same country—say, Italians in Australia— are distinguished from the native-born population and are conscious of this. They are sometimes referred to as an *ethnic group,* although they are certainly not a corporate group. It is almost impossible completely to avoid the use of 'group' for collections of people who do not form corporate groups; what is important is to be clear when it is necessary to use the word in a strict sense.

But a mistake which *must* be avoided is to suppose that any aggregate of persons which is not a group must be a category. A category is not something 'out there'; it is nothing more than the name given to a class of objects that are

[10] E. R. Leach, 'On Certain Unconsidered Aspects of Double Descent Systems', *Man*, LXII, 1962, p. 131.
[11] See pp. 71–80.

perceived by the speaker as having something in common. Categorizing is a way of ordering one's experience. Thinkers sometimes invent new categories, but most of us are content with the ones that we find in the language we learn to speak as children. These include the categories into which we class the persons related to us in different ways by kinship. Some of these *categories*—e.g. 'brother'—describe people who *also* form a *group*. All the people who can be collectively described by any term, whether or not they form a group, are *members of the category* indicated by the term. The curious way in which some anthropologists use the word 'category' has possibly grown out of a discussion by Fortes of Ashanti kinship, in which he wrote that the Ashanti recognized a number of categories called *ntoro* consisting of persons related by descent through the father. It would have been more strictly correct to say that the Ashanti category *ntoro* refers to persons related by descent through the father, and that there are a number of *ntoro*. *Ntoro* members, said Fortes, do not form corporate groups. From that time on many anthropologists have written as if there were two (and only two) significant social aggregates, groups and categories. Some use the phrase 'groups and categories' as a sort of cover-all to be sure nothing has been left out. But to say someone must belong to *either* a group *or* a category is like saying he must live either in London or Wednesday. It is what a philosopher would call a confusion of categories. And it is a confusion that would be laughed at in any other discipline.

SUGGESTIONS FOR READING

D. Forde, *Habitat, Economy and Society* (1934), describes a number of societies in very different environments and shows that, in spite of the limitations that environment may impose on human activities, it is quite impossible to correlate all institutions with environment. This theory is one of many criticized in a long and polemical book, *The Rise of Anthropological Theory*, by Marvin Harris (1968). His critique of Forde is in the final chapter.

L. P. Mair, 'Some Current Terms in Social Anthropology' in *British Journal of Sociology* (1963), surveys a number of the terms in general use.

CHAPTER 2 How Social
Anthropology
Developed

BOOKS of travel are among the oldest forms of literature; some have included, and more have inspired, speculations on the reasons for differences between human societies. People brought up in the European tradition look to the Greek writer Herodotus as 'the father of history'; his is the oldest extant book to be actually called a 'history' (which in his day just meant 'knowing'). Some make him also 'the father of anthropology', and certainly he was not content merely to record what he saw, and what people told him, about the different countries around the shores of the Mediterranean; he asked what made people so different. In discussing his great theme, the attempt of the Persians to conquer the Greeks and their failure, he asked questions such as a social anthropologist might ask: What kind of society in the Greek city-states managed to stand up to the Persians and throw them back into the sea? Why did the social organization of the Persians, who had conquered all their other neighbours, not make them able to subdue the Greeks?

Every age of geographical discovery has seen a burst of interest in the new kinds of society that the explorers have found; we are reminded today by the descendants of these peoples that they were there all along, and were only 'new' to foreigners who had lived for centuries in ignorance of their existence. The explorers and colonizers, however, being accustomed to take it for granted that they were themselves the standard of what people ought to be like, were always prompted to ask why other peoples were so unlike themselves.

The early travellers

The sixteenth century was one such period, the eighteenth another. The French essayist Montaigne (1533–92) was much interested in the apparently paradoxical contrasts between the customs of his own country and others. His essay on cannibals was one of the sources of Shakespeare's *Tempest*. The attitude of Prospero to Caliban, the hardly-more-than-monster who repaid his master's attempt to educate him by trying to rape his daughter, is a paradigm of the cruder form of colonialist attitude, so close to contemporary experience as to be horrifying. A slightly subtler approach to the question of the meaning of physical differences between populations was the theological argument whether people with brown skins who wore no clothes could really be descendants of Adam.

Eighteenth-century Europeans were less certain than sixteenth-century ones that all the advantage was on their side. Interest was now directed to North America and Polynesia. The Indians were taken to represent the pristine condition of man—though Rousseau's 'noble savages' of the golden age of natural man were those same Caribs who the Spanish missionaries had thought could not have souls. Hobbes in the seventeenth century had already thought the American Indians approached pretty closely to his imagined state of nature where every man's hand was against his neighbour and men's lives were 'solitary, poor, nasty, brutish and short'.

Reports of the manners and customs of distant lands now began to be treated not just as bits of interesting information but as data for constructing historical schemes of the development of society. Some writers start the history of comparative ethnography with the Jesuit missionary Lafitau, who in 1724 published a book comparing American Indian customs with those of the ancient world as described by Latin and Greek writers. A little later (1760) Charles de Brosses wrote on parallels between ancient Egyptian religion and that of West Africa—a subject that occupies the attention of a new school of historians today. In 1748 Montesquieu published his *Esprit des Lois*, based on reading and not on travel, and thus became for some the first theorist of our subject. He considered that differences in legal systems could be explained by relating them to differences in other characteristics of the nations which possessed them, population, temperament, religious beliefs, economic organization, and customs generally, as well as to their environment. This could entitle him to be described as the first functionalist.[1]

In Scotland a number of men were seeking to trace the evolution of society from—as one of them put it—'a state little better than mere brutality to that most perfect state... in ancient Greece'.[2] The most famous of them, Adam Ferguson and Adam Smith, based their generalizations, as did Montesquieu, on the widest reading about the institutions of different societies that was available in their day. The idea of such an evolution did not have to wait, as is popularly supposed, for Darwin's discovery of the principle of natural selection in the evolution of biological species, and indeed the influence of Darwin's work was on the whole unfortunate when it led to attempts to fit societies and races—the latter not always clearly distinguished from societies—into evolutionary schemes.

Diffusionism

The nineteenth century saw the beginning of travel for the sake of the observation of different examples of human society. The most famous of the nineteenth-century travellers was Bastian (1826–1905), who engaged as a ship's doctor in order to see the world, and succeeded in visiting a remarkable number of places. He was interested in ideas as such, and particularly religious beliefs, and was struck by the similarities which he found in places far apart. He attributed this to psychological qualities common to all human beings—the 'psychic unity of mankind', which leads people independently to think of similar myths and rituals.

His younger contemporary Ratzel (1844–1904), also a great traveller, opposed his theories root and branch. Rat-

[1] See pp. 32–40.
[2] Lord Monboddo, quoted by D. G. MacRae, *Ideology and Society*, 1961, p. 140.

zel was more interested in implements than in ideas, and he argued that since most people are not inventive, these must have been invented by individuals in a few places and spread over the world by migration. He looked therefore for similarities between objects found in places far apart, but did not seek for further evidence of the migration by which they were supposed to have spread over the world. His theory is called *diffusionism*. It was developed further by his more sophisticated pupil Frobenius (1873–1938), who held that 'culture-complexes'—combinations of objects and items of behaviour—must have been diffused as wholes, since there was no other reason why the items should be found in association. He made it his business to trace the path of their diffusion. This approach to the history of civilization reached its *reductio ad absurdum* with the theory that all the basic inventions were made in one place, namely Egypt.

As we in this century see symbolism more and more as the reflection of universal human experience, at any rate when considering mythology and religious beliefs, we are likely to range ourselves with Bastian against the diffusionists. Not much need really be said about the war of the diffusionists and evolutionists, but it must be mentioned because the writers to whom contemporary social anthropology owes most were still caught up in it. No one today would argue either that *all* social institutions, techniques, and myths were spread through the world by diffusion, or that *every* society has independently evolved every aspect of its own culture. The whole discussion now seems rather unreal, ignoring as it does the obvious fact that the imitation of tools and techniques is something very different from the 'taking over' of institutions or myths. In fact most of the writers whose work has lived have recognized that the history of society must have been a mixture of independent development and the effects of external influences. Most of them, also, have been evolutionists in the sense that they have been more interested in the development of institutions than in the question of their geographical spread.

Theories of evolution

The most famous of the early evolutionists was the American Lewis H. Morgan (1818–81). He was a member of a student society which purported to imitate the rituals of the Iroquois, and this inspired him to spend some time living among the Iroquois so as to find out what their society was really like. In 1851 he published *The League of the Iroquois,* the first description of a political system based on the relations between autonomous lineages, like those later analysed by Evans-Pritchard and others.

In the process of learning the language of the Iroquois Morgan discovered that the names they used to describe kin relationships—father, brother, etc.—were applied to a much wider range of people than they are in English. His method of recording the names by looking at them all from the point of view of one individual, whom he called *Ego,* has become the standard anthropological technique. He was surprised to find that several other Indian tribes had a system of terminology identical with that of the Iroquois, though their languages were quite different. He was so much impressed by this that he started collecting lists of kinship terms from all over the world, and in 1871 he published, in *Systems of Consanguinity and Affinity,* an account of these with a theory explaining them. The extension outside the individual family of the words for parents seemed to him to indicate a confusion about who people's parents were; and as there was clearly no such confusion among the Iroquois, he supposed the terminology must have been carried over from an earlier state of things when there was. This led him to postulate a series of stages in the development of the family from complete promiscuity to monogamous marriage.

Meanwhile other writers were seeking evidence for earlier stages of society in the Greek and Latin, and, in one important case, the Indian classics. Bachofen (1815–87), a Swiss jurist, first developed a theory about societies which trace descent through women. He supposed that they consisted of people who did not recognize male parenthood. On a combination of mythology and the examples in Herodotus he built a picture of a 'matriarchal' society which was a sort of mirror-image of what we are used to; women exercised authority, the left hand was superior to the right, the moon to the sun, female deities were worshipped, and so on.[3] He argued that patriarchal Roman society must have been established as the result of a male revolt against this.

J. F. McLennan (1827–81) believed that apparently anomalous usages could be explained as symbolic representations of actions that had really been performed at earlier stages of social development. In his *Studies in Ancient History* he observed that marriage customs often involved a mock capture of the bride, although she and her family had agreed to the marriage. He concluded that at one time men must in fact have seized their wives by force. Why, he asked? Because they were not allowed to marry within their own tribe (to him a tribe was a roaming band of about a thousand people, like the American Indian tribes) and were at war with all outsiders. McLennan gave us the words *exogamy* and *endogamy* for marrying *outside,* and *inside,* a defined group.[4]

Henry Sumner Maine (1822–88), a jurist who was a member of the Viceroy's council in India, was struck by the similarities between the recorded laws of ancient Rome and ancient India (and later of ancient Ireland). All these were patrilineal societies. This inclined him to think that patriliny was the original rule of descent, but he was primarily interested in the development of legal rules from a starting-point within recorded history. His central theme is the change from societies based on status, where an individual's rights and obligations are given in virtue of his status, and particularly his status in the descent group, and one based on contract, in which he deliberately enters into new relationships for specific purposes. Modern anthropologists recognize that there is room for contractual, or freely chosen, relationships in the simplest societies. Marriage is one, clientship, or voluntary dependence, another. But we still find the idea of the contrast useful, and observe that

---

[3] *Das Mutterrecht,* 1864.
[4] These words, as also the words *polygamy* and *monogamy,* refer to *rules* about marriage, not to actual marriages. See pp. 83–94.

the weight of *ascribed status,* as it was defined in the previous chapter, is much heavier in societies of simple technology. Maine's most famous book is *Ancient Law.* We owe to him the terms taken from Roman law: *agnation* for the recognition of relationship by descent through males, and *cognation* for the recognition of relationship between all descendants of one father and mother.

Edward Burnett Tylor (1832–1917) is often described as the father of British anthropology, though some of us might prefer to trace our paternity to Maine or even Morgan. Tylor's influence at the present day is stronger among American than among British anthropologists. He was greatly interested in religion, which he sought to define as broadly as possible, in opposition to those who supposed that religion must be concerned with gods conceived as separate from and superior to humanity, or must involve a particular emotional attitude towards its object, or required that a system of beliefs should have some other feature in common with the world religions before it was entitled to be put in the same category with them. Tylor offered as a 'minimum definition' of religion 'the belief in Spiritual Beings.' This he expected would be found everywhere, and his expectation was justified. The experience of dreaming, he argued, led people to suppose that they themselves had some non-corporeal part which could be separated from their bodies; while the belief that spirits inhabited inanimate objects was, he thought, an expression of the child's tendency to personify all the objects around him. Like all his contemporaries Tylor thought of humanity in the mass as growing through the ages from childhood to maturity, and of primitive peoples as being still in the stage of childhood.

Tylor also sought to make anthropology scientific by the use of what he called 'social arithmetic', or the tabulation of customs in order to see how they were correlated. Thus he might be regarded as the founder of the 'comparative method',[5] though he did not use this term. In discussing the question whether patriliny or matriliny came earlier, he

[5] See pp. 47–52.

remarked that in matrilineal societies authority was not exercised by women, and therefore he rejected the terms 'matriarchal' and 'patriarchal'. He noted that in the simple societies it was very common for the children of a brother and a sister to marry and gave us the term *cross-cousin marriage* to describe such unions.[6] In the context of exogamy he made observations which anticipate by some sixty years recent discussions on the feud and the circumstances which keep it within bounds, as well as one of the basic generalizations of Fortes' and Evans-Pritchard's introduction to *African Political Systems* (1940). Exogamy, he said, 'cements . . . uncultured populations . . . into nations capable of living together in peace . . . till they reach the period of higher military and political organization'; and 'By binding together a whole community with ties of kinship and affinity, and especially by the peacemaking of the women who hold to one clan as sisters and to another as wives, it tends to keep down feuds and to heal them when they arise, so as at critical moments to hold together a tribe which under endogamous conditions would have split up'.[7]

Tylor introduced into anthropology the term 'survival', though the notion that social usages could be adequately explained as survivals from earlier stages of society was implicit in the theories of Morgan and McLennan. He defined survivals as 'processes, customs, opinions, and so forth, which have been carried on by force of habit into a new state of society different from that in which they had their original home, and they thus remain as proofs and examples of an older condition of culture out of which a newer has been evolved'.[8] By defining the subject-matter of anthropological study as 'culture' Tylor became the founder of a whole school.

Robertson-Smith (1846–94) was one of the scholars who in the nineteenth century began to interpret the Old Testament in its historical context. He also travelled widely in Arabia and so was able to reinforce his theories from observation of contemporary Arab society. His best-known work,

[6] See pp. 87–8.
[7] *Journal of the Royal Anthropological Institute,* 1889, p. 268.
[8] *Primitive Culture,* 5th. edn., 1913, Vol. i, p. 16.

The Religion of the Semites (1889), makes the point that in 'traditional' religions—those not purporting to have been founded as the result of a revelation—ritual is much more important than dogma. There is an obligation to participate in rites, but people are not called upon to express adherence to specific beliefs. Robertson-Smith saw religion as an extension of the social field to include divine beings, relations with whom were patterned on those between living men. Accordingly he saw the essence of sacrifice in the feast shared by the worshippers with their god.

J. G. Frazer (1854–1941) first made the general public aware of anthropology. His *Golden Bough* is still the most widely read book on the subject. Frazer's interests were largely confined to the field of religion. Within that field he assembled a vast mass of data illustrating different themes of myth or ritual, which he found first in the Greek and Latin authors, and then came to see as characteristic of the religions of simple societies all over the world. He showed how universal was the concern of religion with the fertility of men, their herds, and their land; and his theory of 'sympathetic magic' drew attention to the symbolism whereby magical rites imitate the effect they are intended to produce. He interpreted this as the result of a mistaken process of reasoning to which he gave the name of 'bastard science'; such an explanation is no longer found convincing, but in recent years Lévi-Strauss (1908–) in France has revived our interest in the kind of classification by analogy that Frazer was describing.

Around the turn of the century the line of descent of anthropology in Britain began to diverge from that in America. The great figure in the immediate past of America is that of Franz Boas (1858–1942), who was trained in the natural sciences, and turned to the study of human society after an expedition to the Eskimo country which was primarily geographical in intention. Boas' scientific training caused him to look very sceptically at current theories of the evolution of society or the diffusion of culture. He would have none of their conjectures, but he was still interested in discovering how particular cultures grew up rather than how living men organized life in society. He was one of the last scholars to do valuable work in all the different branches of anthropology.

The French sociologists and their influence
In France, meantime, there was growing up a school of sociology which profoundly influenced the leading British anthropologists of the early twentieth century, and caused them to direct their interest wholly to the study of contemporary societies, neglecting archaeology and physical anthropology, which up to that time had been thought of as integral parts of our subject. The French scholars were led by Emile Durkheim (1858–1917) and published much of their important work in a periodical, *L'Année Sociologique*, which they founded in 1898 as a vehicle for their point of view.

Durkheim followed the British sociologist Herbert Spencer in asserting that there was a specifically social aspect of reality which could not be reduced to the behaviour of individual organisms. Social facts, he said, were to be studied as 'things', with an existence independent of the consciousness of the individual people who make up society (*Règles de la Méthode Sociologique*, 1895). The social facts are rules of behaviour, norms,[9] standards of value, expectations that society has of its members, behaviour that corresponds to them, and reactions to deviant behaviour.[10] As far as any particular person is concerned, they are given. He finds himself in a world where there are certain rules, and where he will suffer if he breaks them. Of course people do sometimes break rules, either on calculation or on impulse. This can be called, if you like, expressing their individuality. But the rules themselves do not express anyone's individuality, and social behaviour—the behaviour that is thought appropriate to particular people in particular circumstances—is a response to complex pressures and not the expression of a kind of personality. This is the principle

[9] We owe this word, as part of our technical vocabulary, to Durkheim.
[10] It should be noted that a social norm is different from a statistical norm. A social norm is what people think ought to happen; a statistical norm is what usually happens.

of social analysis that laymen find hardest to grasp, but it is fundamental.

Much of Durkheim's work was concerned with industrialized Europe, but he applied himself also to some of the problems of the simpler societies. In *De la Division du Travail Social* (1893) he contrasted the type of solidarity to be found in societies with a simple and a complex division of labour. In the former, he said, *solidarity* (a word which is difficult to define, but which indicates the way a society is held together) is *mechanical*. That is to say, society is held together by the association of *like* units. He gave as an example the rings of the earthworm. An earthworm lives as one organism, but if you cut it in half it does not die; the head and tail are not organically interdependent. Where the division of labour is complex, solidarity is organic; you cannot cut up the society into independent parts; you cannot even picture how this could be done. The solidarity of such a society is the product of the links between *complementary* units. The solidarity of brothers is mechanical, that of husband and wife organic. Brothers have *like* interests in their common patrimony and should join in defending their rights; but brothers who have grown up together can separate and form independent households; indeed they usually do. But one cannot conceive a household apart from the co-operation of husband and wife.

In his *Formes Elémentaires de la Vie Religieuse* (1912) Durkheim used the results of field studies of the Australian aborigines. Following Robertson-Smith's emphasis on the importance of ritual, he argued that ritual reflects the order of society, and indeed that the god who is worshipped is in fact society—a personification of the rules of conduct and values that the society most cherishes. Periodic rituals bring its members together in a highly charged emotional atmosphere, and thus impress upon them their interdependence and the importance of keeping the rules which maintain it. Although most anthropologists today would say that this approach does not exhaust the study of religion, it drew attention to an aspect of it that had been neglected until then; and every fieldworker now must look out for those aspects of religious ritual—and they are many—that do symbolize social relationships.

Those of Durkheim's contemporaries who are most read by students of social anthropology are Marcel Mauss (on the exchange of gifts and the principle of social relationships that we now call reciprocity) and Van Gennep (on various types of ritual). Their successor in the present generation, Lévi-Strauss, has developed the idea of reciprocity as the fundamental principle of social structure, which Malinowski had demonstrated from his work in the Trobriand Islands.

The work of the French sociologists influenced the two leading British anthropologists of the twentieth century, Malinowski and Radcliffe-Brown, whose theories are so much a part of the body of thought of contemporary anthropology that they are better dealt with in the context of current problems. Malinowski's theories relied more on psychology than Durkheim's, but Radcliffe-Brown, for whom the concept of social structure was central, followed very closely in Durkheim's footsteps.

As social anthropologists have cast their nets wider, have studied societies of larger scale and have sought to draw comparisons between the non-industrialized societies of to-day and those of which there is historical record, they have sought inspiration in the work of writers who treat historical data from a sociological point of view. Chief among these is Max Weber (1864–1920), whose work on different types of political system has suggested many interesting problems to people studying societies with well-developed institutions of government.

Field studies

The idea that anthropologists should go out and find their own data instead of relying on what travellers could tell them became current at the end of the last century. Boas' work among the Eskimo was done in 1883–4; from 1897 to 1902 he was in charge of the Jesup North Pacific expedition, which aimed at establishing the relationship between the aboriginal peoples of North-Eastern Asia and North

America. One product of this study was his interest in the Kwakiutl Indians of Vancouver Island, whom he revisited at intervals for nearly fifty years. His collection of 'texts'—statements made by informants—is said to be the largest ever made for a single society, but he did not have the experience of living continuously among them, and recording actual events. Contemporary with this was the Torres Straits and New Guinea expedition of 1898, in which six British scientists, each an expert in a different field (but none initially trained in anthropology) took part. The anthropological work was done by A. C. Haddon, C. G. Seligman, and W. H. R. Rivers, and all three went on to do independent fieldwork, Haddon and Seligman in Papua, Seligman later in Ceylon and in the Southern Sudan, Rivers among the Todas in Madras. In all these expeditions the anthropologists worked mainly by questioning informants, sometimes through the medium of interpreters. But when they knew the local language they did write down verbatim what their informants said. Boas in particular insisted on the importance of these 'vernacular texts'.

Rivers was the last British field anthropologist to interpret usages that he actually observed as survivals of an earlier stage of society; he built up out of such interpretations a theory that Melanesian society consisted of a mixture of indigenous and invading cultures. The Royal Society awarded him a gold medal for his *History of Melanesian Society* published in 1914. This is worth bearing in mind by anyone who thinks that Malinowski, when he published his *Argonauts of the Western Pacific* in 1922, over-emphasized the importance of looking at customs in their contemporary context.

Nevertheless we owe to Rivers a number of concepts that are still fundamental in the analysis of kinship. He first gave a technical meaning to *descent* as membership of the social group of either the mother or the father, and distinguished *succession* as the transmission of rank or office from *inheritance* as the transmission of property. Rivers held that rules of marriage were the determinants of differences between kinship systems. It was Mrs Seligman who in 1922 pointed out that the most important distinguishing factor was the rule of descent itself.[11]

The next big advance in fieldwork was Malinowski's expedition to the Trobriand Islands. There was an element of chance in this. Malinowski, as an Austrian subject, was liable to internment in the First World War, but he was allowed as an alternative to stay in the Trobriands. This long stay in one little island enabled him to see the actual processes of Trobriand social life, the differences between professed norms and usual behaviour, the kind of social pressures brought to bear on offenders, as well as making an exhaustive analysis of the language. Every anthropologist now is expected to spend at least a year in the society he is studying, preferably two with an interval between to collect himself and find what questions he has forgotten to ask. Few have been able to rival the standard of thoroughness set by Malinowski, whose data can be used by students to-day to answer questions that he himself had not thought of.

The development of knowledge in any field proceeds by the questioning of what is taken for granted at any one time. That is why laymen often find it easier to disregard the knowledge of specialists because 'they don't agree' than to ask what they are disagreeing about or how much common ground they have. But students seeking knowledge sometimes fall into the opposite error of thinking that there must somewhere be one right answer to all the disputed questions. A few of the controversies described in this chapter have been settled by showing that some assumption was contrary to observed fact. But in the main rival theories express different ways of looking at facts. Experience may show that one way is more fruitful than others, but none claims to have attained finality.

SUGGESTIONS FOR READING

Few histories of anthropology confine themselves to social anthropology and few are up to date. One might mention, however, A. Kardiner and E. Preble, *They Studied Man* (1962), which includes essays on Spencer, Tylor, Frazer, Durkheim, and Malinowski, and

[11] 'Asymmetry in Descent', in *Journal of the Royal Anthropological Institute*, Vol. 58, 1928.

H. R. Hays, *From Ape to Angel* (1958), which contains popular biographies of British and American anthropologists. Marvin Harris, *The Rise of Anthropological Theory* (1968), distributes praise and blame on other criteria than would be applied by most British anthropologists. But it illustrates the point made in the conclusion of this chapter, and it is practically up to the minute. M. Fortes, *Kinship and the Social Order* (1970), rehabilitates Morgan, but for very different reasons from Harris's.

Most general books on social anthropology begin with a survey of the development of the subject, and it is useful to see how different anthropologists of today evaluate their predecessors. Books worth looking at from this point of view are E. E. Evans-Pritchard, *Social Anthropology* (1951), D. F. Pocock, *Social Anthropology* (1961), J. H. M. Beattie, *Other Cultures* (1964), and R. G. Lienhardt, *Social Anthropology* (1964). The essay by D. G. MacRae, 'Race and Sociology in History and Theory', in *Man, Race and Darwin* (1960), gives much interesting information about the early evolutionists. The same author's *Ideology and Society* (1961), contains two essays, 'Darwinism and the Social Sciences' and 'Social Evolution before and after Darwin', which treat the work of nineteenth- and early twentieth-century anthropologists. J. W. Burrow, *Evolution and Society* (1966), is also interesting.

Malinowski's theories are discussed from every angle in R. W. Firth ed., *Man and Culture* (1957). Fortes in an essay in his *Time and Social Structure* (1970) gives an evaluation of Radcliffe-Brown's work, and this is further developed in his *Kinship and the Social Order* (1971).

CHAPTER 3

Some Matters of Current Discussion

The concept of function

A good many anthropologists in Britain, and some in America, describe the kind of studies of society that they make as 'functional', and the theory that guides them as 'functionalism'. A number of different meanings have been given to the word 'function'.

In everyday language we speak of a machine, and sometimes of a person, 'functioning' if it, or he, 'works', does adequately what is expected of it, or him; and the noun 'function' means, among other things, a kind of activity that is appropriate to the agency performing it, a meaning that implies that we know what machines or social arrangements are *for*.

We generally conceive of a machine or a living organism as consisting of interrelated parts, each of which must *function* properly if the machine is to keep running or the organism to keep alive, and most of the writers who have made 'function' a key-word in discussions of society have had this analogy in mind. None of them invites his readers to picture society as a machine (though people often write about 'social mechanisms'), but most of them compare it to a living organism. Some push the metaphor further than others.[1]

Herbert Spencer, the first British sociologist (1820–1903) was the first to use 'function' as a technical term for the analysis of society. He saw close parallels between human

---

[1] The word 'function' is also used in a mathematical sense: to say that x is a function of y means that the relation between x and y is constant, so that when y changes x changes. This metaphor has occasionally been used by social anthropologists, but it is not what most of them intend to convey by the word.

societies and biological organisms, both in the way they might be supposed to have evolved and in the way they kept themselves in being. Their existence, he argued, is maintained by the 'functional dependence of parts'.[2] In a society, as in an organism, there is 'a perpetual removal and replacement of parts joined with a continued integrity of the whole'. In this comparison the individual members of the society correspond to the cells of the organism.[3] This is more than a metaphor; Spencer believed that the laws of biology should be equally applicable to aggregations of cells and aggregations of individuals. Societies, he believed, developed through the differentiation of functions as biological organisms had been shown to do. He not only described the functions of different members of a human society as 'duties', but used this word of the functions even of cells in organisms showing the very minimum of differentiation. When he began to draw analogies between the differentiation of function in evolving organisms and in evolving societies, he remarked that an organ increased in bulk as a result of 'actively discharging the duties which the body at large requires of it'; and here the social counterpart of the biological organ was 'any class of labourers or artisans, any manufacturing centre or any official agency'. Railways in his picture of society corresponded to veins and arteries; profits to the excess of nutrition over waste which makes growth possible. By using for both biological and social functions a word—'duty'—which is really applicable only to social relationships, Spencer evaded some of the problems connected with the concept of function that later writers have had to wrestle with.

It will be seen that the writers who have sought to attribute functions to different parts of a social system (to use the broadest possible term) have been far from unanimous in their choice of analogies. To make an analogy of our own,

[2] 'The Social Organism', in *Essays Scientific, Political, and Speculative*, 1884, Vol. I, pp. 1396 ff. The essay was written in 1860.
[3] Readers of literary bent may be interested to note that Marcel Proust in his great novel, when writing of the 1914–18 war, pictures the opposing nations in terms very similar to these, though his biographers do not mention Spencer among the writers who influenced him.

we might say that each has dissected society in a different way.

Whereas Spencer drew his comparisons from the lowest forms of life, later writers made theirs with organs of the human body. Thus Durkheim (1858–1917), when he elaborated his principles of sociological method,[4] said that to explain a social phenomenon one must seek both the cause that produced it and 'the function that it fulfilled'. He preferred the idea of function to that of 'end' or 'aim' because, as he remarked, social phenomena do not owe their existence to the results that they produce. We should look for the relation between the phenomenon we are considering and 'the general needs of the social organism'. Whether it was created intentionally or not is not important. Durkheim adds, however, that even though social phenomena do not come into being because they are useful, they would not continue to exist unless they were useful in some way. Useless social arrangements (a non-technical word may make the meaning clearer) are harmful by the mere fact of being useless; society is burdened with them without getting any good from them. Therefore, we should ask how the phenomena that together constitute social life combine to produce harmony within the society and a satisfactory adaptation to the environment. Examples of social phenomena given in this context are the punishment of crime and the division of labour. Durkheim was primarily interested in the maintenance of *order,* and since most people would agree that order is essential to any arrangement of persons which can be called a society, one could say that his idea of function did not beg many questions.

Of the social anthropologists who drew inspiration from Durkheim, Malinowski developed the conception of function to its greatest elaboration, and even (partly in joke) gave to himself and his pupils the title of 'the Functional School'. His starting-point is contained in Durkheim's argument summarized above. Useless and meaningless customs just do not continue to exist; therefore a student of society, when he is confronted with a way of doing things that seems peculiar at first sight, should ask what it does

[4] *Règles de la Méthode Sociologique*, 1895.

for the people who practise it. This advice is obviously of even greater value to anthropologists working in societies very different from their own than it was to Durkheim's readers, who were only being urged to ask new questions about the world of their own experience.

Malinowski found his answers in the relation of social organization to biological needs. Man, he argued, cannot survive without food and shelter; the species cannot survive unless it reproduces its kind. In this respect man resembles other animals, but he differs from most of them in that he meets these essential needs indirectly through co-operation with his fellows in an organized society; and because he is endowed with speech and conceptual thought, he is able to pass on experience, so that every society has an accumulated heritage of knowledge, values, and rules of conduct which is further developed in every generation. In the possession of this heritage man differs even from the social animals, who do co-operate to meet their basic needs. It is this, indeed, that has enabled him to evolve the roundabout ways of procuring the economic necessities of life, and regulating sex relations and procreation, that we find in every human society. But these roundabout ways necessitate obedience to rules and restrictions, in contrast to a simple response to instinctive drives. Therefore *society*—no longer merely the individual or the species—has further needs. It needs arrangements for the transmission of its heritage of knowledge and moral values, that is some system of education. It needs, also, some source of confidence in the rightness of its rules and the worthwhileness of its continued existence; this it derives from religion.

This scheme of needs has been criticized on the ground that it confuses the needs of an individual organism, which cannot survive without food, or a species, which cannot survive without reproduction, and those of a society, which can survive—that is continue to exist—even if large numbers of its members die of hunger in famines or for some other reason do not produce offspring. Malinowski's most elaborate scheme included other biological needs for which human society makes provision; for example shelter, warmth, freedom of movement. But his actual discussion of the relation of social institutions to biological needs was pretty well confined to those concerned with subsistence and those concerned with marriage and the family; quite rightly, since these occupy the greater part of the life of the simpler societies.

E. R. Leach,[5] a contemporary Cambridge anthropologist, has contrasted Malinowski's use of the idea of needs with Durkheim's. Whereas Malinowski sought to relate *social* arrangements to *biological* needs, what Durkheim did was to draw the same analogy as Spencer between the *biological* function of a *biological organ* and the *social* function of a form of regularly recurring *social* behaviour (what he called a 'social fact'). So far from seeking to interpret social behaviour as a response to biological needs, Durkheim insisted, as was indicated earlier, that social facts were *sui generis.*[6] 'The social can be explained only by the social,' he said; in other words, the explanation of social behaviour is not to be sought either in man's biological constitution or, as is commoner among laymen, in individual psychology.

Radcliffe-Brown, drawing on Spencer, liked to elaborate the analogy between biological systems and social organisms. 'The function of a recurrent physiological process,' he wrote, 'is a correspondence between it and the necessary conditions of existence of the organism.'[7] In social life 'the function of a recurrent activity, such as the punishment of a crime or a funeral ceremony, is the part it plays in the social life as a whole and therefore the contribution it makes to the maintenance of the structural continuity'. More specifically, he said, 'the function of a particular social usage is the contribution it makes to the total social life as the functioning of the total social system'. But he expressly insisted that 'function' should not be used to mean 'aim', 'purpose' or 'meaning',[8] and neither he nor the other writers quoted would have dreamed of equating it with 'duty'. One may note too that he confined his analogy to usages and did not bring in the objects which men make

[5] 'The Epistemological Background to Malinowski's Empiricism', in R. W. Firth (ed.), *Man and Culture,* 1957, p. 123 n.
[6] See p. 26.
[7] *Structure and Function in Primitive Society,* 1952, p. 179.
[8] ibid., p. 200.

and use. Such a treatment assumes that the usage under discussion is *good for* the society in which it is found; and this assumption having been made, the next step is to explain *what good* it does. The proposition that every social usage has a function can then only too easily become the proposition that whatever is, is good, and when people refer disparagingly to 'crude functionalism', this is one of the criticisms that they imply.

Not much attention has been given to the question what kind of social usage we should consider when we are looking for functions; a social usage might be anything from blowing one's nose with a handkerchief to the duty of avenging a slain kinsman. Malinowski's scheme did designate *institutions* as the social arrangements that can be said to meet needs and therefore have functions—and an institution was, for him, a complex of organized activities in which particular persons are expected to co-operate. Other writers have been concerned with what Radcliffe-Brown called *jural* rules, such as those which forbid marriage between persons in certain relationships. Malinowski himself used the rule of exogamy (no intermarriage within a descent group) as an example. He said its function was to eliminate sexual rivalries from a group which is expected to co-operate; others might say with Tylor that its function was to create a network of alliances between different descent groups (which is certainly its *effect*).

It is clear that the people who practise the usages examined by the anthropologist do not ascribe to them functions of this kind. They may say, for example, 'We perform mortuary rituals so that the dead man's spirit will go to the place of spirits and not come back to trouble us'; but they certainly would not say with Malinowski that they perform mortuary rituals to meet the need for reassurance in the face of death. This led Merton[9] to distinguish between 'manifest functions', as the conscious aims of people participating in some prescribed action, and 'latent functions' which are apparent only to the observer.

It is indeed extremely difficult to use the metaphor of 'function' without implying some notion of fitness for ends

[9] R. K. Merton, *Social Theory and Social Structure*, 2nd edn., 1957, p. 51.

which itself implies some idea of purpose. But students of society do not explicitly endorse such ideas. Most of them would repudiate the notion of design in the universe, and all except Lévi-Strauss would hesitate to assume that the institutions of the simpler societies have been deliberately created by the members of these societies. One could then fall back on the Darwinian analogy, once so popular, with species which die out because they cannot hold their own in competition with others better adapted to their environment. But human societies differ from organisms less because, as Spencer and Radcliffe-Brown said, they persist while their members change, than because their members continue to reproduce the species while the society changes. We do not often see societies 'going under in the struggle'; and in the rare cases where this has happened the reason is to be found not in the kind of inadequate adaptation to environment that would explain the extinction of a biological species, but much more crudely in the inadequacy of weapons of defence.

Moreover, though the exaggeration of functionalist theory can lead to the absurdity of assuming that what the fieldworker sees is a system so perfectly balanced that any change must be for the worse, it is certain that it is preferable to begin by looking for 'function' or 'meaning' in social usages rather than assume, as earlier anthropologists did, that, if they are hard to understand, they must be anachronisms that have lost their meaning—'survivals' from earlier states of society. Most of the customs that used to be explained as survivals have proved to have adequate functional explanations; and any fieldworker, however much he may try to exclude from his own interpretations such notions as 'purpose' or 'meaning', will hardly be able to avoid feeling that they are implicit in the attitudes of the people among whom he is working. We should not deny the possibility that certain customs—particularly perhaps rituals—have survived into the present without retaining much meaning, or with their meaning greatly changed; and what is perhaps even more important is that we should recognize social anachronisms in periods of rapid change, such as all societies are experiencing at the present day. But the ideas of survival and anachronism must be used circumspectly, and not as a tool for the invention of imaginary histories.

It may seem that the concept of function has been given too many different meanings to be really very useful. But the attitude towards the study of society which gave it currency is fundamental to modern social anthropology, and that is why many anthropologists who have given up trying to find functions for particular usages still describe their kind of study as functionalism. The assumption they make is that what one is looking for in social behaviour is a system, or systems, or interrelated activities which have, as Radcliffe-Brown put it, 'a certain kind of unity which we may speak of as functional unity'; that what one is primarily interested in is how this system works rather than how it came to be what it is; and that for this kind of study one must see at first hand what actually goes on, not merely ask questions to elicit general statements about what ought to happen. As Fortes pointed out in his inaugural lecture as William Wyse Professor of Social Anthropology at Cambridge, one can see this unity only by living in the society and observing its parts 'working together contemporaneously'.[10] For another contemporary, Gellner,[11] the essence of a functional study is that the usages we are looking at should not be divorced from their context. The question then arises, how wide is the context? For Malinowski the context of any one custom extended all through the society in which it was found (and there was really no reason why it should not extend through the whole world). This insistence on the inter-connections of the facts we were discussing was what made his teaching so intensely stimulating. But as a guide to the fieldworker it was a counsel of perfection, and it becomes more unattainable, not less, as fieldwork methods become more intensive. The fieldworker just has to judge for himself how much context is relevant; there will be critics to take him up if he judges badly. What people mean by a functional study today is selecting a particular prob-

---

[10] *Social Anthropology at Cambridge since 1900*, 1953, p. 25.
[11] 'Concepts and Society', *Transactions of the Fifth World Congress of Sociology*, 1962, pp. 155–8.

lem for intensive examination and looking at it in the context of a wider whole, the structure of which must be understood in its essentials.

Anthropology: science or history?

Much has been written about the relation of history to anthropology. This has been the subject of a good deal of controversy, but the question about which people have disputed has not remained constant; contrasts and comparisons between the two studies have implied very different arguments at different times.

What is anthropology if it is not history? A science, some have replied. Should it be a science? Can it be? Should it try to be? Is the subject-matter of anthropology capable of being treated by the methods of science?

Another set of questions is asked about the *use* of history to anthropology, and here history can mean a number of different things—what any particular anthropologist can find out about the past of the people he studies, what anthropologists can learn from the writings of historians about social institutions that are now out of reach of first-hand study, whether the methods of historical research can be used in societies that have no written records (or for periods of their history when they had no written records).

Spencer, writing in 1873, said: 'What Biography is to Anthropology, History is to Sociology.'[12] F. W. Maitland wrote in 1899, 'Anthropology must choose between being history and being nothing,'[13] a dictum that was repeated in 1933 by Michael Oakeshott. Maitland was concerned specifically with supposed successions of stages in human society.

Spencer's contrast is clearly between narratives of particular events and the search for generalizations, applicable to races in the case of anthropology and to societies in the case of sociology. In each case he was interested in trying to establish laws of evolution, and when he wrote of anthropology he was thinking of what is now called physical anthropology. His view of the relation between history and sociology, however, has its place as the forerunner of later

[12] *The Study of Society*, 9th edn., 1900, p. 57.
[13] *Selected Essays*, 1936, p. 49.

discussions in which social anthropologists have been the protagonists.

Spencer's claim that sociology was a science, capable of formulating laws stating the general characteristics of societies at different stages of evolution, was disputed by historians and others who supposed that any reference to laws must imply some theory of predestination, but predestination without God. In his day historians were readier than they are now explicitly to ascribe the good fortune of their own countries to divine intervention, and to explain historical events by the personal influence of a few great men. But many people still feel distaste for the idea of referring to human relationships in terms of *laws*, because they think this implies a denial of freedom of choice and therefore of moral responsibility. This has led some writers to argue that we *ought not* to try to establish laws, while others are saying that although, if we did establish laws, we could claim the status of a science, in fact we *cannot* do so.

Spencer answered the arguments of his critics by pointing out that the 'laws' of the physical sciences do not assert that any event *must* happen at a given moment; they say that *if* certain circumstances are combined, something will happen. It may be that people accustomed to the popular sense of the word 'predict' have been misled by references to the 'predictive power' of science, which means no more than what has been stated in the preceding sentence. It may be, too, that the nineteenth-century interest in evolution, which *is* a process in time and so in a sense a sequence of events, led anti-evolutionists to suppose they were being told (as indeed Karl Marx was telling them) that the lines of their future history had already been laid down.

The social evolutionists of the later nineteenth century conceived themselves to be following Darwin's example in asserting that human society had passed through the same succession of stages in every part of the world. But what they actually did differed from what Darwin had done in two important ways. To begin with, the process of biological evolution as Darwin described it was not a series of changes through which a single species passed; he described the way in which new species became differentiated from

their parent stock. Secondly, when they said they had discovered 'laws' of social evolution they were using the word
in a different sense from that in which a natural scientist
would use it. Because the human mind is essentially the
same everywhere, they argued (and most scientists would
agree with them on this point), society *must* have evolved
everywhere in the same way; that is, passed through the
same stages. The succession of these stages was what they
called a law of social evolution.

But although Darwin was able to show what had in fact
been the process of biological evolution, he never claimed
to have established a law which made it inevitable that
species should be differentiated precisely as they actually
are. On the contrary, his theory was that species which come
into being by chance perpetuate themselves if they prove
to be better adapted than their rivals to the environment
in which they find themselves. This is usually called the
'theory', not the 'law', of natural selection. It is an explanatory principle of very wide range; if it were called a 'law',
it would still make no claim to predict when a mutation
would give rise to a new species and what the new species
would be. Criticism is usually levelled at the nineteenth-
century attempts to establish 'laws' on the ground that
their 'laws' have proved to be false in the light of further
research; but it might be even more pertinent to remark
that their exponents were not really following the scientific
method that they had made their ideal.

It is the business of philosophers to discuss the validity
of different kinds of generalization. To some of them the
model of the kind of generalization that deserves to be
called a law is found in the physical sciences, and depends
on exact measurement.[14] The simpler parts of the physical
sciences are concerned with what 'everyone knows'—for
example that water will boil if you heat it. This is a valid
generalization which rests on observation, but scientific
measurement gives the exact temperature at which it will
boil and the extent to which this will vary with altitude.
This is *prediction*; but of course the water will not boil at
all unless somebody lights a fire under it.

[14] e.g. Stephen Toulmin, *The Philosophy of Science*, 1953, pp. 50 ff.

As anthropologists seek to make their observations more exact, they have used statistical methods wherever they could, and in this way have been able to measure, in particular societies, the rate of divorce, or the proportion of people who do not in fact follow a rule of conduct that is supposed to be correct for everyone. But they have not yet established any generalizations about society as such that can be expressed in quantitative terms. Some think this is only a matter of time; others think they never will.

Those anthropologists who would like to see their subject classed at any rate among the social sciences recognize that they have produced no quantitative generalizations and few, if any, predictive ones. Therefore they hesitate to claim the names of 'laws' for such generalizations as they have made, and say instead that they look for 'regularities' or 'recurrences' in social behaviour.[15]

In recent years it has also been argued that anthropologists should confine themselves to regularities, and eschew the attempt to find laws, because of the nature of the phenomena they study. The leading exponent of this view was Evans-Pritchard, who, starting from the fact that we have not yet established any propositions 'even remotely resembling what are called laws in the natural sciences', goes on to say that this is necessarily so because social systems are not 'natural systems'; they are 'moral, or symbolic, systems'. Therefore, said Evans-Pritchard, social anthropology 'is less interested in process than in design' and 'seeks patterns and not laws, demonstrates consistency and not necessary relations between social activities, and interprets rather than explains'.[16] This approach to the subject, he maintained, resembles that of the historian rather than the scientist.

Several of his colleagues quickly took up this challenge to the status of social anthropology as a science. Fortes re-

---

[15] This does not save them from being accused of ignoring the importance of human choice. See, for example, Hunter, *The New Societies of Tropical Africa*, 1962, p. 332.

[16] *Social Anthropology*, 1951, p. 62. In a later statement Evans-Pritchard suggests that what anthropologists mean by laws are determined sequences of development in time; these, however, would not be all like the laws of the natural sciences.

marked that the generalizations of social anthropology
should hold good irrespective of time or place, whereas history aims at establishing particular sequences and combinations, and is essentially the study of particular times and
places in the past. He reminded the audience at his inaugural lecture at Cambridge that historians themselves
could not make much of their material unless they posited
'general tendencies' of some kind. To hold that we should
approach our subject in the spirit of the scientist 'does not
imply a belief in mechanical determinism in human social
life or a denigration of man's intellectual and spiritual
qualities . . .'. Social laws refer to ideally isolated features of
social life and can be stated only in terms of probabilities.
The combination of factors that will be present on any particular occasion can never be predicted. But he added:
'The evidence we have is surely incompatible with an
assumption of utter randomness in man's cultural and social
achievements, but this is what we should expect if there
were total absence of law in their occurence.'[17]

Firth at about the same time questioned the possibility
of making distinctions between the 'laws' of a natural and
the 'regularities' of a social system, particularly if it is
agreed that both are 'not invariable principles but statements of probability'.[18] Beattie at Oxford suggested that we
may distinguish systems of social relationships from idea
systems and study them separately, but he did not offer
this as a reason why different kinds of generalization should
be appropriate in the two cases. When one is dealing with
ideas as opposed to events, one looks for *logical* relations
between them, and in this sense one can talk with Evans-
Pritchard of 'pattern'; but since ideas do not *happen* but
exist, the idea of regular recurrence would seem to be as inadequate in relation to them as the idea of law. In practice
Evans-Pritchard himself, though he made studies of the
Nuer system of religious ideas and of Zande notions of
witchcraft, did not confine himself to the field of ideas.

Lévi-Strauss in Paris regards history and anthropology
as cognate, but not because he would reject the name of

[17] op. cit., pp. 30 ff.   [18] *Man*, LII, 1952, p. 38.

science for anthropological studies. He argues, with the historians, that a knowledge of the past is essential for the understanding of any social phenomenon, and, with the anthropologists seeking for generalizations, that only by tracing, where we can, the history of a society can we determine what is in fact its permanent structure—what it is that persists through the changes caused by such events as wars, migrations, and religious schisms. He remarks, further, that historians and anthropologists alike deal with forms of society alien to those of their own experience, and that we need this examination of a wide range of social forms in order to discover what principles of social structure are really fundamental.[19]

The question whether an anthropologist should be interested in the past of the people he studies is connected with the functionalist approach through the argument that we are more interested in the way a social system works than in how it came to be what it is. There is here a confusion that has arisen because there are different kinds of historical data and different kinds of historical research. At the time when Malinowski first advanced his view—in the extreme form that the past is irrelevant to a functional study —anthropologists were making two kinds of historical reconstruction. One was known as 'conjectural history'; certain social usages which did not seem easy to understand were interpreted as relics of previous stages of society, on the analogy of the fossils which have enabled us to reconstruct the history of biological evolution. Malinowski insisted that no social usage was a mere fossil, and the search for interpretations in terms of contemporary significance, which he initiated, amply vindicated this argument. The second kind of reconstruction was the ethnological kind, concerned in tracing, largely by evidence from the distribution of material objects, the way different peoples have influenced one another's culture. This kind of study uses sounder evidence than the first, but it is not evidence that can help to answer the questions that functionalists are asking.

[19] 'History and Anthropology', in *Structural Anthropology*, English translation 1963, pp. 1–30.

But where we can find in records of the past evidence that does bear on the development of the social systems that we are studying, it is absurd to say that we must disregard it; though once we begin working among peoples with a long recorded history, it would be equally absurd to accept the view in which the claims of history are popularly expressed, that *the past* as such must be known in order to understand the present. Obviously we must know what questions to ask of documents and of history books, as we must know what questions to ask of living informants.

Evans-Pritchard set the example in tracing the development of political institutions among the Anuak[20] by means of oral traditions of the way in which kings had succeeded one another, and at the same time Nadel was using written records in his study of the Nupe empire in Nigeria.[21] The argument for the value of historical evidence, and for the study of history in general, for the anthropologist was put by Evans-Pritchard in a lecture given in 1961.[22] Here he says that historians as well as anthropologists 'see the general in the particular', and goes on to explain that it is to sociologically-oriented history that we should look, and that we ourselves should learn 'to treat historical material sociologically'. We should do well to be more critical than we are when we do use documentary sources, and we must not ignore the traditions of their own past history that non-literate people preserve, but learn to weigh critically their value as evidence. We should realize that the simple societies did not remain wholly unchanged in the times before anthropologists could observe them; and we should learn to differentiate between history, myth, legend, anecdote, and folklore. Evans-Pritchard also reminded us that the study of past epochs, when our own ancestors were organized in institutions closely resembling those of contemporary peoples who have not yet been industrialized, can be extremely useful in our pursuit of comparisons and generalizations. He concluded by reversing Maitland's dictum and

---

[20] *The Political System of the Anuak*, 1940.
[21] *A Black Byzantium*, 1942.
[22] 'Anthropology and History', in *Essays in Social Anthropology*, 1962.

saying: 'History must choose between being social anthropology and being nothing.'[23]

Firth has applied the historian's methods to the stories told about their past by the people of Tikopia, checking them against other sources of evidence and, where this cannot be done, weighing their probability in the light of relevant general knowledge. He has not sought to classify these tales under the headings listed by Evans-Pritchard, but has brought together all those which the Tikopia regard as true and as 'having a significant bearing on their social structure and on the organization of their affairs.'[24]

'Comparative' or 'historical' method

Closely allied to the question whether anthropology should be classed as a science or as one of the humanities—for this is the essence of the discussion of its relation with history—is the question whether it should use 'the comparative' or 'the historical' method. Both these phrases can be interpreted in more than one way. What facts do people seek to compare? And what histories do they seek to recount?

It is one of the paradoxes of our subject that the kind of research characteristic of the anthropologists of the nineteenth century has been called *both* 'the comparative' *and* 'the historical' method, and that writers who wished to dissociate themselves from it have also disclaimed both descriptions.

Herbert Spencer's work is sometimes said to have inaugurated the comparative method, consisting in 'the accumulation of customs and ideas gathered from many places and periods, to substantiate developmental schemes arrived at through speculation'.[25]

Tylor sought to introduce greater rigour into the method by making statistical correlations. He examined the 'adhesions'—as he called them—of certain variables which he took to be crucial. He tackled the question whether matriliny preceded or followed patriliny in this way. When he

[23] It could be argued that this implies comparative rather than historical study.

[24] *History and Traditions of Tikopia*, 1961, p. 14.

[25] A. Goldenweiser, 'Cultural Anthropology', in H. E. Barnes (ed.), *The History and Prospects of the Social Sciences*, 1925, p. 215.

presented his new method to the Royal Anthropological
Institute[26] he remarked that it was based on data from 350
societies ranging from the simplest to the most complex. His
key variable was the principle of descent; he distinguished
matriliny, patriliny, and something which was neither, but
which he assumed to be a transitional stage. The customs
which he correlated with these were 'marriage by capture'
and the couvade, the 'farcical proceeding', as he called it,
whereby a husband is required to imitate the processes of
pregnancy and parturition and all the behaviour that is
enjoined upon his wife for the sake of her child's welfare.
By working out the distribution of these customs he came
to the conclusion that the 'maternal' system—the term
which he substituted for 'matriarchal'—preceded the 'pater-
nal', to which it moved through an intermediate stage when
the recognition of paternity was so new that it had to be
ritually asserted.

Clan exogamy,[27] he noted, was found at both ends of the
process, though he might have been hard put to it to say
what happened in the intermediate stage. Indeed this is the
real weakness in the large conjectures of the nineteenth
century about what 'must have' happened. When Tylor
writes that exogamy 'shifts its prohibitions from the female
to the male line of descent, now allowing marriages which
it treated formerly as incestuous, while prohibiting others
which it formerly allowed without scruple', anyone trained,
as is a modern anthropologist, to picture what he reads of
as the real-life activity of real people, will find this rather
difficult to imagine.

Among British anthropologists the comparative method
is associated principally with Frazer, who, like Van Gennep, collected by means of questionnaires data showing the
wide prevalence of certain ritual customs. Later anthropologists, engaged in the intensive study of particular
societies, have criticized this kind of work because it tears
the customs from their context; and Frazer was certainly

---

[26] 'On a method of investigating the development of institutions; applied
to laws of marriage and descent', *Journal of the Royal Anthropological
Institute*, 1889, pp. 24–269.
[27] The rule that people must not marry members of their own clan.

too much inclined to assume that a composite picture could be built up out of separate items from different societies and then held to be typical of primitive society in general. This method is concerned wholly with resemblances and not at all with differences or the reason for them; but it has not been unfruitful. Frazer did establish the universal concern of primitive religion with fertility, Van Gennep the universal tendency to surround with ritual the occasions when the social status of a person is changed. Both called attention to the very widespread occurrence of certain kinds of symbolism, and this is a subject in which social anthropologists are becoming more and more interested.

Van Gennep, however, regarded the comparative method, which he claimed to be practising, as something different from the work of scholars who sought to identify the stages in the development of society. The latter he called the historical method, and he opposed to it the search for regularities independent of time or place. He rather wickedly said of what he called the 'history mania' of the nineteenth century that its adherents were interested in the living only for the light they could throw on the dead.[28]

Boas, dismissing just what Van Gennep dismissed, claimed to be rejecting the comparative method and adopting the historical method. Malinowski, starting from criticism of the 'conjectural history' of the nineteenth century, ended by rejecting the study of history as irrelevant for anthropologists. Boas was interested in the relative importance of diffusion and independent evolution in the development of culture, and held that the comparative method, concerned as it was at that time to establish a uniform line of evolution for all human societies, ignored historical facts that could be ascertained. Boas demonstrated from his own studies that some American Indian tribes had imitated their neighbours, and he held it to be the first task of anthropology to identify the sources of different elements in the culture of the people studied. But Boas did not reject comparative studies because he thought they had been misused. He held that the task of reconstructing cultural history must be undertaken first, but that a second task,

[28] *Le Folklore*, 1924.

which might be even more important, was to examine 'the laws governing social life' which would explain the appearance of similar social usages among peoples between whom no historical connection could be established.

Radcliffe-Brown devoted his Huxley lecture in 1951[29] to an illustration of the comparative method as Van Gennep would have understood it. He began by remarking that both the aborigines of New South Wales and the Haida Indians of British Columbia are divided into two halves which are called by the names of birds, that the pairs of bird species after which they are named are closely similar, and that very similar stories are told among both peoples about events that are supposed to have created hostility between these two species. Confronted with these resemblances, he says, a social anthropologist should not look for their explanation in the past history of the two peoples, but should see them as instances of general phenomena. One is totemism, or the association of human groups with animal species. Another is a kind of division of society into opposing groups, who have no material grounds for hostility but yet are expected to make a pretence of hostility, which he describes as 'a means of integration through opposition'. 'The comparative method,' he adds, 'is one by which we pass from the particular to the general' so as to arrive at 'characteristics which can be found in different forms in all human societies'. The task of social anthropology, which here he explicitly distinguishes from ethnology, is 'to formulate and validate statements about the conditions of existence of social systems and the regularities that are observable in social change'. This, he says, 'can only be done by the systematic use of the comparative method'. He concluded that for a complete understanding of human society a combination of this and the historical studies of the ethnologist would be necessary.

Radcliffe-Brown's range of comparison was indeed all-embracing. He suggested that the opposition between the Yang and the Yin in Chinese philosophy might be treated as a phenomenon comparable to the opposition between Aus-

[29] 'The Comparative Method in Social Anthropology', *Journal of the Royal Anthropological Institute*, 1951, pp. 15–22.

tralian moieties, and he thereby earned the approval of the French anthropologist, Lévi-Strauss, who argued that by extending his comparisons over the widest possible field he had demonstrated a fundamental characteristic of human thought.[30] Other contemporary anthropologists thought sounder constructions might be built on less ambitious premises. Eggan in Chicago suggested that one might begin by comparing moiety structures among American Indians, or the different Hopi villages. Schapera in London pursues this line of argument further. He points out that in recent writings the examples used for comparative purposes have been chosen quite arbitrarily—because there were books about them in English, or—in collections of studies—because the peoples had been described by anthropologists personally known to the editor. What he recommends is to begin with intensive studies of limited areas and proceed from these, first to the comparison of contiguous areas, and later perhaps to the establishment of a comprehensive series of types of social institution. This is comparison for the purpose of classification rather than for the elucidation of fundamental principles of social structure.

Gluckman from Manchester has argued that what a social anthropologist seeks to compare is *process*—the way comparable things get done in different societies. He has been much interested in the question how rebellion may be kept within bounds; another of his examples is the different way in which groups may be aligned in a struggle for succession to office, depending on the rules of succession and the kind of ambiguity that they permit. The kind of comparison which has been made in recent years is the comparison of isolable aspects of social life: kinship and marriage, political systems, cosmologies, witchcraft beliefs, and so on.

Eggan concluded his remarks on the comparative method with a prediction that British anthropologists would in time come to supplement this with the historical method. In the sense that we have become more and more interested in following—where we can—changes over time in social institutions, his prediction has been fulfilled, but it is un-

[30] *Le Totémisme Aujourd'hui*, 1962, pp. 128 ff.

likely that we shall return to the ethnologists' interests in the source of cultural elements.

Another aspect of this debate is the contrast of *synchronic* and *diachronic* studies. A synchronic study is concentrated on a short period of time—the year or so that the average social anthropologist spends in the field. He approaches his work with the assumption that what he is looking for is a system working—'a going concern', as Malinowski used to put it—and that he will look for a meaning of some kind in the usages that he finds and hesitate to explain any of them as mere survivals. Such studies have been criticized on the ground that they lead to false assumptions about the unchanging nature of simple societies. Most anthropologists now supplement their direct observation with such information as they can get about past history. Some of them have been concerned, also, not merely with the sequence of events, but with the ways in which societies change over time. In recent times social anthropologists have returned to the places where they worked some years earlier, or to places where their predecessors had worked, in order to see what changes there have been in the interval. Examples are the work of Firth in Polynesia (returning to the scene of his own fieldwork), and of H. A. Powell in the Trobriands, measuring the changes since Malinowski's day. These may be called diachronic studies.

SUGGESTIONS FOR READING

A survey of the development of the concept of function is given by R. W. Firth under the heading 'Function' in W. L. Thomas Jr. (ed.), *Yearbook of Anthropology—1955*. Malinowski's functional method is discussed by all the contributors to R. W. Firth (ed.), *Man and Culture* (1957), and also by I. C. Jarvie, *The Revolution in Social Anthropology* (1964), a writer who is not fully aware of the way in which theories have developed since Malinowski's time.

The relation of historical studies to social anthropology has been discussed by E. E. Evans-Pritchard in *Social Anthropology* (1951), and in 'Anthropology and History', a lecture reprinted in *Essays in Social Anthropology* (1962), and by I. Schapera in 'Should Anthropologists be Historians?', *Journal of the Royal Anthropological Institute*, 1952. The very different ideas of Lévi-Strauss on this subject are expounded in his essay, 'History and Anthropology', in his *Structural Anthropology* (1963).

Both Radcliffe-Brown and Evans-Pritchard have delivered lectures with the title 'The Comparative Method in Social Anthropology'. The former was published in the *Journal of the Royal Anthropological Institute* for 1951, the latter by itself in 1963. I. Schapera has discussed this subject in 'Some Comments on Comparative Method in Social Anthropology', *American Anthropologist*, 1953.

CHAPTER 4

Social Differentiation

WITHIN any society people are both *organized in groups*—that is to say, they form bodies of persons with common interests and common leadership—and *classified in categories*—that is to say, they are regarded by their fellows as having something in common. A group may be identified by the outsider analysing a society, or it may be labelled by the members of the society and so form a category in their system of ideas. The descent groups or lineages which will be discussed at length in the following chapter are the basic *groups* in many simple societies. The societies in question do not always have a name to describe these groups; where they do, this name is a *category*. Other divisions of the population are also categorized, and people may even have roles assigned to them in virtue of the categories into which they fall, but this does not make such aggregates of persons into groups.

Differentiation by sex

The biological division of humans into male and female is the basis for the most elementary social classification everywhere. In every society the division of roles between the sexes results from the fact that women bear and suckle children, and so are tied to the domestic scene for much of their lives. In those societies where the economy is one of *subsistence production*—where, that is, people get their food and other needs by their own labour from their immediate environment—a large share of the work of agriculture falls to women. Sometimes it is entirely their responsibility; in other places men do the heavy work of clearing the ground of grass before planting. Among the Bemba of Zambia the soil is fertilized by lopping the branches of tall trees and burning them where they fall; this is of course a task for men. There are also some societies in which men and women share in farm work at all its stages. Among peoples who keep cattle, again, it is equally of course the men who drive the cattle to pasture and protect them against raiders and wild animals. Sometimes milking is women's work, but some cattle-keeping peoples believe that women should have no contact of any kind with cattle. Women collect water and firewood, and are responsible for cooking.

Men's tasks are those that call for extra physical strength and agility and that take them away from home—warfare, hunting, herding cattle, sea-fishing, canoe trading. The tasks of government also fall to men. Men exercise *jural* authority—that is, authority in matters concerned with rights and obligations. Households, homesteads, kin groups, political communities, normally have male heads, and a woman is usually expected to have a male guardian, a kinsman if she is not married, a husband if she is, who protects her interests and is responsible for any offences that she may commit. This is what is meant by saying that in societies of simple technology (as indeed in many others) women are always minors. The most important ritual roles too belong to men; it is they who can communicate with the ancestors and other spirits believed to be able to influence human destinies. Women may be excluded from certain rituals; on the other hand, in some societies there are women's rites from which men are excluded.

In most primitive and peasant societies it is not thought appropriate for men and women to associate together outside the home. Even within it men often eat separately from women, and there are societies where men are criticized if they spend too much time with their wives. It is not supposed that men and women who are not spouses could have any interest in associating together for other than sexual purposes—courtship if the woman is not married, adultery if she is.

In the division of roles between the sexes much of the work that falls to men is not manual labour. It consists in a good deal of talking, and since the place for talking can be chosen for its amenities, the talkers may sit in the shade while the toilers stand or walk in the sun. Hence the stereotyped picture of the African or Melanesian male idling while his womenfolk work. It must be remembered that the tasks of maintaining social order and the right relation with the supernatural guardians of society are just as important for social life as the provision of food, even if they are less physically exhausting. It might be worth remembering too that the modern bread-winner, even in our society with its labour-saving machines, probably does a good deal less hand and leg work than his domestic helpmeet.

Differentiation by age

Every society makes some division of its population according to age. This again has its biological basis: children are not ready for adult tasks, old people have not the strength for them. In societies with records, divisions are made on the basis of chronological age, regardless of relative maturity at the beginning or relative senility at the end. In Britain there are fixed ages at which people *can* leave school, get married at all, get married without their parents' consent, contract debts, vote, draw pensions; and, for some of them, ages at which they *must* retire from employment. Also, there is a general notion, however attenuated, that respect is due from the younger members of society to the older.

In the simpler societies there are no records of age, nor are they concerned with such matters as franchise or pensions. On the other hand, they usually attach great importance to seniority, and in societies which are not rapidly changing, people in general are more willing to accept the proposition that a man's wisdom increases all through the course of his life; also, it is often supposed that the old deserve particular respect because they are nearer to death, and so to God and the ancestors.

How then do they know who is senior, except in the very general way that one can tell by appearance? In a good many societies people attain recognition as adults by going through a more or less elaborate ritual of *initiation*; in any given society initiation may be performed for boys, for girls, or for both. The most important effect of initiation is that it qualifies people to marry; in some societies sex relations

are not permitted before initiation. The initiation of girls
is usually accompanied by some instruction on sexual and
domestic life. That of boys may combine instruction in
tribal lore of all kinds with trials of strength and endur-
ance; or the test may be the central feature of the rite, as
with the Nuer of the southern Sudan, where the boys must
submit without flinching to having six cuts made in their
temples, or the Pokot of northern Kenya, where each one
is expected to kill an ox with one blow of a spear.

In societies such as these no one can be initiated before
the onset of puberty, but a given person's initiation may be
delayed for one reason or another; hence all do not attain
social adulthood at the same *chronological* age. But it is the
time of his initiation that fixes a man's seniority for the rest
of his life. Where, as is most usual, boys are initiated in
groups, the set initiated at one time is given a name and
recognized throughout the tribe; the order in which the
names come is known, and so everyone in company with
strangers knows whom he must respect as senior to him and
who, as his juniors, owe him respect. This order is recognized in such matters as the serving of beer at a gathering;
and on formal occasions, and possibly others, in the grouping of men who sit together. Respect for elders means that
one must not openly disagree, still less quarrel with or
abuse them; it is more or less axiomatic that in a difference
of opinion between senior and junior the senior is in the
right. In societies which have not highly developed institutions for keeping the peace, this limitation on the freedom
to argue and quarrel is very important in reducing the
incidence of violence.

Sometimes seniority is measured by other indices, such
as whether a man has children and the (social) age of these
children, e.g. whether they have themselves been initiated.
Women too are sometimes organized in age-sets, though
this is less common.

There are societies in which political and ritual roles are
assigned to the male population as a body in virtue of their
social age.[1] In such societies the *age-sets* formed in a single
initiation period pass together through a series of *age-*

[1] See pp. 117–22.

grades; the set is the body of persons, the grade is the status which they have reached in the course of their journey through life. Very roughly, there may be said to be generally a grade of men of fighting age, often called the 'warrior grade' in ethnographic literature, and a grade of 'elders' who have retired from the fighting forces. In practice no system makes as sharp a division as this suggests, and some have very complicated subdivisions. The general principle, however, is that younger men are called on for tasks requiring physical strength—fighting, police work, sometimes 'public works'—and older men for tasks requiring wisdom—the discussion of public affairs and the arbitration of disputes—and for those ritual duties for which they are fitted by their age itself.

Rank, hierarchy, stratification

Differentiation by age, even where there are no organized groups of this kind, is one way of establishing rules of precedence and of formal respect due to certain members of a society from other members—in other words, of arranging people in *rank* order. The notions of *rank, hierarchy,* and *stratification* have a good deal in common, and the distinctions between them will become clearer as the argument proceeds. Rank may be ascribed on the basis of descent. There is no difficulty to an English reader in the idea of hereditary rank; we cling to our House of Lords, and a speaker at a meeting where any members of this body are present will, if he is formally correct, acknowledge their presence by addressing himself to 'Mr. Chairman, my lords, ladies, and gentlemen'. In the same way in many of the simpler societies persons belonging to certain lines of descent are regarded as superior to others, are entitled to receive formal marks of respect, and may sometimes have other privileges. The clearest case of such differentiation by rank is that of 'royal families'—the descendants of kings and chiefs. A society may be simply divided into 'royals' or 'nobles' and commoners, but there may be much more elaborate ranking systems. In Samoa, for example, every household claims the right to a hereditary title, and all these are ranked in order of precedence on the basis of genealogies that are recited on formal occasions.

Again, among the Kgatla, a Tswana tribe of Botswana, an elaborate system of ranking allocates every man to his appropriate place. The Tswana are politically dominant over numbers of people of different tribal origins. The many Tswana tribes of today have each been formed by the splitting off, at different times, of members of an existing royal lineage to establish independent chiefdoms. Each of these seceding members took with him a band of retainers of mixed origin, people who had, or whose ancestors had, at some time or other attached themselves to his service. Later, more outsiders became subjects of Tswana chiefs; sometimes they were conquered, sometimes they offered their allegiance in return for protection. These differences in origin are recognized by the Tswana, who divide the population into categories with names which can be translated 'sons of chiefs', 'servants of chiefs' and 'refugees'. The sons of chiefs are men descended from chiefs, as all true Tswana are supposed to be. They are ranked in order of their place on the genealogical tree. Every chief has a number of sons, only one of whom will succeed him. The descendants of this man's brothers are ranked in order of the original brothers' status, which derives from the ranking of their mothers (since all chiefs were polygynous in the old days). In each generation a new series of such ranks is created. The brothers of any chief (and their descendants) rank above those of this chief's father and their descendants. In important public discussions people speak in order of seniority, and wherever a number of Tswana are together they know who is the senior, and the rest accept his leadership.

Such a system may be described as *hierarchical*; this word implies relationships of authority and obedience, superiority and subordination, while rank in itself simply implies status. Rank and authority commonly go together, but they need not. The Nuer accept the ranking of their society according to age-set membership, but no Nuer would dream of taking orders from another just because this man belonged to a senior age-set. In England no commoner thinks a titled person has a right to tell him what to do, and though dukes, earls, marquises, and barons are placed in their allotted positions in Westminster Abbey when kings are crowned, they do not defer to one another in this order in everyday life. The army, in contrast, *is* a hierarchy; an officer of higher rank can give an order to any officer of lower rank.

Many societies are said to be *stratified*. Some writers mean by this no more than that their members are of unequal status; others have in mind the metaphor that the word suggests, of geological strata or layers in a cake. If one sticks to the metaphor, one calls those societies stratified where all members of one section are held to be superior to all members of another. The threefold division of the Kgatla just mentioned is an example of this kind of stratification.

A simpler and better known one is the division of a society into full citizens and persons whose freedom is limited in certain respects. In writing of the past history of Europe, people have called the full citizens free men and the others slaves or serfs. The technical distinction between a slave and a serf is that the former is actually somebody's property and can be treated like a thing in two important respects: his owner can kill him without being called to account, and he can be sold as an animal might. The serf, though his freedom is restricted, is not actually treated like a chattel. To most people today, the word slavery first brings to mind the plantations of the Americas and the Caribbean, and the humanitarian revolt against conditions there. This was slavery in a large-scale commercial economy.

In small-scale societies the difference between slaves and serfs is in practice rather blurred; perhaps it is worth recalling at this point that the word 'serf' itself is derived from the Latin word for 'slave'. In the simplest societies slaves were war captives, not objects of commerce. In such societies, where there was no state organization to punish murder, and killing was revenged by the slain man's kin, a stranger with no kin to support him could obviously be killed with impunity. But commonly the slave lived as a dependant in his master's household, probably doing some of the heavy work, such as fetching wood and water, which would otherwise have fallen to the women. Eventually he married into his master's family, and his children, or at least their children, were not distinguished in everyday life from the rest of the society. The Nuer of the southern Sudan used to be constantly raiding the cattle of their neighbours the Dinka and capturing people as well, so much so that about a third of their present population are believed to be of Dinka origin. But there is no division of Nuer peoples on the basis of this difference. In some societies persons of slave origin' are debarred from certain rituals, and usually they cannot succeed to political office. In some, the descendants of a slave remain attached to the descendants of the original owner, and in this respect are treated like property.

But here we come to the difficulty of drawing a sharp line between the statuses of slave and serf. In the territory of some Tswana tribes in Botswana there live a people called Sarwa, all of whom are attached to Tswana headmen and are required to work for them as hunters, herdsmen, ploughmen, and domestic servants. Until fairly recently a Sarwa was not allowed to leave his master without permission, but could be given away by his master, and he had no redress if his master wronged him. Sarwa could not take part in the political assemblies which are so strongly marked a feature of Tswana life, nor were they enrolled in the age-sets in which all Tswana youths were organized for fighting and public services. But English writings about them do not call them slaves.

The distinction between slavery and serfdom generally made by writers on European history is that the slave is actually thought of as an item of property while the serf is not. Hence, it is argued, the limitations on the freedom of a serf are not as great as the limitations on the freedom of a slave. These ethnographic examples show that it would not be easy to draw the distinction so clearly in small-scale societies.

The Bantu kingdoms to the north-west of Lake Victoria provide other examples of the division of a society into first and second-class citizens. The lower-grade citizens here have sometimes been called serfs, sometimes a lower caste, possibly sometimes both; this shows how loosely the words describing social stratification are often used. In these kingdoms, populations of cultivators were ruled by pastoral immigrants. In some of them the two populations became merged, but in others the cattle people kept to their distinctive way of life and treated agriculture, and the people who practised it, as beneath them. The cattle people maintained their separateness by refusing to let their women marry men of the agricultural population. In the kingdom of Rwanda such a stratification was maintained up to the time when it became independent of Belgian rule—and then the cultivators rose up and turned the cattle people out.

Caste and class

The most elaborate system of social stratification is that of the Hindus, which is known as *caste* (oddly enough, from a Portugese word meaning 'race'). The Hindu religion is much concerned with the idea of pollution, and the idea of the caste system is that people who live in such a way as to avoid pollution have higher status than those who incur it. Certain substances are conceived as polluting, and people whose occupations require them to handle these are of low caste. Every caste is called by the name of some occupation, though only a minority of the members of any caste follow the occupation after which it is called. Caste membership is hereditary, and people should not marry outside their own caste. According to Hindu theology there are five great divisions running through all society: Brahmins or priests, Kshatriyas or warriors. Vaishyas or traders, and Shudras or servants; and at the bottom of the scale the 'untouchables', people whose very touch, or even their shadow, is held to be polluting to members of higher castes. This division of society theoretically holds good throughout India. But in practice there are innumerable sub-divisions of these castes, which are ranked in different order in different localities. The cultural expression of the caste hierarchy, however, is everywhere the same, namely that members of a higher caste (or sub-caste) show their superiority by refusing to accept food from members of lower castes. Each caste has its own street in a village. In a small local community there is typically one dominant caste, the members of which own the land. Members of other castes either work for them as labourers, or perform for the whole community services, such as barbering or sweeping the streets, which are thought to involve pollution; in return they are rewarded at harvest time with a share of the produce of the land.

The word 'class' rises as readily to the lips of most of us as the word 'group'. But it too has to be approached with caution if it is to be used as a technical term. Sociologists have pre-empted it to describe certain kinds of division which are characteristic of industrial societies rather than of those most often studied by social anthropologists. Everyone has heard of Karl Marx's theory of class conflict, whether or not he knows what it is. To Marx society was divided into classes defined by their relationship to the means of production; in the simplest possible terms, one class owns the means of production—land, machines, whatever these may be—and the others are exploited by it. The relation in an Indian village between the dominant caste, owning the land, and the rest who work for a share of the rice grown on it would be a typical class division in Marxist terms. Marx identified a division of society into exploiters and exploited at every historical period. But modern sociologists prefer to use other words for the divisions of pre-industrial societies. In complex industrial societies they identify as different classes people pursuing occupations associated with a way of life that distinguishes them from those who follow other types of occupation. Thus we speak of professional classes, labouring classes, and so on. The essential difference betwen a class in the technical sense and other divisions of a stratified society is that divisions into classes are based on occupation and income; where, as in the stratified societies of East Africa—or of the Republic of South Africa or the State of Alabama—they are based on 'race' (that is supposed descent), it is better to use other words. Of course special occupations are assigned in practice to the members of different social strata in these societies too. But whereas in systems of these latter kinds status determines occupation (at least in theory), in a class system occupation determines status, and in such a system there is more room for individuals to achieve a higher status than that of their parents.

Dual divisions

Some societies are divided into two complementary halves. The name given to these divisions is *moieties*, which simply means 'halves', like the French word *moitié*; it is an old-fashioned English word. As the word was first used by anthropologists, it meant a division based on *descent*,[2] or clan and lineage membership. Some North American and some Australian tribes are divided into *exogamous* moieties; that is, every member of the tribe belongs by birth to one of two halves and must marry a member of the other. But moiety divisions are not always exogamous, and even when they are, their principal significance is commonly in the field of religion rather than in marriage relationships. The two divisions co-operate in important rituals, each having its appropriate task and both being indispensable to the success of the ceremony. The Aborigines of the Australian desert perform elaborate rites to ensure the fertility of the animal species they depend on for food. The group associated with a particular animal dance in a manner that is supposed to resemble it, and for the dances they are decked in birds' down, coloured with red ochre and stuck to their bodies with blood. The preparation of the down and of the ritual objects they use is the task of the opposite moiety to that of the dancers; it is they who have to provide the blood from their arms. They must also make the paintings on the ground with blood and coloured down where the ritual requires this.

A number of peoples of Eastern Africa are organized in moieties of a different type. These are based on the principle of *alternation,* expressed in various ways. Among the Turkana of northern Kenya, every man belongs to the opposite moiety from that of his father, but this arrangement does not oppose *all* the men of one generation *to all*

[2] See pp. 71–80.

those of the next. Both moieties are represented in every generation, and every ceremony of initiation creates two new age-sets, one of each moiety. The names of the moieties are Stones and Leopards. Every son of a Stone must be a Leopard, and *vice versa*. When the young men went out to raid cattle—as they did in the old days and may do again— each moiety formed one column, and they approached their objective from two sides. At feasts the meat is divided into shares, one for each moiety, and members of one serve it to the members of the other; they sit apart to eat.

The Arusha, who live high up on Mount Meru in Tanganyika, recognize both an alternating system—this time a division by age—and a twofold division of descent groups. As is characteristic of organizations based on age, the adult men are divided into 'warriors' and 'elders'. But each of these grades has a junior and a senior division, so that men pass through four recognized stages. In this process each group is in competition with that immediately senior and in alliance with the next senior. The members of each group are the formally recognized 'patrons' of that next but one below it, helping its individual members with advice and, most importantly, pressing at the appropriate time for its formal promotion to a higher grade. There is a sense of solidarity, reaching back into the past, among all the members of the series of groups linked by this principle of alternation. Each 'stream', as P. H. Gulliver calls them,[3] claims superior qualities for its members and denigrates those in the other stream; and each claims credit, for unexplained reasons, for fortunate events in past history. Yet their rivalry is friendly; it does not break up the society in conflict, but helps to keep it going. It is a good example of what Radcliffe-Brown called integration through opposition;[4] indeed in some of its aspects it recalls the friendly rivalry of Oxford and Cambridge, which he himself cited as an example.

But Arusha society is also divided into moieties of a different kind. Every man is born into one of two divisions of the whole tribe, but each of these is further divided into

[3] *Social Control in an African Society*, 1963, p. 31.
[4] See p. 50.

two, and so are these again. The significance of these divisions is that, when some quarrel about rights arises, each of the disputants has the right to call on members of his own division to help him pursue his claim. The importance of arrangements of this kind, in societies which do not have magistrates and policemen to enforce the law, as a means of ensuring respect for accepted rules is discussed in Chapter 7.

Among the Ibo in the east of Nigeria the most important duty of the age-grade of young active men is not fighting but communal labour. In one section of the Ibo, age-sets as they were formed were traditionally assigned alternately to each of two moieties. As they were formed at frequent intervals, the 'men's' grade, as it was called in opposition to that of 'elders', contained about a dozen sets altogether. When some public work had to be done—for example the clearing of a road—portions would be allotted to the two moieties, who were expected to compete in speed and efficiency. Each moiety was responsible for the renewal of one of the two earth pyramids at the entrance to the village where its members lived. This work, which involved ritual feasting, was done by each of them in alternate years. In the elders' grade responsibility for the control of the main economic resources was divided between the moieties, one taking charge of oil palms and one of raffia palms.

Associations

Finally, people may be grouped in *associations,* or organizations for special purposes. Such associations are very numerous in western societies. People who follow the same profession, or have the same political views, or like one particular kind of recreation, or want to promote some particular aim such as the abolition of capital punishment, organize themselves in groups to co-operate in promoting their common interests. These are called *single-purpose* associations.

In societies of simple technology, people for the most part pursue their interests by appealing to the obligations of kinship and affinity, or sometimes of political allegiance, and these obligations are usually of a general nature, of co-operation or protection in whatever circumstances call for it. But sometimes people join associations the membership of which is based on neither of these principles. Usually these are *cult* associations; that is to say, their members join in rituals addressed to a particular divinity. Often they have in common certain esoteric knowledge, which is revealed to them when they enter and which they must not reveal to outsiders. This is why they are often called 'secret societies', but this should not be taken to imply that people seek to conceal the fact that they are members. Sometimes these associations have considerable political importance, as in the Yoruba chiefdoms of Nigeria, where they can veto the appointment of a chief. Sometimes membership of such a society gives people the right to call themselves by special titles. This right is earned by providing a feast for those who have already attained to the title sought. As only a wealthy man can afford to give a succession of feasts, the titles are won by persons who are already influential in the community in virtue of their superior wealth. In so far as the beings towards whom these cults are directed are thought to influence particular departments of life, they may be called single-purpose societies.

In societies where there is some development of economic specialization, people who practise the same craft may form an association; these associations too are often bound up with the cult of a tutelary divinity (a 'patron saint'), and they too are characteristic of parts of West Africa.

Where small-scale societies participate in a money economy, a type of association often found is the credit organization or contribution club, the aim of which is to help people to save money to meet specially heavy claims on their resources. The principle of these associations is that members pay the same subscription at regular intervals and each in turn takes out the whole of the fund collected in this way. For the people whose turn comes soon after the foundation of the society, this is a way of getting credit; of course they go on paying their contributions till they have paid it back (unless they default), but they do not pay interest. This kind of association can be found in a remarkably large number of countries. In China, with its long tradition of sophistication in the handling of monedy, the proceedings of such associations were sometimes enlivened by a rule that members could bid for the right to be the first to collect.

The total collection of people with whom any individual has social relations, ascribed or chosen, has recently begun to be called his *network*.

SUGGESTIONS FOR READING

Interesting descriptions of initiation rites for boys are R. W. Firth, *We, The Tikopia* (1936), Chapter XIII; E. E. Evans-Pritchard, *The Nuer* (1940), Chapter VI; J. G. Peristiany, 'The Age-Set System of the Pastoral Pokot', *Africa*, 1951; H. E. Lambert, *Kikuyu Social and Political Organization* (1956); and for girls A. I. Richards, *Chisungu* (1956). A general discussion of organization by age is S. N. Eisenstadt, *From Generation to Generation* (1956). Other references are given in connection with the political significance of age organization (Chapter 7).

B. Barber, *Social Stratification* (1957), interprets the term to mean any kind of inequality and discusses the subject accordingly. The most detailed study of a stratified society in Africa is J. J. Maquet, *The Premise of Inequality in Ruanda* (1961), but later writers have questioned whether the system there was as rigid as he believes. L. G. Fallers, *Inequality* (1974), and P. C. Lloyd, *Power and Independence* (1974), both reject the notion of stratification. A good recent book on the subject of caste is A. C. Mayer, *Caste and Kinship in Central India* (1960). The best description of moieties in operation is P. H. Gulliver, *Social Control in an African Society* (1963).

Cult associations are described in D. Forde, *Yakö Studies* (1964), P. Morton-Williams, 'The Yoruba Ogboni Cult in Oyo', *Africa*, 1960, and S. F. Nadel, *Nupe Religion* (1954). Craft associations in Northern Nigeria are well described in the last-named author's *A Black Byzantium* (1942), also about the Nupe. An interesting description of a Chinese contribution club is M. Freedman, 'The Handling of Money', in T. H. Silcock (ed.), *Readings in Malayan Economics* (1961). A literature on networks is beginning to appear. The concept was first developed by J. A. Barnes in 'Class and Community in a Norwegian island parish', *Human Relations* (1954) and E. Bott, *Family and Social Network* (1957). It is discussed in a collection of essays edited by J. C. Mitchell, *Social Networks in Urban Situations* (1969) and by P. H. Gulliver in *Neighbours and Networks* (1971).

CHAPTER 5

Kinship and Descent

IN societies of simple technology most statuses are *ascribed*.[1] This is another way of saying that a person's place in society, his rights and duties, his claim to property, largely depend on his genealogical relationships to other members. The primary social groups—the ones to be found in all such societies whatever other principles of organization there may be—are all linked by *kinship*, and in many cases their membership is fixed by *descent*. The terms 'kinship' and 'descent' are not identical, and they are not always distinguished clearly enough. People are in one sense kin if they have what is popularly called 'common blood'—that is to say, if they have an ancestor in common. In this sense of course nobody knows all his kin; in a highly mobile society such as ours, it may not even be possible to discover the 'next of kin' of somebody who has no close relatives. The phrase 'next of kin' has interesting implications for the social anthropologist. It is *not* the biological calculation of the proportion of 'common blood'—actually genes—that measures nearness of kin; it is the law of any given society.[2] As Rivers put it, kinship is *the social recognition of biological ties*. Some later writers have gone further—in my opinion too far—and said that kinship has nothing to do with biology. It is, of course, possible to pretend that biological ties exist where in fact they do not, as when a child is adopted. One could perhaps adapt Rivers' definition to say that kinship is the expression of social relationships in a biological idiom. But a society in which the great majority of persons who treated one another as close kin were not biologically related would be a very strange one.

The ties of kinship which are recognized in different

---

[1] See p. 11.

[2] In some countries (of which Britain is one) a married person's 'next of kin' is his spouse. But as anthropologists use the word, at any rate when trying to be precise, spouses are not kin at all but affines.

societies give people claims to land for cultivation, to other kinds of property, to mutual assistance in the pursuit of common interests, to authority over others; and obligations which complement these claims, on those in authority to regard the welfare of those subject to them, on these to obey, on all to co-operate on occasions where the recognition of kinship requires it.

Nobody recognizes kinship with all the people to whom he is linked by common descent. To some extent this is a matter of the passage of time; in all societies, as the common ancestor recedes into the past, he comes to be forgotten and his descendants no longer think of themselves as kin. But there are also differences in the directions along which the members of different societies consider it appropriate to trace their kin, and in the arrangements of people that result.

These may be looked at in two ways. One is to put yourself in the place of an individual, and ask whom he regards as kin and how he arranges his different kinsmen into categories. The other is to stand outside the society you are looking at and see if you can identify corporate groups organized on some principle of kinship.

The first of these methods is the older. It dates back to the time when the American anthropologist, Morgan,[3] discovered the 'classificatory system' of describing kinsmen, in which the terms that we translate 'father', 'mother', 'brother', 'sister', are used of many people outside the speaker's immediate family. The question that interested him was: why do people in the simpler societies arrange their kin in categories so different from those that are used in the industrial societies? The first answers that were given to this question turned out to be wrong, and from Morgan's time until the day before yesterday social anthropologists have been asking what these 'classificatory terminologies' mean. Consequently, quite modern books on kinship introduce the subject by a discussion of this question. The beginner reading such a book is advised to skip this section, and come back to it when he has mastered the part con-

[3] See pp. 21–2.

cerned with the division of society into groups based on kinship.

A little thought will make it obvious that the body of kin who are recognized by one man will be different from those recognized by any other, except his own full brothers and sisters. Hence the *kindred,* as such a body of persons are called, cannot form a continuing element in the structure of society. It is simply the total of the people who are genealogically linked to the man one happens to be thinking about. Its members may, however, have common obligations towards the person to whom they are all linked. In some societies it is the duty of a man's *kindred* to avenge his murder. This used to be the rule among the Anglo-Saxons, and it is, or it was recently, the rule among the Ifugao in the Philippines. A rule of this kind may specify how far—to how many cousins—the obligation extends. But in practice it is unlikely that all of these will turn out on every occasion. Who actually fulfils the obligation will depend on who is within reach; this is true of the collective duties of kin groups of all kinds.

All the people who are related by 'blood' in any way to an individual are his *cognates.* Those who are related to him by marriage are his *affines.* The list at the end of the English Prayer Book of people whom one must not marry is headed 'A Table of Kindred and Affinity'. Of course these two sorts of relationship originate in quite different ways. Affines— married people and their in-laws—may have been kin before the marriage, but very often this is not so. But they often come to be thought of and treated as kin. Hence people sometimes speak of 'affinal kin', though this is not strictly accurate.

Corporate groups—that is continuing property-holding groups—based on kinship are *recruited by descent,* and a clear principle of descent is established by the rule that it is traceable in one line only—either through the males or through females. This is called the principle of *unilineal descent.* Where descent is traced through males only it is called *patrilineal,* or *agnatic*; the latter comes from the word used by the Romans. The Romans did not have a neat word to describe descent through females, in which they were not particularly interested—so we can only call this *matrilineal*; it is also possible, however, to use another word of Latin derivation and speak of *uterine* kin, or those related through females only.

A corporate group recruited by descent is called a *lineage*. If descent is patrilineal, then the child of a legal marriage belongs to his father's lineage. Through his father he has a claim on the productive resources of the lineage, whether these consist in land for cultivation, cattle, a fishing boat, or even possibly a trading business; he can draw on these not only for his own subsistence, but for special needs, such as the payment required to make his marriage legal, or the payment of compensation for a wrong done by him to a member of another lineage. His rank, as a noble or a commoner, will be fixed by his lineage membership; it may entitle him to become a king, a chief, or a priest. It is his duty to obey the senior man of his lineage in such matters as the allocation of lineage resources and to look to him for the settlement of disputes that may arise between lineage mates; and it is the duty of this senior man to further the welfare of his lineage, both in secular matters and by performing the rituals which are held to keep them in the right relationship with supernatural forces. A man ought to stand by his lineage mates in any conflict with outsiders; and particularly to help them in seeking compensation for offences, or revenge if one of them is killed.

In a matrilineal society every person belongs to the lineage of his mother; the question whether her marriage was contracted in due form does not affect his membership, though it may be important in other contexts. In some matrilineal societies, such as the Ashanti of Ghana, women are treated with very great respect, but lineage authority nevertheless always rests with men. Consequently lineage authority rests not with one's father, but one's mother's eldest brother.

Examples of societies with patrilineal descent are the classical Romans, the Chinese, and the cattle-owning peoples of eastern and southern Africa. Examples of societies with matrilineal descent are a large number of American Indian and Australian peoples, many indigenous peoples of Indonesia and Malaysia, the Bantu peoples of central Africa, and the Akan peoples of Ghana.

Sometimes one finds a society where most lineage members live close together, so that lineage and local grouping are largely identical. But it is very common to find in one village or neighbourhood a mixture of people, some of whom have come to live there because of other kin ties with members of the 'owning' lineage. In the co-operation of daily life—when extra labour is needed at harvest time, or to build a house— people look to the whole body of their neighbours and not only to their lineage mates. This kind of co-operation is based on the principle of reciprocity, that every service deserves a return, and he who helps his neighbour can expect the neighbour to help him. It is not an obligation inherent in the relation of kinship.

This is at the bottom of the traditional phrase 'kith and kin'. 'Kith' means 'known', and therefore 'neighbours'; and the different nature of relationships with kith and with kin is aptly (though I feel pretty sure not deliberately) summarized in the clerihew:

> Adam Smith
> Was disowned by all his kith;
> But he was supported through thick and thin
> By all his kin.

Through whichever parent a person traces his descent, he recognizes mutual rights and obligations with the kin of the other. Thus we speak of the importance of *matrilateral* kin in a patrilineal society and of *patrilateral* kin in a matrilineal society. 'Lateral' means 'on the side'; 'lineal' means 'in a line'. If you belong to a patrilineal society, your mother's kin are not, and cannot be, 'matrilineal' kin; they are the members of a different *agnatic lineage* from your own. They are your mother's agnatic kin, and your own kin *on the mother's side*. The relationship of a person with his kin through the parent from whom he does not trace descent is called *complementary filiation*.

A few societies trace descent in the male line for some purposes and the female for others. This is called *double unilineal descent*. Usually the distinction is that people inherit fixed property in the male and movable property in the female line. For the Yakö of the Cross River in the east of Nigeria matrilineal descent has an additional significance. Land is the property of the patrilineages, and so it is agnates who are grouped together in the different wards of a Yakö village. Livestock and currency, tools, weapons, and household goods are inherited in the female line, and it is the matrilineal kin group which is held responsible for the debts of its members. Because it is movable property that has to be distributed when somebody dies, funeral rituals are performed by matrilineal kin. In addition, a number of positions are inherited in the female line. These include membership of some of the associations, each devoted to the cult of a different spirit, which are responsible for the maintenance of order. Also, the priests of the ten village fertility spirits are drawn from matrilineal descent groups. When each of these approaches his spirit on behalf of his own matrilineal group, he draws together people from all the different wards in which agnatic kinsmen are living on their own land; and once a year, at harvest time, all the ten join in a ritual performed for the welfare of the whole village. In this way the recognition of matrilineal descent creates ties among people whom patrilineal descent divides.

The recognition of the importance of unilineal descent as a principle of social structure has been one of the most fruitful ideas in the social anthropology of the last twenty years, and many interesting studies have been made of societies organized on this principle. But students should not suppose that it is characteristic of all simple societies. There are a large number in which descent is not traced unilineally.

Anthropologists are not entirely unanimous about the application of the terms *descent* and *descent group*. The distinction between *descent* and *filiation* has been stressed by Fortes. According to him the relation of a person with his own parents is filiation, and only his relation with his ancestors should be called descent; as in dictionary usage, one's nearest ancestor is a grandparent.[4] Further, and

---

[4] 'The Structure of Unilineal Descent Groups', *American Anthropologist*, 1953, pp. 17–41.

this point is also made by Leach, it is meaningless to talk of descent unless you are talking of a relationship that follows the consistent direction which we picture as a line, and a line must be traced through parents of one sex only; if people trace their ancestry by quoting a father in one generation and a mother in another, there is no such line.[5] Rivers made this point a long time ago. In his *Social Organization*, first published in 1924, he remarked that 'the use of the term [descent] has little sense and consequently little value in the case of the bilateral grouping'. By the latter he meant what today we call a non-unilineal (and therefore non-corporate) kin group. In non-unilineal systems, where people can choose which parent's side they will belong to, there are no distinct groups maintaining their distinctness through time. There is nothing impossible or inconvenient in such a situation; many societies are organized that way. But, said Rivers and now say the Cambridge anthropologists, only a distinct group, recruiting its members by birth on a recognized principle, can accurately be called a descent group; and the only principle that can be recognized is the unilineal principle.

The significance of a continuing group is that it holds and transmits property; and the significance of a descent group is that a member's claim on the property does not depend on where he lives, as long as he does not go, and stay, so far away that people forget him and he cannot prove his membership. In practice there are great differences in the extent to which lineage members live together, though nearly everywhere the ideal is that they should. The members of a lineage who actually do live in close, everyday contact, have been called by Leach the *local descent group*.[6]

Everyone agrees that a lineage is a descent group. But opinions differ about other groups which in Fortes' terms would be said to be recruited by filiation—that is, through the relation of a child to either of its own parents at choice. Such a group is that called the *bilek* family among the Iban

[5] Not all anthropologists are willing to accept this restriction on the use of an everyday word.

[6] 'The Structural Implications of Matrilateral Cross-Cousin Marriage', *Journal of the Royal Anthropological Institute*, 1951, p. 24.

of Borneo.[7] These people live in 'long-houses', as they are called, each one a series of adjacent rooms built on a platform by the side of one of the rivers that are the main means of communication. *Bilek* actually means one of these rooms, as well as the group living in it. The property-owning group consists of the residents of one *bilek*. They own the rice-fields that were first cleared by members of that *bilek*, fruit trees planted by earlier members, a canoe, tools, and valuables. In each generation one of the children born in the *bilek must* live there all its life, but there is no rule to say which; this rule gives the group its continuity by descent, if the word is to be used, as it is used by Freeman, the anthropologist who described these people. Subject to this limitation, every man when he marries can choose between his own and his wife's *bilek* (i.e. that of her parents); and no doubt the wife has some say in the decision. When the choice is made, the partner moving out of his or her *bilek* loses all inheritance rights there. These groups, then, are recruited strictly by filiation; an adult can choose between two groups but cannot be a member of more than one; and some would call them descent groups, though the Cambridge anthropologists would not.

Then there is the *hapu* of the Maori in New Zealand,[8] a local community of several hundred people with its own leader, sufficiently distinct from other *hapu* to be sometimes engaged in war against them. A person may join it if either of his parents is a member. But, like the *bilek* member, if he was not born into the group he can only join it by coming to live in it. Every member of a *hapu*, then, has entered it, if not by birth, by virtue of some kinship tie; and in practice all members are related to one another by some link of kinship or affinity. But does this make them a descent group? Firth would call them a 'bilateral' or 'ambilateral' descent group.

Fortes remarks[9] that they are not clearly demarcated by

[7] J. D. Freeman, 'The Family System of the Iban of Borneo', in J. Goody (ed.), *The Developmental Cycle in Domestic Groups*, 1958.
[8] R. W. Firth, 'A Note on Descent Groups in Polynesia', *Man*, 1957, pp. 4–7.
[9] 'Descent, Filiation and Affinity', in *Time and Social Structure*, 1970, pp. 117–21.

descent as a lineage is; no principle of descent *divides* one group from another. What divides them is the place where they have chosen to live, and the obligations that their choice has involved them in of obeying a chief and joining in wars against other *hapu*. These, Fortes argues, are political and territorial, not descent, boundaries; joining a *hapu* is like becoming the citizen of a country, also a status which can be *ascribed* by birth or *achieved* by choice. Kinship, he says, may give a claim to be admitted to membership of groups of many kinds; but in his view this does not make them into descent groups.

In societies where patrilineal descent is the most important structural principle, the unity of the lineage is usually a deeply cherished ideal. People remember their lineal ancestry for several generations, sometimes as many as fourteen, as do the Tallensi of northern Ghana,[10] though more commonly about five beyond the oldest living generation. They do not recognize that there must have been many more ancestors whose names are forgotten, or give up attempting to trace the line further back. What they do is to link up the last remembered ancestor with one of the mythical persons from whom the whole people think they are descended. Usually the first ancestor, who in the myth either appeared from nowhere or led his people to the land they now occupy, is supposed to have had a number of sons, each of whom became the progenitor of a section of the society. These major divisions of society are called *clans*, and in most societies their number remains fixed. But at the other end of the line, where living men are going about their daily business, lineages are constantly dividing. It has been said that every man is the potential founder of a lineage. The smallest lineage that can exist consists of one man with his children. Sons are expected to respect their father's authority, to live near him, and to accept his decision on the allocation of their joint resources; and only the father has the right to approach the ancestors in ritual to secure the welfare of the group. In such societies no man whose father is alive can have in his homestead a shrine of the ancestor spirits. Such a small lineage, with the members' spouses, is

[10] See M. Fortes, *The Dynamics of Clanship among the Tallensi*, 1945.

called in older ethnographic writings an *extended family*. A *joint family* is a small lineage who actually have a common dwelling and pool their labour and its proceeds. The word was introduced into anthropology from Maine's writings on India.

When a father dies his eldest son succeeds him in the custody of the ancestral shrine, but this man does not exercise authority over his brothers in the economic matters of every day. The brothers, particularly if they are the children of one mother, may go on pooling their resources for a time, but gradually they will establish their autonomy in secular matters; each will become the head of a new lineage consisting of himself and his sons. This is the process of *lineage fission*. Usually lineage members go on co-operating in ritual matters after they have established autonomy in everyday affairs; people sometimes express their common lineage membership by saying, 'We go to one another's funerals.' Thus lineages of lesser *depth* are included for some purposes in lineages of greater depth.

In some societies the whole population can theoretically be placed on a genealogical tree. Although new lineages are always coming into being, their line of descent is still traced back to the founder, who is sometimes called the *apical* ancestor (i.e. the one at the peak). Actually, immigrants may join the society, but they are fitted into the scheme, and given an appropriate place in the genealogy, by some sort of adoption.

Lineage systems of this kind are called *segmentary*, and the process which has just been called fission can also be called *segmentation*. Durkheim used the word 'segment' to describe the rings of the earthworm, all alike. Radcliffe-Brown and others have used it to mean any division of society. But it is more useful to keep the word for this kind of society, in which all the divisions are similar in structure, like the pieces of an orange or slices of a round cake (to vary Durkheim's metaphor). Characteristically these are societies in which there is no other source of authority than that of the lineage heads. The classical descriptions of such societies are those by Evans-Pritchard of the Nuer in the southern Sudan[11] and by Fortes of the Tallensi.[12]

But it is possible for people to recognize unilineal descent even though they do not trace their ancestry so carefully. In such cases one still speaks of lineages, though not of a segmentary lineage system. If people increase in numbers and spread out over a wide area, lineage members lose touch with one another and exact relationships are forgotten. But the common apical ancestor is remembered, and so we find large populations divided into *clans*, the members of which know they must have a common ancestor somewhere but do not think it is important who this was. A clan may include a large number of people. Among the Ashanti of Ghana, with a population of about half a million, there are eight matrilineal clans. Among the Ganda of East Africa with a population of perhaps a million there are thirty or forty patrilineal clans. Members of the same clan are distinguished by the common clan name, and often by the observance of certain ritual prohibitions, sometimes called 'avoidances', connected with particular objects. Sometimes the name of the clan is the name of the object which its members must avoid, or, as others put it, respect.[13] If the clan is called after an animal, its members will not eat the flesh of that animal. But the object of respect or avoidance may be rain, or it may be some material substance such as rope. What is significant is that all members of the clan behave in a special way towards the object, whatever it is, that is their emblem. These emblematic objects are called *totems*, particularly in older writings. The other rule which binds all members of a clan—not everywhere, but nearly so —is that they may not marry one another; this is the rule of *exogamy* (literally 'marrying outside').

When one thinks of a lineage as a corporate group, a body of people with a common patrimony and a common ritual focus in the shrine of the ancestors, one is in fact thinking of the adult male members. Children are not full citizens in any society, and in societies of simple technology women are not either, in the sense that all her life a woman is sub-

[11] *The Nuer*, 1940.
[12] *The Dynamics of Clanship among the Tallensi*, 1945.
[13] See E. E. Evans-Pritchard, *Nuer Religion*, 1956, pp. 64 ff.

ject to a male guardian, kinsman or husband. Both in patrilineal and in matrilineal societies, the joint interests of
brothers are at the centre of lineage organization. If the
system is patrilineal, they transmit these interests to their
sons, and the lineage is seen on the ground as a number of
brothers with their adult sons. Some lineage members may
have chosen to live elsewhere and take no active part in
lineage affairs; this is why Leach considers it important to
distinguish between the lineage as such and the *local descent group*; it is the latter that, in practice, pursues common interests and exercises joint rights.

In a matrilineal system the brothers transmit their rights
to their sisters' sons. It is possible for a body of uncles and
nephews to form a local descent group, but it is not so
easy to maintain rules of residence that will keep several
generations of uncles and nephews together, and this may
be why one does not often find matrilineal societies with a
segmentary system placing the whole population on one
genealogical tree.

It is possible for people to recognize unilineal descent
but not be organized in lineages. Some peoples of Central
Africa, such as the Plateau Tonga of Zambia, inherit clan
membership matrilineally but do not attach importance,
within the body of fellow-clansmen who are their neighbours, to distinctions between those who are genealogically
closer or more distant. In such societies, there exist between
clans reciprocal obligations such as would be more characteristic elsewhere of relations between lineages. Pairs of
clans are linked in a relationship which has been called
'funeral friendship'; when a member of one clan dies, members of the other who are close at hand must come and bury
him, since they are not in danger of that pollution of death
which threatens the lineal kin of a dead man. These people
are performing a service which in some patrilineal societies
is rendered by a sister's son as the nearest kinsman outside
the lineage.

SUGGESTIONS FOR READING

The article 'Kinship' in the London, 1955, edition of the *Encyclopaedia Britannica* is a good succinct introduction to the subject.

M. Fortes, *Kinship and the Social Order* (1970), is an exposition, not always easy, of the development of kinship theory from Morgan through Rivers and Radcliffe-Brown to the views held by most British anthropologists today; it is worth the trouble, as the old-fashioned guide-books used to say. An interesting introductory book is Robin Fox, *Kinship and Marriage* (1967).

The nature of corporate kin groups is discussed by Radcliffe-Brown in his introduction to A. R. Radcliffe-Brown and D. Forde (eds.), *African Systems of Kinship and Marriage* (1950). M. Fortes has expounded the main principles of the theory of unilineal descent, as it was developed by himself and Evans-Pritchard, in 'The Structure of Unilineal Descent Groups'. A comment by Leach on this paper led Fortes to elaborate his theory further in 'Descent, Filiation and Affinity'. Both these papers are reprinted in Fortes, *Time and Social Structure* (1970).

The various meanings which anthropologists have given to the word 'descent' are discussed by M. Freedman in the entry for that word in J. Gould and W. L. Kolb, *A Dictionary of the Social Sciences*, (1964). Certain ambiguities in the use of the word 'kindred' are discussed by J. D. Freeman in 'The Concept of the Kindred', *Journal of the Royal Anthropological Institute*, 1961.

The best-known studies of segmentary lineage systems are E. E. Evans-Pritchard, *The Nuer* (1940), and M. Fortes, *The Dynamics of Clanship among the Tallensi* (1945). L. Bohannan, 'Political Aspects of Tiv Social Organization', in J. Middleton and D. Tait (eds.), *Tribes Without Rulers* (1958), is a shorter account of such a system. In 'A Genealogical Charter', *Africa*, 1952, the same author shows how people revise their genealogical records to make them fit actual situations.

The great majority of the monographs published by social anthropologists since 1940 have been concerned with societies organized on the lineage principle, so much so that students sometimes get the impression that all societies are so organized. It would be vain to attempt to list here all the useful accounts of unilineal societies, but one might mention M. Freedman, *Lineage Organization in South Eastern China* (1958) and *Chinese Lineage and Society* (1966), studies in a field that is relatively new to social anthropologists. Probably the best-known double unilineal system is that described by D. Forde in *Yakö Studies* (1964). S. F. Nadel, 'Dual Descent in the Nuba Hills', in *African Systems of Kinship and Marriage*, is an account of two small peoples in the western Sudan. J. R. Goody, *The Social Organization of the LoWiili* (1956) and 'The Mother's Brother and the Sister's Son in West Africa', *Journal of the Royal Anthropological Institute*, 1959, are concerned with peoples of northern Ghana.

The Iban *bilek* family is discussed in the essay by J. D. Freeman, 'The Family System of the Iban of Borneo', in J. R. Goody (ed.), *The Developmental Cycle in Domestic Groups* (1958). A neighbouring people are described by H. S. Morris, *Report on a Melanau Sago Producing Community in Sarawak* (1953). L. Lancaster, 'Kinship in Anglo-Saxon Society', *British Journal of Sociology*, 1958, answers an anthropologist's questions from the literature that we have on the subject. W. Goodenough, 'A Problem in Malayo-Polynesian Social Organization', *American Anthropologist*, 1955, seeks to classify non-unilineal systems in types.

The pairing of clans in 'funeral friendship' is discussed by E. Colson, *The Plateau Tonga of Northern Rhodesia* (1962), and J. R. Goody, *The Social Organization of the LoWiili* (1956).

The study by anthropological techniques of kinship in western industrial society is the theme of R. W. Firth (ed.), *Two Studies of Kinship in London* (1956), R. W. Firth, *Family and Kinship in Industrial Society* (1964), R. W. Firth, J. Hubert, and A. Forge, *Families and Their Relatives* (1970), and E. Bott, *Family and Social Network* (1957).

CHAPTER 6 # Sex, Marriage, and Family

EVERY human society has rules covering sex relations and the procreation of children, but these are by no means everywhere the same, just as the rules which place a child in a particular descent group differ from one society to another.

It is characteristic of patrilineal societies that women are expected to be virgins at marriage, though this is not always taken so seriously that a man would repudiate his bride because she was found to have lost her virginity. Many African societies regard sex relations before marriage as legitimate but expect them to stop short of complete intercourse; the reason is that what people in these societies really feel strongly about is the procreation of children without the social authorization that is given by marriage. Sex relations themselves, however, must have social authorization, and this is often conferred by a ceremony of initiation which marks the entry upon adult life. Some societies hold such ceremonies for both sexes. In patrilineal societies they are sometimes held only for boys; in matrilineal societies they are usually held only for girls, and the initiation and marriage ceremonies are often combined. These ceremonies, besides formally marking the passage from childhood to adulthood, usually invoke the blessing of spiritual beings on the sex activities of the persons concerned. So it is not surprising that among the Kipsigis of Kenya the offence of making an uninitiated girl pregnant is one of the most heinous that can be committed, and that in the old days the child had to be born in the bush and put to death at once, so that it could be counted as never having lived.

Incest and exogamy

In addition to the rules which, like those of western society fixing the age of consent, are intended to debar immature persons from sexual activity, there are rules which prohibit certain persons as sexual partners and as marriage partners. These are the rules of *incest* and *exogamy*, and they do not always coincide. Incest refers to sexual congress as such; exogamy to marriage, a relationship which cannot be created merely by sexual congress, and includes, in addition to sexual congress, a number of reciprocal rights and duties.

The relationships within which sexual congress is everywhere considered incestuous are those of parent to child and of brother to sister. In western culture incest is thought of as something particularly dreadful, not to be mentioned without a shudder, if at all. We have all heard of Oedipus, who was so appalled when he learned that he had unknowingly married his mother that he put out his eyes. The Elizabethan dramatists liked to ascribe incestuous relations to particularly villainous characters, and later centuries thought that plays with such themes should not be put on the stage. Byron had to leave England when it was said that he was the lover of his half-sister, and this was the source of the Satanic reputation that he rather enjoyed. In some African societies incest is thought of as typical of witches.

Theories about incest are of two kinds. One asks why it is regarded with such horror; one asks why there is a rule against it in every known society. The first question is what philosophers would call a pseudo-problem, because it is not true that the same kinds of illicit sexual congress are everywhere regarded with horror. Incest is often held to be a sin, that is to call down supernatural punishment without the need of any human agent to punish the offenders. But the persons between whom sexual relations are sinful by this definition are different in different societies. They may include people not very closely related biologically, while others as close as first cousin may not only be permitted as mates, but may be regarded as the most appropriate ones. This last point is enough to show that there is no such 'instinctive recognition' that the mating of close kin is biologically undesirable as used once to be supposed.

Westermarck[1] argued that people who grew up together (thinking primarily of brothers and sisters) were so used to one another that by the time they were adult the idea of sexual desire did not occur to them; but this did not account for the strength of the sanctions against incest, nor for the horror felt, where horror *is* felt. Freud accounted for the horror as a built-in mechanism to repress a strongly felt desire (thinking primarily of sons and mothers). A recent writer, considering brothers and sisters only, has suggested that there may be some correlation between the degree of horror felt towards *this* kind of incest and the attitudes in different societies towards intimate play between brothers and sisters while they are growing up.[2]

However, what is more interesting to the student of society is the second question: why sexual congress between persons in certain genealogical relationships is always prohibited, often considered sinful, and often regarded with horror. Within the nuclear family of parents and their own children it is everywhere forbidden.[3] The explanation offered by Malinowski is the one generally accepted by anthropologists. The family is the institution within which the cultural tradition of a society is handed on to the new generation (by the process which in technical jargon is called 'socialization'). This indispensable function could not be fulfilled unless the relations of parents and children were relations reciprocally of authority and respect. Such relations could not be maintained if sexual passions were given free play within the family circle.[4] Certainly such an explanation cannot explain *why* the prohibition of incest came into being, but it is possible to conjecture, with Murdock, that if there were ever human populations which allowed it they must have been in such a condition of disorder that they could not survive in competition with better organized groups.

[1] *History of Human Marriage*, 5th edn., 1921, Vol. ii, Chapter XIX.
[2] J. R. Fox, 'Sibling Incest', *British Journal of Sociology*, 1962, pp. 128–50.
[3] In some societies persons of high rank, such as the Egyptian Pharaohs, are exempt from this rule, but there is none where the rule does not exist.
[4] *Sex and Repression in Savage Society*, 1924.

Malinowski held that the incest prohibition marked the transition from 'nature'—the life of other animals, who have no cultural heritage to transmit and increase with the generations—to 'culture', the mode of life peculiar to man. Lévi-Strauss takès the same view. For him the prohibition of *marriage*—not simply of sexual congress—within the family is the essential criterion of cultural life because it is the beginning of that exchange—in this case the exchange of women between descent groups—which he takes to be the basis of social structure.

In taking up this position he assumes, as Malinowski had also assumed, that exogamy, the prohibition of marriage between members of one descent group, was to be explained as the extension of the incest prohibition to kinsmen who were thought of as in some sense analogous to the members of the nuclear family. There are some difficulties about this interpretation. Also, though marriage between members of a unilineal descent group is nearly always prohibited, marriage may be permitted with persons outside the lineage who are closer genealogically than many of the prohibited spouses.

If one cannot agree with Lévi-Strauss that *incest* is prohibited simply in order to set going a process of reciprocal exchange, one can see the rule of *exogamy* (and other marriage prohibitions) in this light. The rule of exogamy is never the only prohibition. Certain cognates outside the lineage are always forbidden as spouses, and sometimes people who are not kin at all—for example, the children of members of the same age-set.[5]

Since the obverse of any system of marriage prohibitions is the necessity of finding a spouse from among those permitted, this system itself results in the formation of ties running in every direction through the society[6]—what Fortes has called the 'web' of kinship, and others call a network. This is why Lévi-Strauss sees the relation of brothers-in-law as the elementary form of organic solidarity: [7] through the woman who is sister to one and wife to the other, descent

[5] See pp. 56–8.
[6] As Tylor pointed out many years ago; see p. 24.
[7] See p. 27.

groups are linked which would otherwise have no common interest, and might even be enemies. It has been remarked of the Nuer that the prohibitions on marriage which they recognize, taken together, have the effect that a young man looking for a wife is pretty well obliged to find her in some other village than his own. The advantage of this is *not* that he brings in 'new blood', but that every marriage creates a new link between the small village groups, each on its ridge above flood level, a mile or so from the next. It is no accident that in French the word 'alliance' still refers to marriage. Often marriages form the bond of peace between groups that would otherwise take hostility for granted; many peoples, in Africa and elsewhere, say 'we marry those with whom we fight'. *Prima facie* the lineage members, and village-mates too, stand together against the world; the rule that they must not marry their own women, however this came into being, obliges them to extend their field of amicable relations.

Prescribed and preferential marriages

Rules prohibiting certain persons as spouses may be accompanied by rules designating others as particularly appropriate, or even as the only appropriate partners; these cannot of course designate individuals, though in practice at any given time there may be very few members of the appropriate category available. If it is the rule—no matter whether it is sometimes broken—that a man *ought* to marry a person in a particular category, this is called a *prescribed* marriage. If it is just thought *desirable* that a man should find his wife in a particular category of persons, this is called a *preferred* or *preferential* marriage.

There are many societies in which marriage between first cousins is permitted or even sought; where there is a rule of lineage exogamy these must of course be cousins belonging to different lineages. Since a person derives his lineage membership from a parent of one sex, it is usually the child of this parent's sibling of the other sex who becomes his mate. Persons in this relationship—the children of siblings of opposite sex—are called *cross-cousins*; the children of siblings of the same sex are *parallel cousins*. Looking at a marriage from the man's point of view, if he marries a daughter of his mother's brother he makes a *matrilateral cross-cousin marriage*; if he marries a daughter of his father's sister the marriage is *patrilateral*. The latter kind of cousin-marriage is rare.

Prescribed marriage is usually with the matrilateral cross-cousin. The significance of this rule has been discussed with reference to two peoples of the highland region in the interior of Burma, the Kachins and the Purum.[8] The rule is that a man must take his wife from his mother's lineage; she need not actually be his first cousin. The effect of this is that every lineage must have a permanent relationship with two others, receiving wives from the one and giving wives to the other. But since the people who actually marry in this way are the small lineage segments living close together which Leach has called *local descent groups*, it is possible that every group of this kind has a wife-giving relationship, and a wife-taking relationship, with a number of others. This division of every individual's social universe —that is, the range of persons with whom he is likely to be in contact in the course of his life—into lineage-mates and potential affines of two kinds, those whom he may marry and those whom his sisters and daughters may marry, is one way of giving coherence to the social relationships of a small-scale society. Wife-giving lineages are superior to wife-taking lineages, and this establishes the principles by which any individual knows whether he can claim respect from, or must give it to, any other person with whom he has dealings. In Kachin society lineages are ranked, and wife-takers are the vassals of wife-givers.

The rule that cross-cousins must marry is not only interesting as the basis of a particular kind of social structure, but for the light it throws on theories of exogamy and other marriage prohibitions. Although in practice people often marry distant cousins, the fact that they both may and perhaps should marry first cousins on one side, while it would

[8] E. R. Leach, 'The Structural Implications of Matrilateral Cross-Cousin Marriage', *Journal of the Royal Anthropological Institute*, 1951, pp. 23–56. R. Needham, *Structure and Sentiment*. There are cases where it is alleged that patrilateral cross-cousin marriage is prescribed, but these are doubtful.

be a heinous offence to marry a relative equally close or distant on the other, shows that marriage prohibitions in general cannot be explained as an extension to more distant kin of the prohibition of incest.

Prescribed cross-cousin marriage is most commonly found in patrilineal societies. But there are others where it is thought to be 'a good thing'. Matrilineal societies often like matrilateral cross-cousin marriage. It is a way of avoiding conflicts about where a couple should live—a question to be discussed more fully later. While in patrilineal societies a woman usually has to put up with leaving her parents' village when she marries, to go and live at her husband's lineage home, in matrilineal ones a husband is not easily persuaded to spend his married life among his wife's people, and most such societies have to make some kind of compromise. This is unnecessary if the couple are children of a man and a woman of the same lineage; then their home is in the same place. There has recently been some sharp controversy on the question whether, in particular societies, cross-cousin marriage is prescribed or merely preferred. The heat has gone out of the debate as we begin to realize that most people in societies which approve of cross-cousin marriage will say it is the rule, but the same people will not necessarily obey the rule in practice.

No satisfactory theory of the relation between the prohibition of incest and the rules of exogamy has yet been worked out, but it is clear that one cannot regard the rules which forbid the marriage of persons related genealogically in a great variety of ways as just logical extensions of those which forbid sexual congress between brothers and sisters, parents and children. Some forbidden spouses are related in a way that is not analogous to any of these relationships. Some societies allow pre-marital sex relations between persons who are not allowed to marry. As has just been noted, some insist upon the marriage of cross-cousins and many like it; and these may be first cousins, though they need not be. Moreover, although every society singles out certain forms of forbidden sexual congress as particularly dreadful —as sins regarded with horror by men and punished by gods —these are by no means always the same. The Tallensi of northern Ghana, for instance, do not worry about incest between brother and sister; they say this is just so impossible that nobody would ever contemplate it. But they think the unpardonable sin is sexual congress between a man and the wife of a lineage mate—something that many societies permit. Such a couple are by definition not genealogically close (because of the marriage prohibitions); yet, if the definition of incest is a forbidden sexual act which incurs divine wrath, this for the Tallensi is incest *par excellence*.[9]

Some anthropologists would say that the word 'exogamy', since it means 'marrying out', should be kept for the descent group fellow-members of which may not marry. In that case the rules forbidding marriage with certain persons outside the descent group would be described as additional prohibitions.

Although the words 'exogamous' and 'endogamous' express opposite ideas, it should not be supposed that actual communities must be *either* one *or* the other. An Indian caste is endogamous in the sense that it is correct for people to marry in their own caste, but it is divided into exogamous descent groups. The Indian caste rules are the most striking example of endogamy, but one could loosely say that some African tribes are endogamous, in the sense that they do not like their members to marry outsiders, yet each has its exogamous divisions.

What is marriage?

This discussion has anticipated the wider subject of marriage in general and its place in the social structure of small-scale societies. In such societies it is impossible to think separately about marriage and about the procreation of children. Marriage provides a child with a socially recognized father and a socially recognized mother. In most patrilineal societies a child cannot belong to its father's lineage unless its parents have been married in the appropriate way. In a matrilineal society every child belongs to its mother's lineage, but it is still expected to have a socially recognized father.

Marriage has been defined as 'a union between a man

[9] As it was for Hamlet.

and a woman such that children born to the woman are recognized legitimate offspring of both parents',[10] and this is a useful working definition.[11] Marriage creates new social relationships and reciprocal rights between the spouses, between each and the kin of the other, and establishes what will be the rights and status of the children when they are born. Every society has recognized procedures for creating such relationships and rights, and for making it known that they have been created.

The rules of a society may require *monogamy*—that is, that each spouse may have one partner only, as with the Iban of Borneo or the Americans—or permit *polygamy*— that is that one or other spouse may be married simultaneously to two or more partners. The latter rule is more common among societies of simple technology. These words refer to rules about marriage, not to sex relations as such, and the adjectives monogamous and polygamous describe marriages or societies, but not individuals. To call an unfaithful husband or a sexually promiscuous person polygamous is a misuse of language, though people often do it.

Much the commonest form of polygamy is the marriage of one man to a number of women; so much so that this is what most people understand by the word polygamy, though the pedantically correct term for it is *polygyny*. The marriage of a woman to a number of men is *polyandry*.

Although the rights that are created by a marriage are reciprocal—that is, both sides gain something—it is usual to consider this question from the point of view of the rights acquired by the husband. In the simpler societies, and indeed in some industrialized ones, women are never wholly independent. A woman must always be under the guardianship of some man, and when she marries her original guardian hands over some or all of his responsibility for her to her husband. It is correct to say that men dispose of women when marriages are made, although women may be allowed some freedom of choice. The woman's guardian gives to some man the rights over her to which a husband is

[10] *Notes and Queries in Anthropology*, 1951, p. 110.
[11] Though there are rare cases in which it has been argued that marriage can only be said to exist if it is differently defined. See p. 95.

entitled, whatever these may be in a given society. For these the husband makes some return, a return that should be thought of as part of a chain of mutual favours and not as a purchase price.

The rights acquired by a husband differ markedly between patrilineal societies and those which are not patrilineal. In the former the woman's kin give him the means of continuing his line and keeping his name alive, of building a numerous household around him, of being remembered as an ancestor when he dies. It is no wonder that in so many African societies the husband and his kin are expected to give in return a number of cattle—commonly called *bridewealth*—always fixed by convention at a point which strains their resources, and that in some the husband is expected for the rest of his life to behave as an inferior towards the people who have made him such a priceless gift.

Whereas in a patrilineal society a married woman bears children for her husband's lineage, in a matrilineal society the children a woman bears, married or not, belong to her own. In such a society the husband acquires the right to her sexual fidelity and her domestic services, which include a considerable share in the work of growing the food that the family eats. Of course these rights are also acquired by the husband in a patrilineal society. It is not surprising that the gifts or services that the husband in a matrilineal society renders to his wife's kinsmen impose much less of a strain on his resources than would the bridewealth. Goods and services due, as these are, from one party to another in virtue of status relationship are sometimes called *prestations*.

The various rights that a husband can acquire over his wife have been divided into two classes, described by Latin phrases—rights *in uxorem* and rights *in genetricem*. Rights *in uxorem* are rights *over* a woman considered as a sexual and domestic partner; rights *in genetricem* are rights *over* a woman considered as a mother.[12]

----

[12] Latin phrases may jar on some people these days, but whatever is done about this they *cannot* be translated by 'uxorial' and 'genetricial', which mean 'of a wife' and 'of a mother'.

Proxy fathers

In many patrilineal societies it is thought to be so important for every man to have legitimate progeny that arrangements of various kinds are made whereby the children begotten by one man are counted as those of another. These arrangements are all built on the principle that when bridewealth has been given for a woman, the children whom she bears are counted as the children of the man on whose behalf the bridewealth was given. Only if the bridewealth is returned can the woman give children to another man. She may conceive in adultery, or even leave her husband and live with another man, but as long as her husband's cattle are with her lineage her children are his. This means that the boys inherit from him and not from their actual father, and he claims the bridewealth that is given for the girls. Anthropologists distinguish the legal from the actual (natural, biological, physical) father by the names *pater* and *genitor*. Where the genitor is not a mere adulterer, but a man in a socially approved relationship to the wife, we may call him a *proxy father*.

The commonest relationship of this kind is that created by the *levirate* (from the Latin *levir,* a husband's brother). In many patrilineal societies a man's heir is his next brother, who *succeeds to* his responsibilities and his status generally as well as *inheriting* his possessions. He thus becomes the guardian of his widows as well of his children, and is expected, particularly if a widow is young and has not yet borne many children, to 'raise up seed', in the biblical expression, to his dead brother by cohabiting with her. This is an expression of the principle that a marriage made legal by bridewealth is not dissolved even by death; it can only be broken by the return of the marriage cattle. This principle operates often in another way; a widow who does not want to cohabit with her dead husband's brother is often not forced to, but if she chooses to live with another man the children she has by him are still counted as her husband's.

A more remarkable kind of proxy father is that created by the institution that has been called 'ghost-marriage' by Evans-Pritchard, who observed it among the Nuer. The

Nuer, and some other African peoples, believe that every man has a right to marry and found his own line of descent. It is the duty of his agnatic kin to provide cattle, from the herds which they own in common, to enable him to do so. But sometimes a young man dies before his marriage arrangements have been completed; or a man has only daughters, or his sons die before they grow up. It is then the duty of the nearest kinsman to 'marry a wife to his name'. The children of this marriage will count as the dead man's children; and since most Nuer cannot afford to marry more than one wife, this husband in his turn will die without heirs, and a kinsman will have to make a 'ghost-marriage' for him. Evans-Pritchard reckoned that there must be as many ghost-marriages as ordinary marriages.

It is also possible sometimes for a woman to provide bridewealth cattle, and so establish the right to count another woman's children as hers. It is usually barren women who do this. Such women often practise as diviners, and so may attain considerable wealth in cattle paid them in fees. The woman-husband nominates a man to cohabit with her 'wife'; she has the same legal rights as any husband, and can claim compensation if the wife commits adultery. It should not be thought that the Nuer are peculiar in this respect; other well-known examples are the Zulu and the Yoruba-speaking people of Dahomey.

The family

Marriage lays the legal foundations for the family, but the family can exist without marriage. A family is a domestic group in which parents and children live together, and in its elementary form it consists of a couple with their children. This is often called the *nuclear* or *elementary* family. Societies in which this does not exist as a domestic group are very rare.

Evans-Pritchard made a classification of types of family which would be useful for many patrilineal societies.[13] The *natural family* consists of parents, whether married or not, and their children. If the parents are not married their relationship is one of *concubinage*. The *simple legal* family

[13] *Kinship and Marriage among the Nuer*, 1951, pp. 108 ff.

consists of a married couple and their children (and so may be also a natural family). The polygynous family is a *complex legal* family; it has been described as a number of separate families linked by their relationship to a common father. A *ghost-family* consists of the ghost (the pater), his wife, their children, and the kinsman who became their genitor in virtue of his duty towards the ghost. (Evans-Pritchard did not invent a name for the family set up by the bridewealth paid by a woman.)

Among the peculiarities of matrilineal societies (and they do have peculiarities, they do not merely seem peculiar to westerners) is the fact that with them the family does not always, or at all times, constitute a domestic group. The most remarkable example is the traditional marriage system of the Nayars of the Malabar coast in southern India. These are the people for whom a special definition of marriage has seemed to be necessary if they are to be regarded as possessing that institution. The Nayars were not only matrilineal but also polyandrous.[14] Every Nayar girl was ritually 'married' before puberty to a man of a lineage linked to her own, who after this ceremony need have no further contact with her. The performance of this rite authorized a girl, when she became nubile, to have sexual relations with men who visited her in her home for the purpose. If she became pregnant, one of these was expected to acknowledge paternity by paying the midwife for her delivery, but he had no responsibility for the maintenance of the child; this rested with its mother's lineage. Its biological paternity must often have been in doubt.

Such a system was only practicable because the Nayar men were professional soldiers, and expected to be away from home during a great part of their lives. It cannot quite be squeezed into the definition of marriage that has been given. Yet it does provide children with legal parents. The girl was not legally entitled to be a mother unless she had been through the ritual marriage. The range of men she might receive as husbands was limited by lineage exogamy, and by prohibitions against relations with men of

[14] E. K. Gough, 'The Nayars and the Definition of Marriage', *Journal of the Royal Anthropological Institute*, 1959, pp. 23–34.

lower caste. A father of appropriate rank must be forth-coming to establish the caste status of the child, a matter of as great importance here as lineage membership in a patri-lineal society.

Another society in which the family need not be a domes-tic group is the Ashanti, where husband and wife after marriage go on living among their own kin; for this reason the Ashanti like to find their spouses in the same village, in contrast to peoples who prefer to marry outside the village and so spread their network of affinal ties as widely as pos-sible. Fortes has described how an Ashanti village at sun-set is full of little boys carrying steaming dishes on their heads from mother to father—sometimes exchanging be-tween two houses, if in each house there is a woman mar-ried to a man in the other. Thus, when they are first mar-ried, spouses live among their lineage kin, and the husband does not have to suffer the disadvantages of a 'stranger' subject to the authority of a kinsman of his wife. But every man wants to establish a home of his own—a substantial house that has cost money to build—where his wife will live with him. Many men achieve this during the time that their children are growing up. But in a study made by Fortes three-quarters of the wives in an old-fashioned vil-lage, and nearly half the wives in a village that was strongly influenced by modern ideas, chose to live their whole life among their own kin.[15]

In most matrilineal societies the family constitutes a domestic group, and there results a conflict between the domestic authority of the father and the *jural* authority[16] of the lineage head, who would normally be a brother of the mother. This may be resolved by rules that require a couple, or their children, to live in different places at differ-ent stages of their lives. Thus in the Trobriands a boy grows up in his father's house, but when he marries and sets up house he is expected to live in the village of his mother's brother, where he has a claim to land; so, unless he marries

---

[15] 'Time and Social Structure', an essay in a book with the same title published in 1970.

[16] i.e. authority in matters of rights and duties: distribution of property, guardianship of minors, giving of women in marriage, and the like.

a daughter of his mother's brother, his bride is removed from
the vicinity of her kin just as in a patrilineal society. Among
the Yao and Cewa of Malawi, when a man first marries he
must live at his wife's home, but later he may be allowed to
remove her to a village of his own matrilineal kin. So by
the time his daughters are old enough to marry he will be
the head of the homestead to which their husbands come.
Among the Bemba, near neighbours of the Cewa, it used
to be thought correct for a couple to live in the village of
the wife's parents until they had married daughters of their
own living with them. Then this whole body of people
might move away and found a new village.

In societies where descent is the most important principle
of social grouping, there are usually rules about where a
young couple should live (though these may not always be
kept, and it does not follow that a couple will live all their
lives in the place where they first set up house). It would
seem logical that a new family should live near the kin from
which the children would take their lineage membership,
those of the father or mother as the case might be. On this
assumption writers early in this century divided types of
marriage into *patrilocal* and *matrilocal*; some have also
written about patrilocal and matrilocal *societies*. Nowadays we use words like this to describe neither marriages
nor societies, but *rules of residence*. In patrilineal societies
the position is usually clear: a young husband takes his
bride to the homestead or village of his father. But matrilineal societies are much more complicated because, while
the children belong to their mother's lineage, it is not immediately obvious which of her male relatives the young
couple should attach themselves to: it may be her father, it
may be that mother's brother who is her lineage authority.
Where it is definitely the mother's brother, some people
have called the rule *avunculocal*.[17] Others have tried to get
out of the difficulty by saying *virilocal* and *uxorilocal*,
meaning 'with the husband's people' or 'with the wife's
people'. Though it is necessary to be able to understand
these words when you meet them, it is not really necessary

[17] Occasionally, as among the Trobriands, they live with the mother's
brother *of the husband*.

to use them much; they are convenient when one is stating the rule in a given society, but one can get on quite well without saying that a particular couple have 'married uxorilocally' or are 'living avunculocally'.

It should always be remembered that many people do not live where the accepted principles of their society would require them to. Particularly in patrilineal societies, people will often be found living in a local group to the head of which they are attached by other than agnatic ties.

Affines

A marriage creates relationships of affinity between people who may have been strangers or even enemies before. I have already quoted the saying, 'Those whom we marry are those with whom we fight.' This may mean no more than the principle that lineage kin should not fight with one another, while they should stand together to defend their interests against outsiders. But a marriage is often a way of sealing a peace between hostile groups. In such circumstances there is likely to be a certain constraint between the spouses and their new affines, and there are often prescribed rules of behaviour which in one way or another limit the possibilities of awkward situations. One form of prescribed behaviour is *avoidance*, or, as we more commonly call it nowadays, formal respect. This is usually required at the outset from each spouse in relation to the other's parents. In South Africa a Xhosa bride is expected to show respect to all her husband's senior kinsmen by keeping away from the parts of the homestead associated with men. The right side of every dwelling is the men's side, and the cattle kraal is a place of men; so a young woman has to make great detours around the homestead to get from one part to another. If she meets one of these men on a path she must move off into the grass. She must not speak their names or even words that sound like them. In a matrilineal society it is the husband who is a stranger in the homestead and must behave as such, but young husbands rarely seem to be subject to such stringent rules as young wives. For both, the restrictions are relaxed as the years go by.

Wherever a married couple live, there is always much

visiting between affines, and in this context also rules of respect must be observed towards affines of a senior generation. Sometimes there are 'avoidances' in the strict sense of the word; a person must refrain from using the name of a senior affine, must not come face-to-face with a senior affine of the opposite sex, must avoid sexual references in the presence of such a person. In patrilineal societies men may be expected to show respect to their affines in a positive way, and particularly in the standard of hospitality offered them. A visiting in-law must be offered a meal. Among numbers of East African peoples you cannot offer him less than a fowl, a rare delicacy where people seldom eat meat; if he turns up unexpectedly and you haven't got one, you must borrow or buy.

The rules of the Nyoro of Uganda express quite clearly their sense of the indebtness of the husband to the lineage who have given him his wife. They on their side are expected to treat him politely when he visits them—cook special food for him and have a young woman wait on him while he eats it. But he has to behave with the submissiveness of a youth in the presence of his elders, call his father-in-law 'master', and must not argue with him or even raise his voice in his house. It is his duty to pay visits of respect to his parents-in-law every two or three months, and on such a visit he must always bring some present; if they ask him for help in some job such as building, or taking produce to market, he must give it.

Nyoro explain the constraint of this relationship by saying that it is a matter of dealing with 'outsiders'. As I remarked earlier, kith can repudiate you, kin cannot. Affinal relationships are at the outset relationships between kith. They are not 'given'; they are a matter of choice. It may be unlikely that they would be broken off, but it is not impossible; therefore people must be especially careful in such relationships not to give offence. This explanation would hold good for most rules of respect towards affines. They apply in a context where causes of offence may well arise, since spouses often quarrel, and when they do the wife's kinsmen are likely to take her part.

But there is another way of dealing with this kind of delicate relationship—a relationship which requires people to be on friendly terms although circumstances may give rise to tensions between them. This is what anthropologists call the *joking relationship*. Parties to such a relationship are allowed and expected to behave towards one another in ways that would be considered outrageous in every other context. Insult and obscenity are permitted, and the victim is obliged to take it all in good part. One would not expect this kind of behaviour to be legitimate between persons of different generations, since respect for elders is one of the fundamental rules in all simple societies; and it is usually characteristic of the relations between a man and the brothers and sisters of his wife. Radcliffe-Brown has called it an attitude of 'mutual disrespect'[18]. Examples may be found in places as far apart as North America, East Africa, and Fiji.

Mother's brother and sister's son

But there is in very many patrilineal societies a one-sided relationship characterized by 'privileged disrespect'. This is the relationship between a man and his mother's brother, in which the younger man is not only entitled to behave towards the elder with what would to anyone else be quite unbecoming familiarity, but may also help himself to his property. Among the Tsonga of Portuguese East Africa, a nephew who arrives when food has just been cooked may eat it up and leave none for his uncle. Among the Nyoro a nephew who is refused food may stamp on the stones that are used to stand pots on over the fire that is made on the ground, and this is a form of cursing which will make it impossible ever to cook on that fire again.[19] A sister's son is sometimes also entitled to seize and run off with a part of the meat when his mother's brother is making a sacrifice. Such usages are found in Polynesia as well as in Africa.

Although anthropologists habitually write of *the* mother's brother and *the* sister's son, most uncles have many nephews

[18] 'On Joking Relationships', in *Structure and Function in Primitive Society*, 1952, p. 92.
[19] J. H. M. Beattie, 'Nyoro Marriage and Affinity', *Africa*, 1958, p. 20. In this case the licensed disrespect is accompanied by strict rules of respect in other contexts.

and most nephews many uncles. Occasionally, however, as in parts of Southern Africa, it is the rule that every brother is paired with a particular sister, and so is *the* mother's brother to her children.

The special position of the sister's son was at one time interpreted as a survival from the matrilineal stage of society which was supposed to have everywhere preceded the patrilineal, and his claim on his uncle's property could with some show of reason be considered as a relic of the time when he was his uncle's heir. But, as Radcliffe-Brown pointed out, where the mother's brother is the lineage authority he is treated with the same respect as the father in a patrilineal system, and a relationship marked by an unusual degree of familiarity can hardly be thought of as a survival of its opposite.

Radcliffe-Brown's original interpretation was what is called the 'extension theory'. In societies based on kinship, he said, people group their kin into categories towards whom and from whom particular kinds of behaviour are appropriate. This categorization is based on analogies between kin within the immediate family and more distant relatives. The principle on which these were ultimately based is 'the social equivalence of siblings'. The behaviour appropriate between parents and their children was extended to the siblings of both. In patrilineal societies the father is the source of authority and discipline and so must be treated with respect, and similar respect must be given to both his brothers and sisters; the father's sister has fallen out of the picture in more recent arguments, but Radcliffe-Brown did adduce instances where she exercises authority over her brother's children and is much feared by them, and the Tikopia provide a further example. But the mother's brother, as the sibling of the tender, indulgent mother, is expected to treat his sister's children with the same indulgence that she does, and so are his ancestors even; that is why he can steal their sacrificial meat. Radcliffe-Brown related this explanation to the fact that in a great many societies all over the world the word for mother's brother etymologically means 'male mother'. The term 'male mother' *does* of course express the social equivalence of siblings. Later, however, he saw the 'joking relationship' as a means of mitigating potential hostility between the lineages which are linked by a marriage.

The explanation in terms of family sentiment would have been expected rather from Malinowski, for whom the family provided 'the initial situation' for the learning of social behaviour. Malinowski did his work in a matrilineal society, and in his descriptions of it he had much to say about the indulgence of fathers towards children over whom they did not hold authority. Homans and Schneider's interpretation of cross-cousin marriage[20] is derived from a combination of these two writers' theories.

A recent study of the mother's-brother/sister's son relationship relies rather on the principle of complementary filiation. This was published by the Cambridge anthropologist J. R. Goody in 1959.[21] He begins by following Malinowski's principle that 'it is sometimes valuable to state the obvious', and reminds us that mothers are just as tender and indulgent in matrilineal as in patrilineal societies. Next he asks whether the stealing of the sacrificial meat, which is the *nephew's* action, can really be interpreted as an expression of indulgence by the *uncle*.

Most contemporary anthropologists in Britain reject the approach which begins with the family and moves outwards, and prefer to look for explanations in the nature of unilineal descent groups. Such groups are property-holding corporations; claims to share the property of the living, and inherit that of the dead, are derived from membership of them, and this kind of common interest is a source of tension rather than of the harmony that should prevail between brothers. One of the group may resent the way the property its laid out by the man in control of it, or question the fairness of his share in the inheritance. If the corporate property of the group includes a claim to office, particularly kingship, there is bound to be competition for it; among some East African peoples the potential heirs were actually

[20] G. Homans and D. Schneider, *Marriage, Authority and Final Causes*, 1955.
[21] 'The Mother's Brother and the Sister's Son in West Africa', *Journal of the Royal Anthropological Institute*, 1959, pp. 61–88.

expected to fight for the kingship, if necessary killing their brothers.

With kin outside the lineage there is no such competition, and this is one reason why their relationship is expected to be an easy and friendly one. Rivals for office seek the support of their matrilateral kin, who cannot oust them from their position, and who give support because they can expect to be rewarded with subordinate offices if their candidate is successful.

In other contexts too the mother's brother (or the sister's son, depending whether you are looking upwards from the junior generation or downwards from the senior) is, as Goody has pointed out, the closest kinsman who does not belong to the lineage. When the LoWiili of northern Ghana make sacrifices to their ancestors it is because they wish to appease their anger; but because they are afraid of this anger, they get a sister's son, whom the lineage ancestors cannot harm, to approach them by making a 'peace offering', the reception of which will show whether the ancestors are willing to be placated. It is as a reward for this service, at any rate in this case, that the sister's son gets his share of the meat. The 'snatching' Goody interprets as an assertion of what he calls a 'residual claim'. In systems of unilineal descent siblings are *not* equivalent, because either the brothers or the sisters are debarred from transmitting lineage property to their children. The one who cannot transmit property Goody calls the 'residual sibling'. When a man snatches property from a member of his mother's lineage he is in a sense acting on her behalf, asserting what Goody calls her 'submerged rights'. He *must* do this in an aggressive manner, because he is in fact an outsider to the group within which claims are recognized. In a matrilineal society the brother is the 'residual sibling', and the 'submerged claim' is the one that a man could make through his father. But since men, unlike women, control property in matrilineal as well as in patrilineal societies, fathers do manage to hand over property to their sons by giving it while they are alive; hence there is no need for 'snatching' in a matrilineal society. Goody expresses this as a recognition by the father of his son's 'residual claim', whereas

Malinowski saw it as an evasion by the father of the rules of a matrilineal society.

Kinship terminology

It is now time to return to the question of kinship terminology. Lewis H. Morgan gave the name *classificatory* to the mode of grouping of kin into categories which he found to be characteristic of so many small-scale societies. There is nothing to be surprised at in the fact that people do label, or categorize, the persons who are related to them by ties of 'blood'; brother, cousin, uncle, are all labels of this kind. Every language provides them.

What Morgan meant by a classificatory system was one in which names which apply to *lineal* relatives (e.g father, mother, son, grandson) may also be used for *collateral* relatives. In such systems a father's brother is called 'father' and his sons are called 'brother'. Morgan ascribed this practice to a failure to distinguish one's own line of descent from collateral lines; at the time when these terms came into use, he thought, people cannot have known who their fathers were, so they gave the name to a number of people any of whom might have been the speaker's father. He knew that the Iroquois among whom he had lived had no such difficulty, and this was what led him to explain this kind of terminology as a survival from days when groups of brothers were married to groups of sisters.

Rivers found the explanation of features of these systems in rules prescribing or allowing marriages with different relatives. In what is known as the Omaha type of terminology, a type found among several American Indian tribes and in parts of East Africa and New Guinea, a man uses the same term for his mother and for the daughters of his mother's brother. Rivers explained this by conjecturing that in the old days in these societies a man would expect to marry the daughter of his wife's brother. This woman would then become the step-mother of his sons. So the sons were brought up to anticipate the creation of this relationship (an event which was by no means certain) by calling her 'mother'.

When anthropologists turned to the principle that

customs would be best explained in terms of their contemporary significance, they began to see these systems, as we do today, as ways of grouping relatives according to the behaviour to be expected of them by the person using the terms. All men called 'father' must be treated with respect, and all such men have some degree of authority over, and also responsibility for, all men whom they call 'son'; the special relationship which exists in most patrilineal societies between men who address one another as 'mother's brother' and 'sister's son' has been discussed.

The standard way of recording the terminology of any society is to get hold of some member of it who understands what you are after and ask him 'What do *you* call X or Y (the father, sister's son, grandson, etc. (naming the persons concerned) of the informant)?' This is done along with the drawing up of genealogies, so that the questions are not completely abstract but are directed to actual cases. Then the scheme of kinship terms is drawn up with 'Ego' in the middle.

This mode of operation led almost inevitably to the 'extension theory'. Once it was recognized that everyone did in fact distinguish between near and distant relatives who were all called 'father', new explanations of the wide application of such terms had to be sought. Malinowski, and to some extent also Radcliffe-Brown, thought of the extension of terminology and the extension of sentiments in much the same way. A child grows up in a home with its parents and siblings, it learns the appropriate relationship terms for them, and as other kinsmen appear on its horizon it extends the terms over a wider and wider range. Someone once remarked in his seminar that most English infants say 'Dada' whenever they see a man, and have to learn later that the name is appropriate in one case only. It was also observed that, in the dwelling of an extended family, a child is more likely to learn first that several men are called 'father', and later that one of these has a specially close relationship to himself.

Radcliffe-Brown explained the classification of lineage kin on the principle of the *unity of the sibling group*, and that of affinal kin in terms of the *unity of the lineage group*.

He used this principle to explain the peculiarities of the Omaha terminology (which is not peculiar to the Omaha, but has been found to be one of the typical ways of classifying one's lineage kin). In a patrilineal society every person is related through women to a number of different lineages; in fact there must be an infinite number, but the ones that matter are the ones that he is aware of and that he comes in contact with, so that it is of practical importance to classify them by terms indicating the relationship. In the Fox tribe of American Indians, an example of Omaha type terminology who have been studied in some detail, the significant lineages are those of a man's wife, his wife's mother, his own mother, and the mothers of his two parents. He groups together, and so describes and addresses by one term, all the men of his mother's lineage, whatever their generation, all the men of either grandmother's lineage, and all the men of his wife's lineage. The only way to translate these terms into English is by using our name for the closest relative in each of the categories—'mother's brother', 'grandfather', and 'brother-in-law'. But this should not lead us to suppose that the terms refer primarily to these close relatives and only in some metaphorical sense to more distant ones. If this had been recognized in Rivers' day he need not have had recourse to conjectures about old-time marriage customs.[22]

The recording and analysis of these systems is an important part of fieldwork. The list of terms, with their application, gives us the skeleton of the social structure, and shows how the people concerned see the world of their social relationships. The roles associated with the relationships to which the terms apply can always be described by the people who use them, though the observer will get a fuller picture of the expectations attached to them by hearing comments on the way individuals play them. The observer, too, can detect such structural principles as lineage unity, of the implications of which the members of the society are not conscious.

SUGGESTIONS FOR READING

Malinowski's views on the function of incest prohibitions are ex-

[22] *Structure and Function in Primitive Society*, 1952, pp. 70 ff.

pounded in his *Sex and Repression in Savage Society* (1924). The somewhat similar theory of C. Lévi-Strauss on exogamy is to be found in the introduction and Part I of his long book *Les Structures Elémentaires de la Parenté* (1949) (English translation 1969). The views of Lévi-Strauss on cross-cousin marriage have been criticized in G. Homans and D. M. Schneider, *Marriage, Authority and Final Causes* (1955), and defended in R. Needham, *Structure and Sentiment* (1960). E. R. Leach has discussed the subject from another point of view in 'The Structural Implications of Matrilateral Cross-Cousin Marriage', *Journal of the Royal Anthropological Institute*, 1951 (republished in *Rethinking Anthropology*, 1961).

M. Fortes, 'Analysis and Description in Social Anthropology', in *Time and Social Structure*, 1970, discussess the jural implications of marriage in matrilineal and patrilineal societies respectively. E. K. Gough, 'The Nayars and the Definition of Marriage', *Journal of the Royal Anthropological Institute*, 1959, is more valuable for its description of the Nayar system than for its attempt to devise a form of words that will entitle the Nayars to claim the institution of marriage.

A. R. Radcliffe-Brown and D. Forde (eds.), *African Systems of Kinship and Marriage* (1950), contains an introduction by Radcliffe-Brown, some of which is now rather out of date in its treatment of the subject, and nine ethnographic accounts by different authors.

A good discussion of the distinction between *pater* and *genitor*, and the possible ways in which one who is not the *genitor* of a child may become its *pater*, is to be found in E. E. Evans-Pritchard, *Kinship and Marriage among the Nuer* (1951). This book also discusses the significance of the bridewealth payment and its relation to marriage stability. The question of the circumstances in which people defer the payment of bridewealth is one of a number of interesting topics discussed in M. Fortes (ed.), *Marriage in Tribal Societies* (1962).

Any anthropological monograph must treat family and marriage in detail, and there would be little value in giving a long list of them here. An article which has been used as a source in this chapter is J. H. M. Beattie, *Nyoro Kinship, Marriage and Affinity* (International African Institute Memorandum, 1958). J. R. Goody (ed.), *The Development Cycle in Domestic Groups* (1958), discusses the ways in which family configurations change as children grow up and found their own families. This is also the theme of M. Fortes, 'Time and Social Structure', in the collection of essays with the same title published in 1970.

Joking relationships are interpreted by Radcliffe-Brown in an essay in his collection, *Structure and Function in Primitive Society* (1952). The special relationship between mother's brother and sister's son is discussed with reference to the Nyoro in the article by Beattie just quoted, and with reference to the peoples of Northern Ghana in J. R. Goody, 'The Mother's Brother and the Sister's Son in West Africa',

Journal of the Royal Anthropological Institute, 1959. This and a number of other essays by Goody have been republished in *Comparative Studies in Kinship* (1969).

Radcliffe-Brown's views on classificatory terminology are given in his introduction to *African Systems of Kinship and Marriage*, as well as in the essay 'The Study of Kinship Systems' in *Structure and Function in Primitive Society*.

CHAPTER 7

Politics Without the State

THE nineteenth-century anthropologists who sought to trace the history of society from its original condition had in the back of their minds an assumption that man was at one time as it were socially naked, and later began to clothe himself with institutions—proceeding, for example, from complete promiscuity to regulated marriage.

We should be more inclined today to suppose that there must have been institutions of some kind as long as there have been creatures who qualified to be described as men. One current definition of man is 'a tool-making animal'; one might guess that people claimed property in their flint implements as soon as they discovered how to make them, and along with property there must go rules about who can dispose of it, who can inherit it, what is to be done if people dispute over it.

But the nineteenth-century hypothesis might seem more plausible in the field of *political* institutions. We know from the study of history how these have developed over the centuries in various parts of the world. Whereas in the field of domestic relationships we now feel confident that the individual family has always been recognized, we cannot say of the various types of government observed in small-scale societies that any of them has 'always been there'.

What is politics?

Morgan dealt with this subject by dividing the political evolution of humanity into two stages; though unlike some more recent writers he thought both had government. The earlier, he supposed, was 'founded upon persons, and upon relations purely personal'; that means, of course, kinship. He called this 'social organization', and this may be the

reason why to many American anthropologists today social
organization means kinship, whereas in Britain it means the
total organization of society. Morgan held that the idea of
property arose only later, along with the idea of territory as
the basis of a common government. He gave the name
'political organization' only to a government claiming
authority over a definite territory, and this he called the
state.[1] Brought up, as were all his contemporaries, on Latin
and Greek, he knew that *polis* originally meant city.

Since his day some anthropologists have equated government as such with the state, but have argued that people
who have no government still have political systems; while
the most recent discussion of the subject in Britain maintains that, if government is appropriately defined, every
society will be found to have it.[2]

Maine, like Morgan, believed that the conception of
political allegiance owed to a territorial authority arose
fairly late in the history of mankind, and made a change in
human relationships so dramatic as to deserve the name of
revolution.[3]

Schapera has pointed out that there are no societies in
which membership of a political unit (what he calls a
political community) depends solely upon kinship, and
none in which all persons who are linked by kinship are
subject in virtue of that link to a common authority. His
illustrations come from the kind of societies that Morgan
would have described as having social but not political organization: the Australian aborigines or the Bushmen of
south-western Africa. Morgan himself naturally had American Indians in mind. These are peoples who neither keep
domestic animals nor practise agriculture, but live by hunting wild animals and collecting wild berries and roots; thus
their technological level is the simplest possible. They move
about in very small bands, each politically distinct in the
sense that it recognizes no external authority, and all members of the band are, or are considered to be, kin; it is

[1] Lewis H. Morgan, *Ancient Society*, 1958 edn., pp. 6–7, 71.
[2] See especially M. Fortes and E. Evans-Pritchard, *African Political Systems*, 1940, and I. Schapera, *Government and Politics in Tribal Societies*,
1956.
[3] *Ancient Law*, 1930 edn., p. 144.

characteristic of these societies of smallest scale that they
do not conceive of any relationship between two persons
which cannot be described by a kinship term.

But the fact that the band think of themselves as being
all kin does not preclude their believing they have joint
rights over a territory, and in fact this *is* what they believe;
they may allow outsiders into their territory, but they claim
it as their own and nobody else's. Moreover, the argument
that in these societies kinship is the sole basis on which
government rests is vulnerable from another direction, in
that all persons who are related by common descent do not
belong to the same band, or, as we can now put it, the same
territorial unit. Bands are exogamous, so that the men must
get their wives from other bands. But the women who
marry *in* accept the authority of the leader of the band they
join, and the women who marry *out* are no longer subject to
the authority of the leader of the band they have left.

The study of political systems has been developed in
recent years largely with reference to Africa, because that
continent provides examples of states (defined as something
more than territorial units) such as could not be paralleled
in the fields favoured by the earlier anthropologists, with
their preference for hunting bands and small island populations. The collection of studies by pupils of Malinowski,
published in 1940 with the title *African Political Systems*,
contained two introductions, one by its editors Fortes and
Evans-Pritchard and one by Radcliffe-Brown, which gave
definitions of a political system and also of government.
Unlike Morgan, Fortes and Evans-Pritchard held that all
societies do not have government; for them, only states
have government, and this is characterized by 'centralized
authority, territorial administration and judicial institutions'. But, again unlike Morgan, they maintained that
every society has a political system, and that this operates
within a territorial framework.

What then did they understand by a political system?
The definition which was given by Radcliffe-Brown was a
functional one in the sense that he asked, in effect, what it
is that political institutions *do* in a society, and how we
identify them where we do not find the clearly recognizable

characteristics of the state. His answer was that a political system is 'that part of the total organization' (of a society) 'which is concerned with the maintenance or establishment of social order, within a territorial framework, by the organized exercise of coercive authority through the use, or the possibility of the use, of physical force'.[4] The political system, then, is what supports the system of rights and obligations that any society must have if it is to be a society at all (since a society *is* a body of people linked together by mutually recognized rights and obligations).

Schapera's more recent discussion of the subject rejects a definition which makes the command or use of force the sole criterion of a political system. He points out that the leaders of Bushman and Bergdama bands do not command force for the punishment of offenders, yet their authority is recognized. This is an argument which one must accept as logically valid. But confronted with the proposition, 'Political systems need not rest on the control of force', one cannot help reflecting that only the very smallest can do without it. More significant, however, is Schapera's reminder that the organization of public activities and the taking of decisions on behalf of the whole community are also political activities; in his view they do more for the maintenance of social order than does the use of force in support of just claims. He then argues that every society recognizes certain roles which can be described as governmental; there are certain persons whose 'recognized and regular activity' it is 'to attend to the conduct of public affairs'.[5] The body of persons who have a common set of officials, and who do not recognize any authority above them, he calls the *political community*—'a group of people organized into a single unit managing its affairs independently of external control'.[6]

Schapera's argument is a valuable reminder to students of political systems that they should not overlook the decision-making functions of government in the preoccupation with its law-and-order functions. But it remains true that in those societies which Fortes and Evans-Pritchard

---

[4] *African Political Systems*, p. xiv.
[5] *Government and Politics in Tribal Societies*, p. 208.
[6] ibid., p. 8.

call 'acephalous' ('headless') it is extremely difficult to identify a political community recognizing a single set of common leaders or organizers.[7]

Questions of the nature of authority, what makes it legitimate, when obedience may or should be refused, how to prevent those who hold it from abusing it, have engaged men's minds for many centuries. As a result, the words 'politics' and 'political' have become encrusted with associations, and it is vain at this date to try to fit their different uses into a logical scheme. But it may be useful to mention some of the ways in which they are used in anthropological discourse.

The most comprehensive phrase is 'political system'; contemporary anthropologists in general assume that every society has a political system, though ethnographic accounts of the small island societies do not always make it clear what this is.[8] As has just been pointed out, anthropologists may classify political systems in different ways, some saying that every political system is a governmental system and some holding that some political systems are not. It is also necessary to distinguish between government, which is a process, and *a* government, which is a set of recognized offices.

The word 'politics' is sometimes used to mean the study of government. But a political system implies a wider field of activities than those we have in mind when we think of government. Within a political system students of 'politics' in this sense often distinguish 'politics' from 'administration'. When this distinction is made, 'politics' refers to any kind of contest to gain power within the political system, whether by fighting an election or trying to poison your competitors; and 'administration' means the conduct of public affairs by the people who have acquired legitimate power by getting into office. 'Politics', again, is the process of discussion and manoeuvring which goes on before a decision is taken, 'administration' the carrying out of the decision. In these senses 'politics' as an activity can be observed in bodies which are not in themselves political, such

---

[7] See L. P. Mair, *Primitive Government*, 1962, Chapter 2.

[8] A noteworthy exception is J. Singh Uberoi, *Politics of the Kula Ring*, 1962.

as a church or a university; but in the ordinary use of language one would not describe the competition for religious privilege, or the struggle for a change of syllabus, or the aims with which these contests are pursued, as 'political'. Accordingly some might regard as too broad the definition which says that 'political relations must be described in terms of how particular rights and privileges are maintained or promoted'.[9] But there is no need to choose one of these definitions and reject the rest. Each suggests different questions which can profitably be asked if one is looking for that part of a social system which deserves to be called its politics or its government.

Some types of political system

It would be a tedious and unrewarding enterprise to try to enumerate all the different ways in which small-scale societies organize their political life, and even more so to attempt to classify them into types.[10] But it is interesting to consider some of the varieties that anthropological study has revealed. The distinction made by Fortes and Evans-Pritchard between those peoples which look to a single head as a source of authority and those which do not (the acephalous societies) is useful as a starting-point.

A community may look to a single head either when it is very small, and the head is in direct contact with all its members, or when it is very large, so that only a system of authority extending from a single centre could hold it together. Populations that recognize common rights and obligations but do not look to a single authority may be thought of as falling between the two. Some tiny states, however, actually include populations no larger than the typical Nuer and Dinka tribe which recognizes no chief.

Schapera's example of the smallest political unit is the

---

[9] A Sommerfelt, *Political Cohesion in a Stateless Society*, 1958, p. 174.

[10] The discovery of a type of African political system not mentioned by Fortes and Evans-Pritchard is triumphantly proclaimed from time to time. Their book contains a paragraph which could be taken to imply that the classification into two types of the eight societies described in it could be imposed on all African societies; if they did not hedge this statement about with qualifications, this was because they were not interested in classification into types as an end in itself.

Bushman band of fifty to a hundred persons moving together from one water-hole to the next. This is what is called a 'face-to-face' community, in which every member is known to every other. In the evening all the men gather round a fire in the middle of the camp, and decisions for community action emerge from their informal talk. The chief is the leader, not in the sense that he can overrule the opinion of the other men (which would be impossible since he has no means of compelling them to accept his wishes), but in the sense that he is expected to organize the activities that have been decided upon; he tells the hunters where they are to go, when they bring back meat he divides it, he leads them in their moves from one water-hole to the next and in attacks on neighbouring bands, and he conducts negotiations with other bands on such matters as permission to enter his territory, or the conclusion of a marriage with one of their members, or the organization of a joint ritual.[11]

In such a band there is a good deal more authority and organization than one would find among some populations of hunters and gatherers. An extreme example of the absence of authority, whether for settling disputes, punishing disobedience, organizing common activities, or defence against outsiders, comes from Tanzania, where the Hadza neither claim ownership of territory nor recognize any leadership. There are no rules stating what people must, or even should, camp together on their wanderings, and people move freely from one camp to another. So there is no need for decisions as to when and where a camp as a body should move. Individuals forage for themselves and often eat the food they find at once, on the spot; so there is no need for organized hunting or rules for the division of food. One band does not seek to keep others out of its territory, nor do they try to keep out other tribes, to whom they have lost much of their hunting area. One could hardly say they did not *need* any organization for defence, but it may be that the food supply would not maintain in one place numbers large enough to be so organized. Quarrels do break out and may lead to blows, but they are 'settled' by one of the disputants moving away. It would be difficult to identify a

[11] Schapera, op. cit., pp. 85–6.

political system here; and perhaps we may come to find our selves saying that there are societies of very small scale which have no such system.

An acephalous society

The classic example of an acephalous political system is provided by the Nuer of the southern Sudan as they were thirty years ago. Each kin group, and each village, was autonomous, and the respect of individuals for the rights of others was secured through the recognition that a man who was injured had the right to seek redress by force, and would have the backing of his kin and village-mates in doing so. Homicide was an injury to the lineage of the victim, and they were entitled to revenge it by killing the killer or a close agnate of his. Homicide also had serious ritual consequences. When a man had been killed it was believed to be dangerous for his lineage and that of the killer to come into contact. This condition of ritual danger was created automatically by the act of killing; so no homicide could be disregarded. This state of quarantine, or latent hostility, is a *blood-feud*; in most writing on the subject, anthropologists have simply used the word 'feud', which actually has a much wider significance. (It should be noted here that the connection between this word and the word 'feudal', which many anthropologists have used of primitive states, is purely accidental; 'feud' comes from a word meaning 'foe', 'feudal' from a word meaning 'fee'.) If in fact every killing had been avenged by another, the quarantine between lineages, and between the villages in which members of feuding lineages lived, would have lasted for ever and made all social relations outside the village impossible. But the Nuer agreed that a feud could be brought to an end by the offer of a payment of cattle in compensation for the offence and by a formal ceremony of reconciliation. Evans-Pritchard finds in this rule that compensation can be offered and ought to be accepted the criterion of a common 'rule of law'; he gives the name of 'tribe' to the divisions of the whole Nuer population within which this rule is recognized. Fighting between tribes was war; a man who killed another in war had to be purified from the ritual consequences of his act, but there was no question of offering compensation. It sometimes happened that a number of feuds between members of a tribe whose homes were far apart, so that the ritual separation did not inconvenience them, remained unsettled for a long time, and people might give up the idea of settling them and instead begin to see themselves as belonging to two separate tribes. In the sense that they recognized a 'common rule of law' a Nuer tribe might be called a 'political community'; but it would be hard to identify any person with recognized responsibilities for co-ordinating public activities throughout the tribe.

Age organization as a basis of political authority
Political functions may be distributed among the male population according to *age*. In political systems so organized the most significant distinction is often that between men of fighting age and those who are too old for fighting. In those characteristic of eastern and southern Africa men formally enter upon warrior status and formally pass out of it at fixed times.

It is unfortunate that the terms used by different anthropologists in describing age organizations are not uniform, but those given here are in fairly general use.

It is important to note that what is significant is not chronological but *social* age. A man is recognized as an adult when he is formally admitted to adult status, not when he reaches a certain birthday; he is eligible for admission at puberty, but his admission may be delayed for one reason or another. A formal procedure of admission, generally called *initiation*, is characteristic of many societies besides those which make age a criterion for the distribution of political functions. Particularly among the latter, initiation involves a period during which the youths are separated from the normal life of the village, and subjected to hardships and ordeals, including usually the operation of circumcision which gives the mark of adulthood. During this period the one who is to be their leader is chosen by the older men in charge of the initiation. It is common for initiations to be held in a number of successive years, at the end of which either there is a 'closed period', or else one 'set' of warriors is declared to be 'closed' and boys initiated later belong to the next 'set'. Whichever is the practice, a distinctive name is always given to each set, and this indicates to every man in the society his status in terms of seniority in relation to every other.

An *age-set* may be taken to mean the youths who have been initiated during a single period, whether this is marked by a special proclamation or continues for a fixed number of years. Those who actually went through the ceremonies together will then be called a *sub-set*. Some writers, however, use the word *age-set* to describe the youths initiated in one year, and call the named body a *generation*.

The members of one age-set commonly pass together through the *grades* first of warrior and then of elder. The *set*, then, is the body of men, the *grade* the status in which they are at any given moment. It may be helpful to think of the simple illustration of a train made up of four carriages. Each of these represents a sub-set, and the whole train is the complete set. The order of the sub-sets remains unchanged, as does the order of seniority depending on the year of initiation; the whole train moves as one, and all stop together at each station, first the warrior grade, then the elder grade (or intermediate stations in more complicated systems).

In the age systems characteristic of Eastern Africa, the warriors are mainly responsible for offensive and defensive fighting, but they may be called upon to execute decisions of the elders by bringing accused persons before them, and if necessary by seizing property awarded in compensation. The elders are expected to spend much of their time in the discussion of public affairs, for which purpose they gather at a recognized place, often in the shade of a big tree. It is also their duty to perform public ritual, a duty thought to be particularly appropriate to the old, who are nearer to the ancestors and will soon be ancestors themselves.

In West Africa age-sets and associations with voluntary membership may be combined in the political systems of both stateless societies and states.

The Yakö of the Cross River area in the east of Nigeria illustrate one kind of distribution of political responsibili-

ties between age-sets and other forms of association.[12] The
large village of Umor, with a population (in 1935) of 11,000,
was divided into four wards. The men of each ward (300–
600 households) were organized into age-sets, which shared
among them such public services as the protection of houses
from fire during the day-time when most people were
out working in their fields, and the clearing of weeds from
the paths between village and farmland and from the
springs that provided the village water supply. Authority
to allot this work to the different sets, and call them out for
it, rested with the head of the ward. This man had to be a
member of an association of 'Elders' or 'Leaders' (*Yakamben*), to which all heads of lineages belonged, but which was
open to anyone who could afford the fees paid on admission.
It might include about one-third of the men in a ward. The
head was appointed by the free choice of his fellows, which
was not limited by any lineage claims to the office. Nor did
seniority give a claim; a man who was not too old to be
active was usually chosen. He was expected to maintain
order within the ward by persuading disputants to settle
their quarrels. Another association, *Ebiabu*, which was also
divided into age-grades but within which membership was
voluntary, was available to coerce people who failed to turn
out for work allotted to their age-sets, to bring before the
ward head people who refused to come and listen to charges
against them, and to stop brawls. The ward head was always
a member of *Ebiabu*, and as such had the right to call it together at the house of its own elected head. Most of the
leaders were also members of *Ebiabu*. There existed also in
each ward a branch of an association known as *ηkpe*, which
offered to its members the protection against thieves and
adulterers of a Leopard Spirit whom they honoured. Members of *ηkpe*, an organization of foreign origin, were not
admitted to the formally recognized ward associations; in
their turn they saw themselves as protectors of the common
man against abuse of authority. Daryll Forde, to whom we
owe our knowledge of the Yakö, calls them a 'reluctantly
tolerated opposition'.

The most important *Yakamben*, including the ward

[12] See C. D. Forde, *Yakö studies*, 1964, pp. 135–64.

heads and their deputies, were members of a village-wide association called *Okengka*. This was devoted to the cult of an officially recognized Leopard Spirit, and purported to call on this spirit when some dispute arose which could not be settled by agreement, particularly if it concerned persons from different wards. It was believed that to disregard the judgment of this Leopard Spirit would bring disaster upon the offender.

All the priests of village shrines, twenty-four in number, belonged to yet another council to which men might appeal for the settlement of disputes. Their authority was effective because it was believed that they could withhold from those who rejected it the benefits that their spirits conferred upon the virtuous. The council of priests could summon *Yakamben* and heads of other associations to discuss with them matters of public interest; they could authorize other associations to take action against people who had offended them; and they could 'ex-communicate' a member of the village by planting their staves in front of his house as a sign that he must stay inside on pain of punishment by the spirits.

Other associations too claimed to act with the authority of the spirits they worshipped to punish particular types of offence. One was concerned with the stealing of standing crops or palm-fruit from trees. It offered its protection in return for a payment to the spirit, and set its mark on the property it had undertaken to protect. If this was disregarded, it was the association, not the owner of the property, that was held to have been wronged, and it was their duty to bring the offender to justice before the Leaders' or the priests' council. Yet another association dealt with disputes over land rights.

This is perhaps an extreme case of the diffusion of responsibility for the protection of recognized rights.

It should not be supposed that kinship ceases to have any political importance wherever political functions are allocated on some other basis. If we contrast political systems based on age-sets with those based on descent groups alone, we see that in the former more aspects of public life are organized outside the descent groups, but it does not follow that the descent groups lose all their political functions. Whether this happens depends partly upon the extent to which the age-sets in the warrior grade are effectively used to enforce the reference of disputes to the elders for decision, and this must have varied from time to time within every society, as well as between different societies.

Moreover, it is not necessary to think of the age-sets as seeking to wrest from the descent groups their power to redress wrongs done to their members. A study recently made of the Arusha of Mount Meru in Tanzania by the London anthropologist Philip Gulliver[13] shows how age and lineage organizations operate side by side in seeking to secure the settlement of disputes and righting of wrongs by peaceful means; for this is a society in which direct retaliation or 'self-help' is not approved. The Arusha system of age organization is one of the few such systems in East Africa to have been observed in actual operation by the modern technique of intensive fieldwork.

Among the Arusha the elders of each small local group are summoned to meet in council whenever there is any matter to discuss. Such questions may be matters of organization, such as the formation of a new age-set, or matters of dispute, concerning land boundaries or claims for debt or compensation for injuries. A leading part is taken in the discussions by men called 'spokesmen', who have been chosen by the members of each age-set as its representatives. They are chosen for the qualities of wisdom and skill in negotiation—since the Arusha are a people who do not recognize any kind of chief or ruler with authority to give binding decisions in matters of dispute. Though their voice carries weight by virtue of their personality rather than of their office, they are the only people who are thought of as having a duty to take part in all public discussions whether or not the subject is of any particular interest to them. This role—whether or not it goes with an office—is one very commonly found among peoples who do not recognize any office that confers authority upon the holder.

The interesting characteristic of the Arusha is that each lineage too has its 'spokesman', selected by members of the

[13] P. H. Gulliver, *Social Control in an African Society*, 1963.

lineage in the age-grade of elders, and formally installed at a ceremony where he is presented with a staff of office. Some of these, but only a minority, are also age-set spokesmen. When a claim for debts or damages is disputed, both sides are represented by their lineage spokesmen, who first put the case of their lineage member and then seek to negotiate an agreed solution.

There are, then, two possible ways of pursuing a claim, either before the assembly of elders of the locality or at a meeting of the lineages of the two disputants. Theoretically the different bodies have what might be called different jurisdictions. The local assembly of elders deals with disputes among persons belonging to the locality, and not with any quarrels they may have with people outside, while the assemblies of kinsfolk handle disputes among agnatic kin. Of course there are some people who would take a leading part in the discussion whether the meeting was one of elders or of lineage members. The spokesman of the elders is bound to carry weight in a meeting of his lineage, and a lineage spokesman is listened to in a meeting of elders. In practice, a man who is pursuing a claim takes it to the body where he thinks he has the best chance of winning support for it.

This system shows an intimate interlocking of political functions based on age and on lineage.

SUGGESTIONS FOR READING

R. G. Lienhardt, *Social Anthropology* (1964), argues in his chapter on politics that the most important contribution of social anthropology to this subject has been the analysis of political organization in stateless societies; he gives an excellent account of the balance of power which maintains order in such societies. The initial discussion of segmentary political systems is to be found in the two introductions, one by Radcliffe-Brown, one by the editors, in M. Fortes and E. E. Evans-Pritchard (eds.), *African Political Systems* (1940). I. Schapera in *Government and Politics in Tribal Societies* (1956) surveys the views of some earlier writers and offers a different definition of a political system. L. P. Mair, *Primitive Government* (1962), discusses the applicability of Schapera's concepts to segmentary societies. *African Political Systems* contains brief accounts of the societies whose political structure is described at length in E. E. Evans-Pritchard, *The Nuer* (1940), and M. Fortes, *The Dynamics of Clan-*

ship among the Tallensi (1945). Other short descriptions of acephalous political structures are collected in J. F. M. Middleton and D. Tait (eds), *Tribes Without Rulers* (1958).

The best description of a society where age-sets still have political significance is P. H. Gulliver, *Social Control in an African Society* (1963), on the Arusha of Tanganyika. Accounts of other East African age-systems reconstructed from old men's memories are H. E. Lambert, *Kikuyu Social and Political Organization* (1956), and G. W. B. Huntingford, *The Nandi of Kenya* (1953). Age organization in Nigeria is described in D. Forde, *Yakö Studies* (1964), and G. I. Jones, 'Ibo Age Organization', *Journal of the Royal Anthropological Institute*, 1962.

CHAPTER 8

Primitive States

THE commonest form of political system among the societies studied by anthropologists is that which every writer on political theory would recognize as a state. This is the type of political system which alone, in the view of Fortes and Evans-Pritchard, deserves to be called a government. A ruler who is recognized as supreme makes his authority effective through territorial agents chosen by himself. Such a system provides, as Radcliffe-Brown said it should, for the maintenance of internal peace by the settlement of disputes, and for defence against external aggression as well as the prosecution of aggressive war. It organizes public works, a function performed by the Ibo age-organization but not by the other types of system discussed up to now. It provides for the performance of the rituals held to be necessary for the common welfare. The collection of tribute, which is characteristic of all states, and is necessary to enable the officials to carry on their activities, is an aspect of government not found in the other types of political system that have been described.

Very small populations, sometimes no more than the inhabitants of a couple of villages, are sometimes organized in this way. It is not easy to say why this should be; but what can be said with confidence is that this is the only system that can integrate a large population into a single political community recognizing the same body of authorities with the same rights, and with some notion of matters of common interest to be organized and regulated on behalf of them all. The 200,000 Nuer, the 900,000 Dinka, and the six million Ibo are ethnic groups, united by common culture and a sense of common identity which differentiates them from their neighbours, but they are not political communities.

A discussion of the differences in detail in the organization of different states could be extended to fill volumes, but differences of detail are more important to specialists than to the student interested in a general grasp of principles of social structure.

A typical African state

The following could serve as a description of a 'typical' state in eastern and southern Africa. A particular lineage is recognized as having the right to provide the ruler, and this claim is supported by a legend (the *mythical charter*)[1] associating them with the origin of the nation; their founding ancestor is believed to have first entered the country over which they rule, emerging from the earth or from a river, or descending from the sky, or to have led the people there from some other place, miraculously overcoming difficulties on the way. By virtue of this descent from the founding ancestor, the ruler is often held to be able, and to be alone able, to approach the line of his ancestors with prayers for the well-being of the whole people, and it is one of his principal duties to offer these prayers on appropriate occasions. In more elaborately organized states, however, there may be a specialist priesthood. Then the responsibility of the ruler is limited to seeing that the priests and temples have the resources that they need and sending offerings on appropriate occasions.

The authority of the ruler is made effective through the appointment of subordinates, each responsible for part of his territory. These may be his kin, or they may be commoners whom he rewards by such appointments for loyal service. Sometimes such offices come in practice to be regarded as hereditary; the extent to which power is actually concentrated in the hands of the ruler can be measured by asking how far he can really impose his wishes in the appointment of subordinate officials.

The headquarters of the subordinate official is a replica in miniature of the royal establishment, and he exercises the same rights over people under his authority as the ruler does over the whole population. He can call on their labour

[1] As Malinowski called it.

to keep his homestead in repair, and to hoe extra fields for him, and he is entitled to a share of their produce in tribute. His duty is to hold court and decide cases in dispute among persons under his authority, to collect the tribute due from them to the capital, and to summon the manpower required at the capital for building, cultivation, or war, unless this last is organized on some other basis.

This qualification refers to a type of state found in southern Africa, where men are recruited into age-regiments and can be called upon at any time, not only for fighting but for other public purposes. Tswana regiments, for example, were turned out to round up missing cattle. During the time when the crops were growing on the land near their homes the Tswana sent their cattle away to graze in distant parts of the country; then, after harvest, they were brought back to feed on the stubble. A good many might stray away during the move, and a regiment would be called up to go and find them. When cash came to be more useful than direct labour, some chiefs sent regiments down to Johannesburg to earn at the mines money to be spent on public ends.

Both the ruler and his subordinates hold positions of privilege. They receive tribute in kind and in labour, and they are able to live in greater comfort (within the limits imposed by a subsistence economy) and with a higher standard of conspicuous consumption than the generality of their subjects. Rulers usually have a claim to those natural products of their territory that are rare, and, as such, valuable, and also to those that are most valuable in external trade. Ivory and the skins of certain wild animals are typically royal property. The Tallensi chiefs (men with little political authority) claim the right to all shea-butter trees in their territory. In the gold-bearing parts of Ashanti chiefs used to claim a third of all gold found by their subjects.

Before these small-scale states were incorporated into wider political units, these claims on the resources of the country and the labour and produce of its population provided the economic basis of the state. We should ask next whether the ordinary citizen derived from the existence of the state benefits which made it worth his while to accede to the claims of rulers and their subordinates.

Certain benefits were commonly recognized. The first of these was the existence of institutions for the settlement of disputes; this was explicitly valued wherever centralized government had been established. The governmental system (provided, of course, it was working properly) afforded protection against violence within its territory and attack from without. The prosecution of successful war brought glory to all citizens and wealth to some—those whose performance had been thought worthy to be rewarded with a share of the booty. The ritual performed by the ruler, or financed by him, guaranteed the good will of the spirit world towards his subjects, and was indeed usually considered indispensable to their well-being. The surplus wealth of ruler and chiefs enabled them to reward services and assist the needy, and this they were expected to do. Those who were called upon for labour expected to be rewarded with food, and more lavish food, particularly in the provision of meat, than they would have at home. A centralized government, on however small a scale, offered prospects for social advancement through services which found favour with authority, and this was the principal form of social advancement in a non-commercial society, where people could not rise in status through economic efforts alone. The power, and the display, of rulers and chiefs was a matter of pride to the majority of their subjects, though at any given moment some of them might be smarting under harsh punishment, or grumbling at the tribute taken from them or the labour imposed upon them.

There were, moreover, definite expectations attached to the role of ruler or chief, and these were publicly stated on solemn occasions, notably during rites of accession. These rites typically included mimed performances of the actions characteristic of a ruler, and exhortations to him to rule in accordance with established norms. Thus a Ganda ruler at his accession shot arrows towards all four points of the compass to signify that he would conquer his enemies; at the accession of a king of Bunyoro a trial was enacted to remind him of his duty as the source of justice; a Tswana chief was reminded that his subjects were 'people and not dumb cattle' (and so could express resentment if he inspired it).

As Beattie has pointed out,[2] the power of any ruler is diminished by the very fact that he has to delegate it. He can never be sure that his subordinates will carry out his wishes in full measure, and exactly in accord with his intentions. It does not necessarily follow, of course, that their modification of his intentions will be deliberately made in the interests of the people under his authority, or will in practice work out in their interests. This can happen, however, particularly in the case of unpopular innovations. Thus some Tswana chiefs were persuaded by missionaries to impose severe penalties for the seduction of unmarried girls, but their laws became a dead letter because nobody would enforce them.

No African ruler has ever been expected to take decisions in matters affecting his subjects without consulting anyone else, and among the counsellors whom chiefs were required by custom to consult were some whose duty it was to let him know the reactions of these subjects. Among the Bantu it was customary for the ruler to have as his chief adviser a man not of his lineage—that is, a commoner who was expected to be, among other things, a mouthpiece of popular dissatisfaction. This chief counsellor, or, as he has often been called, prime minister, was of course a very important person and one of the richest in the country; his circumstances were not such as to make him easily put himself in the place of the humble supplier of tribute or labour. But he was expected to listen to people who thought they had been wronged—particularly by unjust punishments—and to remonstrate privately with the ruler and persuade him to make amends without publicly admitting that he was at fault.[3]

The councils with which affairs of state were discussed were variously constituted. They might consist, as among the Ganda, of all the leading subordinate chiefs, or, as among the Tswana, of all adult Tswana men (but not any

---

[2] J. H. M. Beattie, *Bunyoro, an African Kingdom*, 1960, p. 28.
[3] See, for example, Schapera, *Government and Politics in Tribal Societies*, 1956, pp. 150 ff.

member of the other peoples who had come under Tswana rule); such popular assemblies could not easily be held among most African peoples, but the majority of members of every Tswana tribe lived in a single town near one of the rare sources of permanent water, and so the men could easily be summoned to the council-place.

West Africa provides us with examples of more elaborate systems. That of Abuja, a kingdom in the north of Nigeria, has been described in detail by M. G. Smith[4] as it was in the nineteenth century. The king was obliged by custom to consult certain officials, each of whom held a position described by a specific title. These were the eighteen officials of the palace and the four senior officials who had governmental authority in the country at large. The latter included the Madawaki, or army commander, and the officials with ultimate responsibility for tax-collection, the organization of police and prisons, the control of markets and the provision of supplies to the army and the royal capital (in Abuja, a Muslim state, justice was dispensed by specialists learned in the Koran, who were not supposed to participate in political discussions). Since he depended on his officials to carry out any decision that he might make, the king would in any case have had to secure their support. But proposals which they put forward might be rejected by the household officials, in which case the decision rested with the king. Administrative posts were commonly filled by the promotion of household officials—but their appointment had to have the agreement of the four seniors. Thus there was room for a good deal of political manoeuvre, in which the king did not necessarily have the last word.

Clearly this kind of arrangement for balancing royal claims to autocracy is worth more to the members of the official hierarchy or ruling class than it is to the population at large. Their principal recourse, in the days of fluid political and administrative frontiers, was evasion. Within a kingdom individuals could move from one chief's area to another; and on a larger scale, groups could secede, and either make themselves independent or seek the protection of another ruler. The ultimate safeguard against oppres-

[4] *Government in Zazzau*, 1960, especially pp. 36–42.

sive authority was the desire of rulers and their subordinates alike to keep up the numbers of their following. This is not to say that people in societies which had never heard of democratic freedoms did not put up with a good deal before deciding that they had had enough.

The struggle for power

What is 'politics'? In his discussion of the manoeuvring that the rules of the Abuja system make possible Smith emphasizes the distinction mentioned earlier between politics and administration. The latter is the exercise of authority within recognized limits; the former, according to Smith, includes both competition for positions carrying authority and attempts to influence decisions in public matters, and also any action of a person endowed with authority that goes beyond the recognized limits of his right to command. Authority itself, in the political sense, has been defined as the legitimate use of power; the right to command implies the right, and the ability, to punish the disobedient. Of course there may also be moral authority, which does not rely on physical power, but on religious belief and on the sentiments inculcated in the process of bringing up children; authority within kin groups is of this kind, and this is why most anthropologists regard kinship and political organization as analytically separable aspects of society. Politics in Smith's sense would include intriguing for one's own, or a friend's, appointment to an official post; it would also include any action that might be described by the term 'abuse of power'. Perhaps the most characteristic expression of 'politics' in this sense, in the field that social anthropologists study, is the competition between princes for succession to a throne. It is rare for the rules of succession to designate one man as the heir apparent, and even where they do so there may often be doubt whether the rules have been correctly followed. The Zulu rule was that a chief must be the eldest son of the 'Great Wife'—the woman whom his father married after he had himself become chief, to whose marriage cattle the whole nation had contributed. There was little room for argument here, but the working out of the rule itself could lead to a struggle for power. If a chief succeeded late in life his legal heir might well be a child when he died. Then a regency would be necessary. Probably a younger brother of the dead chief would become regent; he might consolidate a following before the heir was old enough to succeed, and be unwilling to surrender power when the time came.

But it was very commonly the rule that any son of a chief could succeed him, and sometimes any son of a man who had been chief at an earlier period was eligible when a new one had to be chosen. Some peoples had 'kingmakers' —a small body of senior officials who were expected to know the dead king's wishes, and also to select the candidate whom they thought best endowed for the responsibilities of rule. But it is unlikely that they made their choice on grounds of personal merit alone; they must have considered the popularity—that is, the following—that different candidates could command. The rule in Buganda, as described by the missionary Roscoe[5] from the accounts of old men who remembered the pre-colonial days, was that the princes were lined up in the public space before the royal palace, and the dead king's prime minister went down the line till he came to the chosen one, picked him out and presented him to the people. But when he had done so, he invited anyone who was dissatisfied with the choice to challenge it in combat. In the neighbouring kingdom of Ankole the tradition was that the successor must fight for his throne till he had defeated all his rivals and captured the sacred emblem of kingship, the drum Bagyendangwa.[6] Theoretically the unsuccessful rivals should have been killed, and this would have effectively eliminated the possibility of revolt during his reign. We do not know what actually happened to them, though we do know that some kings eliminated possible rivals at a later stage in the reign by having them put to death.

Where it is the rule that any man whose father has been chief may succeed, the competition is liable to be keener because the descendants of an unsuccesful candidate are for

[5] J. Roscoe, *The Baganda*, 1911, pp. 189 ff.
[6] See K. Oberg, 'The Kingdom of Ankole in Uganda', in M. Fortes and E. E. Evans-Pritchard (eds.), *African Political Systems*, 1940.

ever disqualified from the succession; in fact there must be many such in every generation. In societies which have such a rule, one often finds that two or three lineages expect to provide the ruler in turn. The Shilluk of the Upper Nile are an example; it has become customary there for the Reth to take under his protection and patronage a young man from one of the alternating lineages, and in this way secure for himself the friendship of at any rate one of them. Many of the Yoruba kingdoms in the west of Nigeria have a similar rule. Where there is a choice of candidates there is also a recognized procedure for making the choice. But it is not to be supposed that the competitors just wait passively for the decision; they must do what they can to further their own chances.

It was a very common rule in pre-colonial Africa that princes—potential rivals to the ruler—must be kept at a distance from him. Sometimes they might be appointed to chiefdoms in distant parts of the country; but it was perhaps more common for them to be excluded from political office altogether. In widely separated parts of Africa (e.g. Nigeria and the Upper Nile) the wives of rulers went home to their own kinsmen to give birth, and their sons were brought up among their mothers' kin. This kept them out of court intrigue, but it also gave to each an opportunity of winning a following in a different part of the country, with his mother's lineage, who could not compete with him but could expect to profit by his success, as its nucleus.

There can also be competition among commoners for royal favour—in particular for appointment to those offices which bring prestige and wealth to their holders. Where a central authority was firmly established, this form of political action consisted essentially in pleasing those already in authority, but since it was held to be a mark of worthiness for promotion to attract a large following, competition for the king's favour could also be, as was suggested earlier, a safeguard for the subjects of a chief against oppressive rule.

One could even find an element of 'politics' in this sense in the rise to prominence of the informal leaders found in non-centralized societies; for no man attains to a position of influence without seeking it. In the age-based societies of

Kenya we are sometimes told that quite young men might be appointed to the grade of elder if they showed wisdom beyond their years. This statement has been interpreted to mean that every lineage had to be represented among the elders, so that if a young man became the head of a lineage through the death of everyone older, he would have to be promoted. It is possible though that men built up for themselves positions of leadership which were formally recognized in this way.

There may also be political struggles between rulers and their most powerful chiefs. Max Weber (1864–1920), the German sociologist whose work has influenced many contemporary anthropologists, argued that in a system where subordinate authorities are rewarded for the work they do by a share in the resources of the area they administer, they are apt to treat this area as their own property, and may successfully establish a claim to hand on their official position to their heirs.[7] Then, if the ruler wishes to maintain his authority and insist on his right to appoint his subordinates, he must challenge this claim and break the succession. Records of the clan membership of the ten 'great chiefs' of Buganda in the period before British occupation suggest such alternation at different times in the balance of power between kings and their chiefs.[8]

Many anthropologists have described such a system as 'feudal', thereby transferring a European word to an African context. For historians this word describes a period in the history of western Europe during which a number of changes in political relationships took place. Historians criticize our use of the word because the political systems we describe do not seem to them to resemble closely enough the conditions of western Europe at the point they choose as marking the essence of 'the feudal system'. Marxists use the word 'feudal' to describe a stage of society between that based on slave-labour and that based on private ownership of capital.

Of course we cannot expect that any African political

[7] M. Weber, *The Theory of Social and Economic Organization*, translated by A. M. Henderson and Talcott Parsons, 1947, pp. 351 ff.
[8] See M. Southwold, *Bureaucracy and Chiefship in Buganda*, 1961.

system should correspond in detail to any one western European feudal system. But we could usefully use the word if we were agreed as to what are the essential characteristics of feudalism. At present this is not the case. Max Weber, whose use of 'ideal types' was an attempt to characterize the essentials of different political systems without getting lost in the details of particular cases, defined feudalism as a system in which the administrative staff are maintained by fiefs, and a fief as 'a set of appropriated governing powers . . . granted primarily to particular qualified individuals by a contract' in which 'the reciprocal rights and duties involved are primarily oriented to conventional standards of the honour, particularly in a military connection, of a distinctive social group'.[9] If anthropologists were to adopt this definition the use of the term would probably have to be restricted more narrowly than it has been hitherto.

Where the superior power is weak, or none is recognized, political competition may consist predominantly in the attempt to secure a following. The clientship (*ubuhake*) system in Rwanda, as its working has been reconstructed by the Belgian anthropologist Maquet,[10] illustrates this. The Rwanda recognized a single ruler, who appointed his own chiefs to collect tribute and labour on his behalf. But every member of the ruling Tusi population gathered to himself followers, who entered into a specific relationship with him, offering services in return for protection. As we know from records of the neighbouring kingdom, Burundi, some of these chiefs tried to set themselves up as independent rulers; the king of Burundi then sent *his* clients to plunder their possessions and reduce them to submission. Only a man whose following was strong enough to resist the king's could have succeeded in such an attempt.

A society where this kind of competition has been described in great detail is that of the Pathans in the Swat valley on the north-west frontier of India.[11] Here the land is owned by the descendants of immigrant conquerors, the

[9] ibid., p. 351.
[10] J. J. Maquet, *The Premise of Inequality in Ruanda*, 1961.
[11] F. Barth, *Political Leadership among Swat Pathans*, 1959.

Pakhtuns, who divided it among themselves when they entered the valley some four hundred years ago. They constituted a single large lineage, subdivided into the descendants of sons and grandsons of the founder. The conquered territory was said to have been divided into shares for these separate descent groups by a holy man who was appealed to to settle quarrels between them. This myth (for even if the story is true, it is a myth in the sense that it is appealed to as justification for an existing state of affairs) describes the essence of Swat politics as they were observed in 1954. Land is lineage property; agnates quarrel over land; holy men are called in to settle disputes if people for whatever reason prefer not to fight them out.

Whereas African chiefs were interested in the control of territory, much of which was not cultivated, primarily for the sake of the population in it, on whom they could call for services and tribute, the Pakhtuns of Swat are interested in the control of cultivable land as such; they are landlords in the accepted sense of the word. Their wealth is derived from rice grown by landless persons on contracts made with Pakhtuns. Every extension of a man's holding of land directly increases his wealth. One way to extend one's boundaries is to remove his neighbour's landmark; in other words, to plough an extra furrow in every season. A weaker neighbour may not dare to protest; a weaker neighbour is one who has a smaller following. But there might be protests; and until a few decades ago there was also occasion for dispute because the original settlement made by the holy man was held to involve a periodic redistribution of all land so as to give every lineage its fair share of the best kinds.

Since there is no superior authority which can impose a settlement in disputes, these are very often settled by the relative strength of the parties; hence the actual numbers of a man's following are all-important. Not every landowner can make himself a leader; the landowners of a small area choose as their chief the most prominent man, judging by the same qualities that win the chief his following.

These qualities are the same that are admired in all turbulent societies: generosity and courage. Every chief maintains a 'men's house' in which his followers gather to spend their leisure hours. From time to time he gives feasts there, and the poor landless villagers depend upon these for a large part of their subsistence. The chief gains his followers by offering this hospitality, and he gains the means to offer hospitality by using his followers to maintain or extend the area of land under his control. The Swat attitude towards the obligation incurred by accepting hospitality differs from what has been recorded of many African and Oceanic peoples; it is not a matter of being unable to repay a gift, but of the almost sacred bond of loyalty created by 'eating a man's salt'. Attendance at the man's house is a public declaration of allegiance, and when a dispute is boiling up it is by going to the man's house that people rally behind their leader.

In a large village there may be rival men's houses, and any man may attend the men's house of a neighbouring village. People choose the men's house of a leader whose hospitality is lavish, and whom they respect for his readinesss to avenge insult or injury. Revenge in Swat is not limited to the exaction of an equivalent for the offence received; it should be pursued as far as the injured party is able, and if possible until the offender's side are driven to beg for peace. Success in pursuing revenge gains a man honour and followers. But revenge is not pursued through pitched battles; it is for the purpose of extending control over land that chiefs number their following. Disputes over land are of necessity disputes between lineages; therefore no obligation to support agnatic kinsmen can come to be recognized as a general principle. Loyalty to agnates is expected only within the minimal agnatic group—a father with his sons. It is assumed that sons will always stand by their father, so that the greatest blessing is to have many sons; but Barth has recorded cases where sons ranged themselves in the opposite camp to their fathers. As for brothers, as soon as the father dies, and his lands are divided, they become rivals. It is interesting, nevertheless, to see where common lineage ties do, or may, form a bond of alliance. If a man has gone as far as he can in extending power over the land claimed by his nearer collaterals, he may begin to encroach on that of more remotely related lineages (it must be remembered that all Pakhtun lineages are supposed to be genealogically related). But since any member of a more distant lineage feels that he has a better claim to its land than the outsider, they will be likely to unite in opposition to him; for some of them this will mean transferring their support from his bloc of allies to the opposing one.

A more general reason for the instability of alliances is that many men are ambitious, and no one of these likes to see anyone else get too strong. Rivalries develop within a successful alliance; and since these cannot be fought out in an explicit contest for leadership—since allies are regarded as equals and do not recognize one of their number as leader—they can only be resolved by the defection to the other side of men who hope to wield greater influence there.

Where the governments of newly independent African countries have decided that they canot afford to tolerate organized political opposition, they frequently appeal to an alleged African tradition that decisions in affairs of state, though freely discussed beforehand, must not be questioned once the discussion has been concluded and action agreed upon; and this supposed principle is quoted in many of the books that have been published on contemporary politics. This is not a statement to be supported or contradicted; it is a statement to which it is impossible to attach meaning in the context of pre-colonial Africa. The essential difference between the modern African states and those that have been described in this chapter is in the nature of the decisions that their rulers were expected to take. These were *ad hoc* executive, once-for-all decisions on such questions as who was at fault in a dispute, when a warlike expedition should be mounted and against whom, who should be appointed to some office. Such decisions, once taken, cannot easily be reversed; they may well be criticized, but it would be absurd to conceive of an opposition party dedicated to undoing them. Something of the kind, however, may be said to have happened when Tswana tribes repudiated decrees inspired by missionaries. But in general it is not until governments make themselves responsible for functions that were unknown to the pre-colonial rulers, notably the direction of economic policy, that they become involved in the kind of decision that does not finally settle any question and that can be made a subject of continuing debate.

SUGGESTIONS FOR READING

I. Schapera, *Government and Politics in Tribal Societies* (1956), and L. P. Mair, *Primitive Government* (1962), discuss small-scale states in southern and eastern Africa respectively. Recommended West African studies are R. S. Rattray, *Ashanti* (1923), C. K. Meek, *A Sudanese Kingdom* (1931), on the Jukun of Northern Nigeria, S. F. Nadel, *A Black Byzantium* (1942), on the Nupe of Northern Nigeria, and M. G. Smith, *Government in Zazzau* (1960), a combined historical and analytical account of the Emirate of Zaria. R. E. Bradbury, *Benin Studies* (1973) and W. J. Argyle, *The Fon of Dahomey* (1966).

The political significance of clientship is discussed in J. J. Maquet, *The Premise of Inequality in Ruanda* (1961), and in L. A. Fallers (ed.), *The King's Men* (1964), a collection of essays on Buganda. Max Weber's ideas on bureaucracy are applied to Africa in L. A. Fallers, *Bantu Bureaucracy* (1956), on Busoga in Uganda, and M. Southwold, *Bureaucracy and Chiefship in Buganda* (1961), as well as in *Government in Zazzau*. F. Barth, *Political Leadership among Swat Pathans* (1959), shows how rivals for power build up followings, and this question is discussed in more general terms in F. G. Bailey, *Stratagems and Spoils* (1969). J. P. Singh Uberoi, *Politics of the Kula Ring* (1962), shows how the small Melanesian communities linked by the *kula* ceremonial exchange have something in common with a segmentary political system as this is understood in Africa. J. M. Gullick, *Indigenous Political Systems of Western Malaya* (1958), is one of the few non-African studies.

Marc Bloch, *Feudal Society* (English translation 1961), describes forms of political organization in many ways like those that anthropologists study.

CHAPTER 9　　Law

LAW is a subject which can be treated in more than one context. It is certainly an aspect of government, since the basic responsibility of government is recognized to be the maintenance of law and order; and some discussion of the settlement of disputes has inevitably been brought in in the chapters on politics. But since it is concerned with rules of conduct and the forces which operate to secure respect for these rules, it also belongs to the wider field that social scientists call *social control.* People have tried to separate laws from other rules by various criteria, some of which obviously cannot be applied to most small-scale societies, though others might. Thus, if one thinks of laws as rules enacted by a superior authority, one must say that some societies lack them, because, with very few exceptions, rulers in pre-literate societies do not enact laws. They issue commands—'Go out and bring in tribute', 'Send the army against the enemy in the north', 'Put this man to death'— but they do not make rules for the conduct of social relationships, saying that what was permissible yesterday will be forbidden from tomorrow, or that the procedures for making marriage legal, or the lines along which inheritance should run, are to be changed.

But one might argue that laws are to be distinguished from other rules by the way in which they are enforced, and this would lead one to ask whether they are or are not to be found in all societies. On this question social anthropologists have held different views.

An earlier chapter discussed the question whether any society could be said to lack a political system, and answered it in the negative. But it recalled that Fortes and Evans-Pritchard, who showed us how to recognize a political system where there was no ruler, asserted that some societies had political systems but not government. Similarly Rad-

cliffe-Brown, who provided these writers with a definition
of a political system, held that to have a political system did
not necessarily entail having law.

What is law?

This proposition, which had already been advanced by
earlier writers than Radcliffe-Brown, has engendered much
controversy, some of it very tedious. In considering the
arguments that have been used, it is important to realize
that when people say 'law' they do not mean quite the same
thing as they do when they say 'laws'. A good deal of confusion is caused if one slides without noticing it between
the singular and the plural. 'Laws' are rules, and if you set
out to distinguish laws from other rules you are talking
about different kinds of rules. But 'law' means the whole
process by which rules that are recognized to be binding are
maintained and enforced, including the motives and values
that influence judges, and all the manifold social forces
that prevent the majority of people from having to come
before a judge at all.

When Radcliffe-Brown wrote, 'Some simple societies
have no law, although all have customs which are supported
by sanctions', he was thinking of a specific way of enforcing
rules, and also by implication defining laws and rules enforced in this way.

But when Evans-Pritchard wrote that within a Nuer
tribe 'there is law',[2] he implied that law exists where people
agree that certain actions infringe the rights of others, and
also agree that injuries can be made good, and so disputes
formally settled and the parties reconciled, by the payment
of compensation. By implication he here defined law in
terms of an institution, the procedure of compensation and
reconciliation; if a Nuer is injured by a member of another
tribe he is held to be justified in retaliating, but there is
no procedure for ending the quarrel, and therefore, on his
argument, no law.

[1] 'Primitive Law', in *Structure and Function in Primitive Society*, 1952.
[2] M. Fortes and E. E. Evans-Pritchard (eds.), *African Political Systems*,
1940, p. 278.

What kind of rules are laws?

Some earlier anthropologists had not only argued that the simpler societies had no law but only custom, but had also maintained that custom differed from law in being obeyed automatically without any need for enforcement. The writer who most strongly combated this view was Malinowski, who from his first published work, twenty years before Radcliffe-Brown wrote the sentence I have quoted, insisted that law was to be found in every society, however simple. His purpose was to attack the idea, which was by no means universally held but was favoured in some quarters, that 'primitive man' was entirely dominated by customs which he never thought of disregarding. Malinowski's great contribution in this field was to draw attention to the importance in social life of the principle of 'reciprocity': the fact that every man depends on many others and must meet his obligations towards them if he wants them to meet his own claims upon them. This is true of every society, but above all true of the 'face-to-face' societies where people depend directly on their neighbours' co-operation in every vicissitude of life. The value of this contribution was only obscured by his many different attempts to set up a definition that would clearly distinguish law from custom. Other writers too have sought a definition that would identify law in societies that lack the institutions which readily come to mind as 'legal' to most of us. One of the latest books on the subject refers to 'the vast amount of words that have been spilled out in increasingly fruitless controversy'. One reason for the controversy has certainly been a confusion of the type just mentioned between 'law' as a particular type of rule and 'law' as a way of enforcing rules and seeing that people get their rights. 'Law' as a way of making new rules belongs rather to the field of politics.

Of course every society has rules that it calls 'laws' and others that it calls 'customs'. Both are matters of knowing how people expect you to behave and what you can expect of them. Where there are what Malinowski called 'codes, courts and constables' people recognize that you can do many things that other people won't like, but only some of them will get you into trouble with the police; that you may have many grievances against other people, but you can only go to law about some of them. The difficulty of definition arises where there are no courts or constables. Some writers on that type of society play safe by referring to 'customary law'.

Certainly every society has some rules of a kind that we would not hesitate to call laws when they apply to ourselves. Even the Hadza, whom I quoted as an example of minimal organization, have a rule that if you want to marry you must give your mother-in-law some strings of beads, and if you want to stay married you must give her meat whenever you bring any home; otherwise she will marry her daughter to a better provider, and there is nothing you can do. Most readers will I think regard this as a different kind of rule from the rules of the gambling game that Hadza play whenever they have nothing to do. If you are thinking of a number of such rules you are more likely to call them 'laws' in the plural. Nevertheless, both lawyers and anthropologists who have made collections of such rules in different societies are more likely to call their books by such titles as *Sebei Law* or *Zuni Law* than to use the plural.

Are we then—is it necessary?—to frame a definition to tell us which of these rules are laws and which not? Such definitions are constantly being offered, examined, and rejected. What is called the Austinian definition of law—'the command of a sovereign'—obviously cannot apply where there is no sovereign, and it has been rejected by lawyers in modern states as well. Some American writers have said that law is whatever you can expect a court to enforce; but that is no good where there are no courts.

Radcliffe-Brown took a definition from the American jurist Roscoe Pound: law is 'social control through the systematic application of the force of politically organized society'. This brings his definition of law very close to his definition of a political system; indeed it could be said that they are two sides of a penny, and there is no harm in that if it is agreed that the most rudimentary political systems are concerned with the elementary need for the maintenance of order and the protection of recognized rights. But here we have slipped across the boundary that divides 'laws' from 'law' as the means of enforcing rules. In Radcliffe-Brown's mind the link was that rules which deserve to be called laws are those which 'politically organized society' would enforce. But the fundamental rules of all societies are the same. They safeguard life and limb, rights in wives, and rights in property. The Nuer defend their rights by 'self-help'—by going out with a spear and a band of friends and taking the compensation or revenge that they consider due to them. Radcliffe-Brown did not regard this as a legal action; it was not part of a judicial system. But the injuries that led a Nuer to retaliate were just the same as those for which a Tswana sought redress in a chief's court. If the Nuer have no law while the Tswana have, the rules that you must not steal a man's property, or kill him, or run away with his wife, or neglect to pay him what you owe him, are laws for one but not for the other. Which is absurd.

The anthropologists who have contributed most to the study of law in the last two decades are the American, E. A. Hoebel, and the South African (teaching in Manchester), Max Gluckman. Hoebel expands Radcliffe-Brown's definition in a manner that would grant the possession of law to the Nuer, and to other peoples where public opinion allows and approves retaliation although there is no court to authorize punishment. Indeed Hoebel would say that there *is* a court: what we call 'the bar of public opinion'. Hoebel writes: 'A social norm is legal if its neglect or infraction is regularly met, in threat or in fact, by the application of physical force by an individual or group possessing the socially recognized privilege of so acting.' Would that cover the Hadza's obligations to his mother-in-law? I wonder.

Gluckman dealt with this difficulty by showing that a distinction between types of society is a different matter from a distinction between different types of rule. Courts and constables are legal (or judicial) *institutions,* and they are possessed in some form by every society that recognizes a ruler, and some others as well, such as the East African age-organized societies where the settlement of disputes is the duty of elders as a body. Societies without courts, says Gluckman, have *rules of law* but not *legal rules*. He calls such societies *a-legal*. The rules he refers to are those that Radcliffe-Brown called *jural*. The word comes from the Latin word *jus,* meaning a right, whereas 'legal' comes from the Latin *lex,* meaning a law in the sense of something enacted ('the command of the sovereign'). So justice by derivation means giving people their rights rather than enforcing laws, and this is somewhere in people's minds when, as they often do, they contrast justice and legality.

Pospisil, an American anthropologist trained in law, who has worked in West Irian, finds law in rules for which there is no physical sanction and writes: 'Law is conceived as rules or modes of conduct made obligatory by some sanction which is imposed or enforced for their violation by a controlling authority'.[3] Sanctions may include ostracism, ridicule, avoidance or denial of favours. Radcliffe-Brown knew of all these sanctions, but he regarded them as unorganized, and therefore not legal. What makes a rule legal in Pospisil's eyes is that it is a controlling authority and not an injured individual who imposes the sanctions. Even this definition does not cover the Hadza and his mother-in-law (unless taking away your wife is a 'denial of favours'; even then the elder lady does not appeal to a controlling authority). But is not marriage a legal relationship?

Gluckman tells us that both the concepts and the procedure of Lozi law have close counterparts in European systems. Another anthropologist, Paul Bohannan, insists that we do violence to the societies we observe if we try to fit their ideas into our categories. Our legal language, he says, is as much a 'folk-system' as any of theirs. But even he cannot get away from the necessity of writing in a language that can be read by others than the few literate Tiv (the Nigerian people of whom he writes). He does, however, use other words than those of professional lawyers, and that certainly helps us to look with fresh eyes at the 'law-ways' of the Tiv.

Hoebel, on the other hand, argues that *if* western jurisprudence has worked out legal concepts that *really are* fundamental, anthropologists should make use of these to order their data. He recognizes that there is often much confusion in the language of legal analysis, but he finds in

[3] L. Pospisil, *Kapauku Papuans and their Law,* 1958, p. 257.

the work of one American writer, W. N. Hohfeld, a schema which does not depend on the usual technical vocabulary, and which both he and Gluckman consider could be applied to any system. Hohfeld argued that basic legal relations were always between pairs of persons, and he divided all legal relationships into four pairs. The first two are those that anthropologists would find most useful. If A has a claim on B, B has an obligation towards A (a pair of words that have already appeared often enough in this book). If A has a *privilege*, that is a relationship between him and anybody else you can think of; a privilege is something nobody can stop you doing. Here at last, by concentrating on the nature of the rule rather than the nature of the sanction, we can accommodate Hadza marriage.

Trouble cases

Hoebel's great contribution to the study of primitive law, however, consisted in asserting the principle that law cases are 'trouble cases'. He made this assertion in the context of an American Indian tribe, the Cheyenne, who would earlier have been thought to have no legal institutions, and therefore, in Radcliffe-Brown's eyes, no law. He recorded all the 'trouble cases' that came his way and deduced both Cheyenne law and Cheyenne legal institutions from what he saw. He found that many procedures that didn't look at all like those of courts of law had the same *function* of dispute settlement. For example, when he extended his study to the records of another Indian tribe, the Yurok in California, he found that they dealt with disputes by sending messengers to and fro between the two parties until some agreement was reached as to who was at fault and what compensation should be paid. He says the two go-betweens 'rendered a decision for damages', but admits that what actually happened may not have been quite so cut and dried.

Recent work by anthropologists has concentrated on the careful recording of cases, as far as possible in the context of what is already known about the disputants, their relative status, and the events that led up to a 'trouble case'. P. H. Gulliver, a London anthropologist who has done much work of this kind in Tanzania, maintains what is implicit in Hoebel, that when we are studying law what we should really be looking for is *the process of dispute settlement*. By a dispute he means a quarrel that has reached the point where the man who thinks he is injured demands some kind of third-party intervention to establish what his rights are and give him the satisfaction due to him. He reminds us that 'settlement' does not necessarily dispose of the issue. But once a *quarrel* has been treated by either party as a *dispute* something has to be done.

There are two main ways of dealing with a complaint that somebody has broken the law. One is to persuade or compel him to make restitution to the person he has wronged. The other is to punish the lawbreaker; if that method is chosen, it could be argued that he is making restitution to the community as a whole, being held by his action to have injured them all. This division corresponds to the distinction in modern jurisprudence between torts and crimes; and there has been a good deal of discussion about the way small-scale societies divide offences between these two categories. Sir Henry Maine wrote that 'in the infancy of jurisprudence the citizen depended for protection against violence or fraud not on the law of crime but on the law of tort'.[4] He referred to the familiar fact that in small-scale societies many offences that we are accustomed to see treated as crimes are dealt with by compensating the victim. But his way of putting it suggests that the distinction between civil and criminal cases is one that could be recognized in any society. Bohannan pointed out that the Tiv language does not permit such a distinction to be made. The Tiv have only one word that can be translated 'breach of norm'; this word, *ifer*, he says, means 'that wrong of which the accused stands accused'.[5] This is part of his argument that we should not try to describe the institutions of alien peoples in the technical language that fits our own. But if one looks, not at what people say but at what they do, one can certainly distinguish between these two ways of treating a case, and the words crime and tort are convenient for doing so.

4 *Ancient Law*, 10th edn., 1912, pp. 380–1.
5 *Justice and Judgment among the Tiv*, 1957, p. 119.

Radcliffe-Brown followed Durkheim in his discussion of the grounds on which different societies adopted one or other of these two ways of dealing with breaches of their rules. An act which is treated as a crime, he argued, is one that is held to injure society as a whole by its very enormity; it is the feeling of moral indignation aroused (in some societies) by murder, for example, that leads people to feel that restitution to the family of the victim is not enough. But in these days, when governments are constantly making rules the breach of which is an offence against them and not against any private citizen—such as bringing whisky into the country without paying duty or riding a bicycle without lights—it is difficult to argue that all crimes are held to be such because of the strong sense of injury that society feels when they are committed.

Certainly, there is a marked contrast in this respect between small-scale and large-scale societies. In the latter, a very great number of offences are punished by the state, including some, such as theft, which clearly injure particular individuals. In the former, even homicide is conceived as an injury to the slain man's kin, for which they should accept compensation if it is offered; and if the killer is himself killed, this is in vengeance by the people directly injured and not in punishment by a wrathful society. So Radcliffe-Brown, discussing primitive law, remarked that simple societies recognize very few crimes. The examples he gives are all offences punished by death or banishment, and most of them are actions that could also be called sins—that is to say they are believed to offend spiritual beings and by doing so to bring pollution on society. Incest is often regarded as such an offence. Some societies expel or kill people accused of witchcraft, an activity which in their eyes is the most abominable of sins. But Radcliffe-Brown drew attention to one particular crime which has no such religious association—'the crime of being a bad lot'. In fact this does not always refer to the whole range of actions which might give a man such a name; it is recorded of several societies that they expel incorrigible thieves. It is true also of most centralized societies that offences against the ruler himself are severely punished, often with death.

But the principle which covers the majority of breaches of rule is that it is the injured individual who matters, and that what is important is for him to be compensated. Among the pastoral Turkana of northern Kenya there is no agreed scale of compensation, and an injured man who can muster support from his friends will go on seizing cattle until he considers he has taken enough. The Nuer recognize a fixed number of cattle as due in compensation for a homicide; the amount is larger if the slain man is an aristocrat—that is to say, is living in the part of Nuerland that 'belongs' to his descent group. But it is a mistake to interpret this, as is often done, as meaning that for the Nuer 'law is relative'. Homicide is a wrong that must be avenged or compensated, whoever is killed; there is nothing relative about that rule. The fact that a big man's life is valued more highly than a little man's does not mean that it is less wrong to kill a little man.

Usually one finds that settled agriculturalists are less turbulent than cattle people who move about with their herds. For cultivators who have no cattle, one explanation may be that they have no possessions which can be readily seized and carried off in compensation. But many farmers are also cattle owners, and one society of such people, the Arusha, expressly forbid self-help and private vengeance. Gulliver has suggested that this is because their country is so densely settled that the disorder it could create would be intolerable.[6]

One cannot divide societies neatly into those in which disputes are fought out, and those in which they are argued out before an impartial authority which decides who is right and what is to be done. The latter type indubitably have legal institutions; some of the former might be said to go only part of the way. Thus, among the Luhya of western Kenya, the heads of descent groups were traditionally held to be responsible for the actions of their members, and if someone was involved in a dispute the elders of the two groups got together and tried to agree on a solution. Except within the narrowest descent group, no solution could be imposed unless the parties agreed. In the case of a dispute

[6] *Social Control in an African Society*, p. 220.

between members of a larger lineage it was not considered permissible to fight the matter out, but if no reconciliation could be attained the weaker party numerically (who could not have won in a fight) moved away and broke off relations with the rest of the lineage. If the disputants belonged to different clans, and the elders failed to find an agreed solution, there would be fighting, though the elders were still expected to intervene as soon as there was an opportunity.[7] This is the kind of proceeding that led a District Commissioner in quite another part of Africa—Sierra Leone— to say that African disputes were settled by 'diplomatic rather than judicial methods'.

Then there have been societies in which rulers held courts and decided cases, but left it to the injured party to collect the redress awarded them. Among the Nkole of western Uganda the kinsmen of a slain man were allowed to seek vengeance, though only after the ruler had authorized it; and even among the Ganda, in the most highly organized kingdom of eastern Africa, blood-feuds were sometimes pursued.

Primitive judicial processes

But even in African societies where the authority of the ruler's courts was unquestioned, and no resort to force was considered legitimate, the decisions of the courts were concerned as much with reconciling the parties as with awarding damages or punishing offences. This was at one time taken to indicate that there was something peculiar about African ideas of law. J. H. Driberg, an anthropologist who had been a District Commissioner, held that they were focused on the notion of restoring equilibrium; an offence disturbed the balance between two groups, and this must be righted by an appropriate payment from the offender's side. This view has been criticized by Gluckman. Gluckman points out that in a small-scale society where the people involved in disputes are usually near neighbours and will still be so after the court has decided the case, a different approach is necessary from that followed in a large-scale one,

[7] G. Wagner, *The Bantu of North Kavirondo*, summarized in L. P. Mair, *Primitive Government*, pp. 53–6.

where people who have fought a lawsuit can usually manage, after it is over, to keep out of one another's way. Gluckman reminds us that we too have legal institutions devoted to the reconciliation of parties to a dispute—the solicitors who work for a settlement out of court and do what they can to bring together quarrelling spouses or kinsmen.

Much of his elaborate analysis of the cases at which he was present in the court of the paramount chief of the Lozi, in Zambia, is directed to showing that despite the apparent differences in their procedure, Lozi judges have just the same conception of the nature of law as European ones, and indeed have a vocabulary that can be readily translated into European legal terms. To a superficial observer they appear to listen to a great deal of evidence that an English judge would consider irrelevant. They clearly do not narrow down the matter to be judged to a single question: Has the accused broken this particular law, or has he not? They are not expected to come to the matter 'unprejudiced', with no prior knowledge of the people who are to come before them; on the contrary, the more they know, the better.

Gluckman argues that this is an appropriate attitude in the circumstances of Lozi society. In this small-scale society the people between whom disputes arise are bound together in half a dozen different ways. Their relationships are, as he puts it, *multiplex*. The headman of a village is its religious as well as its political authority; he is the source of rights to cultivate land and to fish in ponds and dams; and since anyone who wants to live in a village must establish a claim in virtue of kinship with someone already living there, he is also the kinsman of everyone under his authority. When a suit is brought against a man for a wrong done in one of his roles, the judges consider how he has behaved in all of them, and they examine the behaviour of his accuser in the same way. The suit itself, though it is brought as a complaint on a specific issue, is bound to be one aspect of a total quarrel; the nature of the continuing relationships between the litigants makes this inevitable. So the judges, instead of shutting their eyes to everything except the question they were asked, consider and give judgement on the total balance of rights and wrongs. Thus, Gluckman argues, they are applying the same principle that European judges do when they compare what somebody has done with what a reasonable man might have been expected to do; but they are extending it to the whole field of the multiplex relationship between the disputants. The Lozi 'reasonable man' is more than an undifferentiated human being behaving in a reasonable way in a given situation. He is, as Gluckman puts it, 'the reasonable and customary occupier of a specific position'.[8]

Other points that anthropologists have observed in the dispute settlement procedure of small-scale societies are how courts are organized, how parties, elders, and witnesses behave, what arguments people use and which of them carry conviction, and, not least interesting, what kind of manipulation or stratagem is most effective in different societies. The answers do not always give as close parallels as Gluckman has found among the Lozi between the methods of small-scale and large-scale societies, particularly in the matter of establishing the truth.

Thus Gulliver, in his study of the Arusha, shows how a dispute may be taken, according to its nature, either before the village elders or before the lineage heads of the two parties, and how a clever litigant will calculate where he is likely to find the most support and appeal to that body even if it is not strictly speaking the appropriate one to deal with his case. He shows that witnesses and even judges are expected to be partisan; members of the same age-set should support one another, for example. It is not assumed that interested parties will speak the truth. 'An argument by one party is not necessarily expected by Arusha to be wholly truthful and straightforward. They realistically expect attempt at deceit, and are wary of false diversions; and the discovery of these fetches little resentment. Notables no less than others are prepared to lie and deceive on behalf of their own side, and a later admission of the truth is not thought to bring discredit.'[9] Gluckman might perhaps argue that it is just because our courts expect a quota of dishonesty that lawyers perfect the art of cross-examination.

[8] Op. cit., p. 155.
[9] *Social Control in an African Society*, 1963, p. 229.

Of the Arusha, however, Gulliver remarks that the elders in charge of the proceedings do make it their business to maintain orderly discussion, allowing parties and witnesses (or, more accurately, supporters) full freedom to state their case, of course including much that a British judge would dismiss as irrelevant; and that this is what is most important, for the settlement here emerges from the discussion as parties begin to make their own suggestions on which they will eventually agree.

From a very different part of the world, Surinam, the Dutch anthropologist A. J. Köbben describes how claims are asserted and disputes dealt with by the Djuka. The Djuka are a tribe of 'Bush Negroes', people whose ancestors escaped from slavery on the plantations in the eighteenth century and settled in the interior. Djuka disputes are discussed by village headmen and elders. These 'judges' align themselves *before* the 'trial' on one side or the other; some of them may change sides as it goes on. This is not a matter of kinship solidarity; they may be close kin of either, or both. They are influenced by general considerations of reason or morality as the discussion proceeds, but are apt to give more credence to the evidence for their own side. Yet the Djuka recognize the idea, and the value, of neutrality, at least to the point of accusing the other side of interested judgements. In asserting their rights the Djuka sometimes follow an ingenious method called 'I caught you'. A man puts up with an injury and says nothing about it until he finds himself in a position where he has the advantage of his adversary; say, the latter, or one of his kin group, wants to marry a girl of the victim's kin group. 'I caught you there,' he says; and refuses to consent until the injury has been admitted and compensation paid. This might be described as a kind of non-violent self-help.

Rights in land

It is obvious that legal rules are the rules of behaviour in different institutions, and that such rules have already been implicitly described in earlier parts of this book, in such contexts as marriage, descent, inheritance, or political allegiance. In relation to the economic aspects of social life the most important legal concept is that of property. This is another concept which Bohannan considers to be so peculiarly European that it cannot be usefully applied to non-European legal systems, but I would suggest that it is sufficiently general to be applicable anywhere; the only danger arises from assuming that 'property' means a totality of rights which cannot be divided and must be held by one individual. Ideas about property in movable objects do not differ much from one part of the world to another, but the rules relating to land are different where it is not a saleable commodity from what we find in wholly commercialized societies. The essential difference is that in the former case a number of people may have rights over the same piece of land.

The Tiv system described by Bohannan[10] is one of the most remarkable illustrations of this principle. The Tiv are organized in agnatic lineages, and every lineage member can claim land for a farm in an area over which his lineage as a whole has rights. But the Tiv as a people are engaged in a process of steady, slow migration, each lineage pushing into the lands of its neighbours, who in their turn move on. So 'lineage land' is not a fixed area with boundaries on a map. The place where a man can claim land to farm is next to that which his brothers are farming. The land is allotted by the head of the extended family who live in one compound (a ring of huts with a clear space in the middle). Hence, this man has a right in this area additional to the right of his juniors who cultivate it. Every man has a right to *enough* land for his dependents to get food from, and he asserts this by asking his neighbour (who is also a lineage mate) for land. This is practicable because at any given time there is an area of land lying fallow. The neighbour agrees, and, if necessary, asks *his* neighbour for land, and the process goes on until there has been in effect a redistribution of the land in accordance with the need of the existing set of families. No one is on record as ever having refused such a request. But it is important that a request must be made; nobody can simply move in in the exercise of a 'group right'. Once a man is farming land it cannot be taken from him,

[10] P. and L. Bohannan, *Tiv Economy*, 1968, Chapter 6.

nor can the field allotted to any one of his wives be taken from her.

In societies with chiefs the answer to the question 'Who owns this land?' would usually be 'The chief owns the land' —'and everything in it' would often be added. The conclusion drawn from this might be that the chief was a despot, a sort of super-landlord, against whose exactions his subjects had no protection; on the other hand, in one famous instance, that of Buganda in East Africa, large estates were allotted in freehold title to political authorities who could be described in the Ganda language as 'owning' them but who had previously had by no means the rights of landlords.

Gluckman's study of the Lozi provides us with a starting-point for this discussion, for he has enumerated the various meanings that they attach to the word which he translates as 'ownership'—*bung'a*. *Bung'a*, he says, refers to rights of whatever kind that attach to a particular status. Thus a husband is *bung'a* of his wife, not because he has bought and could sell her, but because he has authority over her. 'A headman,' Gluckman writes, 'has *bung'a* over his clothes, over his village land (over which the king has superior *bung'a*), over his own gardens in that land, over his wife, over his kinsmen, over his children.' When the Lozi want to indicate the precise nature of the rights implied in each case, they do it by specifying the status to which it applies, as wife, child, brother, subject.[11]

The quotation from Gluckman refers to three different meanings of *bung'a* in relation to land. The king's superior *bung'a* is that ownership that is generally ascribed to rulers; it is expressed in the right to claim tribute and service from the inhabitants of his country, and in the right to nominate some of his subjects as village headmen with their own type of *bung'a*. Remember the phrase 'The chief owns the country *and everything in it*'; he claims tribute and service as a political superior, not as a landlord charging rent in return for the use of his land.

The village headman's *bung'a* entitles him to say whether a newcomer may join his village and what land this man is

[11] Gluckman, *The Judicial Process among the Barotse*, 1955, p. 300.

to have for planting; and to stop outsiders from fishing the village ponds. His right over his own gardens is the same as that of his subjects over theirs—to have his neighbours respect his boundaries, to be undisturbed in cultivation as long as he is a loyal subject of his superior, performing his political duties and not plotting treason, and to pass on the gardens to his heir.

If, then, one moves from the point of view of the headman to that of the ordinary villager, one sees that three different people have *bung'a* over the land that the villager cultivates. He himself has rights of occupation which he can transmit to his heir; the village headman has the right of allocation which he exercised when the cultivator joined the village (or his predecessor did for the cultivator's predecessor); and the king has the overriding right to depose the headman, tell him to move his village, or appoint another one. An English lawyer might not regard these last rights as property rights at all; but to the Lozi they *are* expressions of the king's 'ownership' of the land. A Ganda once put the position succinctly when describing the authority of a territorial chief. Having recognized that such a man has authority over a definite area of land, including the right to admit or refuse newcomers, he said, 'He doesn't rule land, he rules people.'

In relation to any piece of land, then, rights of different kinds are exercised by different people. The Lozi are atypical in that land rights are acquired solely by village membership and not by membership of a descent group. Where descent groups own land as their corporate property, yet another type of right exists. This is the potential claim which any member has on the lineage land even if in practice he chooses not to live there.[12] The logical corollary of the existence of such claims is that individual members of a land-owning lineage cannot dispose of their rights without regard to the views of their fellow-members. It is on the whole true that nobody in the pre-commercial days ever wished to abandon altogether any rights in land that he

[12] Such claims are not usually maintained by women in patrilineal societies who marry into other lineages; it is for their husbands to provide them with land.

might have; where there is no alternative livelihood to farming, there can be nothing for which one would wish to exchange land. But people often have rights of occupation over land that they are not actually cultivating; it may be land that ought to be resting, it may be land that has become surplus because there are fewer in the family than there used to be. If an outsider seeks to use this land, as frequently happens in areas of dense population, the occupier must get the approval of the right-holding group—or at least of its recognized head—before he agrees to this. This is what has given rise to the popular idea that African land was traditionally 'communally owned'. Literally understood the phrase is perhaps correct; but if it is taken to imply that individuals have no rights at all in specific areas, it is wholly misleading. It might be more helpful to think of rights in land as being divided into rights of *use* and rights of *administration*.

The admission of outsiders to lineage land may be initiated from either side. If the outsider *asks* for a plot it must be because he is short of land, but if the rightholder *offers* one it is because he needs something else. His wife is sick and the spirits demand a sacrifice; or his father-in-law is pressing for outstanding bridewealth cattle; or he is required to pay a fine. He has to borrow from a neighbour, and as a pledge he offers land for cultivation. He is entitled to redeem the land at any time; there is no such calculation as is made in a commercial mortgage, of value of land in relation to value of loan, or of a time-limit for repayment, and no equivalent of foreclosure. Where an outsider is received as a tenant, there is similarly no question of a rent calculated in relation to the value—or the yield—of the land. The outsider is expected to give the rightholder a gift at harvest time—probably some beer brewed from his new supply of grain—but this is essentially an acknowledgment of his relationship of dependence. Often the tenant becomes an affine by marrying the rightholder's daughter or sister, and these tenant relationships are frequently maintained through the generations. Pledges too are often left long unredeemed. It may be that in the course of years the question whose ancestor was the original rightholder is forgotten and that in this way land passes from one lineage to another. But at the time when these transactions are made people are usually careful to have witnesses; sometimes they bring a young boy to witness the transaction, so that there may be somebody to remember it when the original parties are dead.

In general, it is true that small-scale agricultural societies think of land as inalienable. There is not a prohibition against the sale of land; this is just not thought of as possible, and many of the African chiefs who agreed to sell land to Europeans did not realize that they were committing themselves to the renunciation of all rights in it. Some ethnographic accounts of particular peoples tell us that with them land sales were traditional. Thus it has been stated of the Kamba of Kenya that when they were in process of taking possession of their present country the man who had cleared a patch of virgin soil would 'sell' it, giving his lineage mates the first refusal, and move on further. The Kikuyu, in their long debate with the European settlers in Kenya, maintained that they had 'bought' their land from the Dorobo forest people whom they found in occupation, and so had as good a claim to title as the Europeans who bought farms from the government.

Of these examples one can say with confidence that whatever the transactions described may have been, they cannot have been at all like sales as these are understood in societies where people live by buying and selling. It is not too much of a paradox to say that, unless everything can be bought and sold, nothing can be. What we see in these two Kenya examples is that in certain circumstances people abandoned certain claims on land for a consideration. The Kamba man who did not intend to stay in the first place where he cleared a field handed it on, perhaps, to someone who made him a return for his trouble in clearing it. The Kikuyu, when they began to cut down the forests where the Dorobo lived by hunting, placated them with presents of goats, in return for which the Dorobo moved further into the forests and refrained from shooting poisoned arrows at them. It is hardly possible to conceive of the Dorobo, who did not even cultivate their land, regarding it as a saleable commodity.

With the entry of the small-scale societies into the world of commerce, the cultivation of cash crops and the general extension of money transactions, the ways in which people in these societies have considered it permissible to dispose of land have changed considerably. But there has not, of course, been a clear, simple switch from 'communal' to 'individual' tenure, such as many people anxious for rapid economic development would like to see. Ashanti farmers buy and sell cocoa land, but still think it would be shameful to part with the family food farm. Bantu in South Africa who have been allotted individual holdings take advantage of their undisputed ownership of economically valueless land to go away and earn wages, but they would never have dreamt of selling their holdings, even before the *apartheid* policy made it impossible for them to settle in town. There is a sense in which rights to land still give, in most parts of the world, a security that is not guaranteed in any other way. This explains both the traditional principle that land was ultimately inalienable and the attachment to it at the present day.

SUGGESTIONS FOR READING

Some writers on law are quite sure what law is and discuss the legal rules characteristic of different societies. This is perfectly permissible, since a certain quota of rules, concerning particularly rights to property, and marriage (as determining succession to property) are necessary for any social order. It has often proved possible to describe the law of a small-scale society in a manner which would be a guide to their judges, as well as to any outside authority responsible for supervising the judges' decisions.

The classic study of this kind is Maine's *Ancient Law* (Everyman edn., 1917) which is discussed in Chapter 2. Books of this kind by anthropologists include I. Schapera, *A Handbook of Tswana Law and Custom* (2nd edn., 1955), J. F. Holleman, *Shona Customary Law* (1952), P. P. Howell, *A Manual of Nuer Law* (1954). C. K. Meek, *Law and Authority in a Nigerian Tribe* (1937), about the Ibo, is largely concerned with political systems, but has some chapters on law in this sense.

Malinowski's views on primitive law, and the various definitions of law which he offered at different times, are summarized and discussed by I. Schapera, 'Malinowski's Theories of Law' in R. W. Firth (ed.), *Man and Culture* (1957). Radcliffe-Brown's views on the subject are summarized in an encyclopaedia article, 'Primitive Law', which is reproduced in his *Structure and Function in Primitive*

Society (1952). Both these writers were concerned with law enforcement rather than with legal rules. H. I. Hogbin, *Law and Order in Polynesia* (1934), with an introduction by Malinowski, applies the latter's theories to ethnographic literature on the South Sea Islands. A number of writers have discussed the procedures for settling legal claims in societies where there are no courts with final authority. Among these are R. Barton, *Ifugao Law* (1919), P. J. Bohannan, *Justice and Judgement among the Tiv* (1957), K. N. Llewellyn and E. A. Hoebel, *The Cheyenne Way* (1941), and A. L. Epstein, *Matupit* (1969).

M. Gluckman in *The Judicial Process among the Barotse* (1955) analyses the handling of a large number of cases by Lozi courts and argues that, despite differences in procedure, they follow essentially the same principles as would western judges. He examines the vocabulary they use in trying cases and in discussing law in the abstract, and maintains that they have concepts corresponding to all those that are most fundamental in English jurisprudence.

A number of studies of land laws have been made, not all by anthropologists. The older literature for Commonwealth countries is summarized in C. K. Meek, *Land Law and Custom in the Colonies* (1946). Monographic studies of single societies include I. Schapera, *Native Land Tenure in the Bechuanaland Protectorate* (1943), V. G. J. Sheddick, *Land Tenure in Basutoland* (1954), and J. F. M. Middleton, *Land Tenure in Zanzibar* (1961). Studies showing how land rights have changed with new commercial opportunities—a theme of Meek's book—include P. H. Gulliver, *Land Tenure and Social Change among the Nyakyusa* (1958), C. Allan, *Customary Land Tenure in the British Solomon Islands Protectorate* (1957) and A. I. Richards ed., *Subsistence to Commercial Farming in Present-day Buganda*.

The Organization of Production

LIKE law and politics, economics is an aspect of social organization that small-scale societies have often been thought to lack. Those who conceive economics as essentially concerned with money and prices are on firm logical ground in saying that there can be none in societies which do not exchange goods for money and so cannot make exact calculations of price. But this is as narrow a view of economics as the view of politics which holds that there cannot be politics without the state. There are many wider definitions of its field. Some have called it the science of choice. This would make it embrace probably the whole of life, certainly the whole of politics. In fact economics is concerned with the way people manage their resources (mainly but not entirely material) and particularly the choices they make between different uses of these—'the allocation of scarce means to competing ends'. Raymond Firth, a leading student of the economics of small-scale societies, has called it 'that broad sphere of human activity concerned with resources, their limitations and uses, and the organization whereby they are brought in a rational way into relation with human wants'.[2]

Of course everyone recognizes that small-scale societies produce, exchange and consume goods. But some people nevertheless deny that their members make 'economic' calculations. It is argued that they have no foresight, no notion of relative values, of refraining from present consumption for the sake of the future, and in fact that their ideal man is not at all like a business tycoon. This is a matter of practical

---

[1] For suggestions on the revision of this and the following chapters I am indebted to Dr. Maurice Bloch.

[2] *Primitive Polynesian Economy*, 1939, p. 4.

importance to many economists who are interested in the problem of increasing productivity in the low-income countries of the world; some of them ascribe their difficulties to the people's 'lack of economic sense'.

An examination of this question does not find a place as a matter of course in all contemporary ethnographic monographs. All social anthropologists are expected to find out how the people they study get their livelihood, what sources of food they have, what use they make of the natural resources of their environment, how labour is organized and tasks distributed, what possessions they prize most. Details of technique are generally left to students of culture, and some of these have earned the description that was originally applied to certain writings of a famous economist—'spineless platitudes about manure'.[3] Social anthropologists sometimes calculate how much time is given to different kinds of work. A calendar of seasonal activities, or at least a description of the variations in routine in the course of the year, is obligatory in a modern fieldwork report. But more sophisticated analysis calls for the way of thinking of the trained economist, and only a few anthropologists have acquired this. The work that these few have done, however, can and should be understood by all students of small-scale societies.

Such societies are commonly said to have a 'subsistence' economy. This does not mean that they produce only enough for a bare subsistence, but it does mean that they expect to use what they produce in meeting their own needs, and not in trading for other goods which are acquired through the medium of money, as in the typical 'exchange' economies of the industrialized world. Anthropologists have long distinguished three main types of subsistence economy: that which depends on hunting wild animals and collecting wild fruits and roots, that which depends on domestic animals and that which depends on agriculture—or on agriculture and animal husbandry together. These different types used to be thought to represent successive stages of human development. Nowadays it would be better to regard them

[3] R. W. Firth, *Elements of Social Organisation*, 1963, pp. 130–1.

as forming a logical scheme in which one can distinguish different levels of technical knowledge.

Judged by the number of people they will support on a given area of land, they do represent different levels of efficiency. The archaeologist Gordon Childe argued that this was the only objective basis of judgement—the same by which biologists evaluate the fitness of other animal species—their capacity to maintain and increase their numbers. Without settled agriculture and animal husbandry, not only could the world's population never have reached its present alarming numbers but there could have been no cities, and none of the intellectual and artistic achievements that city life has fostered.

But settled agriculture is still not everywhere so obviously 'best' that everyone has adopted it. There are still a few wandering food-gatherers and rather more nomad herdsmen. Are we to suppose that they are not intelligent enough to change to a clearly preferable way of life?

A more convincing explanation is to be found in *ecology*; this word refers not only to the environment in which people find themselves but to people, techniques, and environment as forming a single system. A given environment can support a given density of population. Intensive agriculture will support a larger population on a smaller space than any other form of food production, but not all land can be intensively cultivated. Desert peoples such as the Australian Aborigines, or the Bushmen of the Kalahari, get a living from land that could not be cultivated or even grazed by cattle. Of course it is true that before the Australians took over the Aborigines ranged over land that has turned out to be very good for grazing, but there didn't happen to be cattle or sheep among the local fauna—ecology again.

And then arises yet another question—why *should* the food-gatherers have taken to herding or agriculture? It was assumed for a long time that their life was an unremitting struggle to get enough food to keep alive. But anthropologists who have actually lived and travelled with them in recent years have found that this is very far from the truth. Richard Lee calculated that the working week for a !Kung

Bushman was twelve hours at times when people could get their food near their camps, nineteen hours when they had to go further. As for sufficiency, the Bushmen depended more on vegetable food than on the animals they hunted, and their diet in calories was well above what has been taken by nutritionists as the necessary minimum. Of course they were short of animal protein, but so are poor people in every kind of economy.

These Bushmen do not envy what some might consider the higher standard of living of their agricultural neighbours. Perhaps they are actually nearer to the mythical 'savage' who lies under the tree and lets the fruit drop into his mouth. They have to go and get it, but they know it will be there. 'Why should we plant,' one of them asked Lee, 'when there are so many nuts in the world?' And in a severe drought in 1965, the tables were turned when people from settled tribes, whose crops had failed completely, joined Bushmen bands in foraging.

Every other form of subsistence is harder work, though cultivators have a slack time between harvest and sowing. Civilized man prides himself on the invention of labour-saving devices. The food-gatherers do not have to invent such devices; they just refrain from modes of subsistence that cost more labour. They do not even try to control their own food supply.

Gordon Childe argued that the various techniques for deliberately producing food *made possible* a great increase in population. Some agricultural economists would be more inclined to say that increases in population *force* people to devise means of improving the food supply. We cannot hope to know what happened fifteen thousand years ago. But in the world today, where many different techniques are practised side by side, where ideas *are* exchanged and professional experts seek to improve cultivation methods for the sake of better food yields, it is more practicable to ask why we find these different modes of subsistence, and we may well find the answer in the question how much extra labour different people find worth while. We should remember, too, that within the three broad divisions I have mentioned there are many different varieties of technique.

Some hunters use bows and arrows, some blowpipes, others nets; some hunt on their own, others in bands. Grain cultivators must harvest their food at one time and store it; root cultivators may dig it out of the ground as they need it. Some farmers depend on the rain, others irrigate their land. There are all kinds of different farming implements.

A specialist in 'material culture' could be interested in these implements for their own sake. To a student of society what is interesting about techniques is the kind of co-operation the use of them requires. A student of economics, with 'scarce means' in mind, might see a relation between different means; and among his 'scarce means' he would include *time*. Only fairly lately did economists coin the term 'leisure-preference'. To them it describes the behaviour of people in industrial societies who would rather work shorter hours than earn more. As we learn from the Bushmen and many other peoples at a much lower standard of living than our own, leisure-preference is significant anywhere in the world; as it prevents *some* food-gatherers from taking to farming (some of them do), so it prevents some cash farmers from making improvements that would cost them more labour, unless they are very sure that the benefit will be worth it. Anthropologists have learned not to ascribe this kind of calculation (it *is* a calculation) to the inherent laziness of inferior peoples. People *allocate* their time; 'savage' or civilized, they never reckon to do *nothing at all* when they are not working for their living.

Economists enumerate as the 'factors of production' land, labour, and capital. Anthropologists argue a good deal about what, if anything, can be called capital in non-commercial economies. But there is no doubt that both land and labour are essential for subsistence, and another 'factor', which the economists would probably include under 'land', is water.

One can sometimes see how systems of property rights and the organization of production are affected by the relative scarcity of these different factors. Systems of land rights such as were described in the previous chapter would not arise where there was no scarcity of land, and different systems develop with increasing scarcity. The Tiv, as Bohannan describes them, found room to expand by making requests to their neighbours that nobody would refuse. Peoples who are more crowded, such as the Ibo in Nigeria or the Kikuyu in Kenya, recognize arrangements whereby outsiders can be allowed to enter, in a dependent status, on the land of other rightholders. Where land is scarce, men who leave their village take care to arrange for a relative to cultivate it, so that nobody can say it has been abandoned and is free to be re-allotted.

Water is scarce among herdsmen, who travel in search of it; and among some cultivators, who store it and use it to irrigate their fields. Note that scarcity is not simply a matter of the natural environment; it is the water stored in tanks that is scarce. Herdsmen grant a prior right to waterholes to the people who dig them and keep them in repair. Where crops depend on tank irrigation, as they do, for example, in Ceylon, the area that can be planted, and so the size of the village, is limited by the amount of water that the tank can hold. It is essentially rights to water, not rights to land, that pass by inheritance, though of course the land you plant must be what is watered from your strip of ditch. Such a system cannot work unless the water flow is controlled, and unless the tank is kept in repair and the ditches cleared. So it requires closer control by some village authority, and better organized co-operation between villagers, than is necessary where there is no water storage.

For examples where labour is the scarce factor we have to look at pastoral peoples, and here again it is the mode of operation and not the environment as such that creates this situation. Herdsmen need labour for herding, for milking, for making butter, for cleaning utensils, for taking milk to market if they sell their milk; and the female part of the labour force also has to care for children. The nomad Fulani, who move with their flocks to and fro along the southern fringes of the Sahara, allot his own share of the herd to a man as soon as he is married. If there are very few animals he and his wife may manage them. But in any case he will expect their numbers to increase. So as to be able to give his own time to other occupations than herding, whether it is repairing the ropes that tether the cattle or paying his respects to an influential man, or inquiring around to find where the good grazing is this year, he must have a young boy to go out with the cattle. His wife needs a girl whom she can send to market or leave at home with younger children. So in practice a man must go on keeping his herd with his father's or elder brother's until some years after he theoretically has control over it.

The conception of labour as a scarce factor throws some light on the importance that patrilineal peoples attach to the rights over children that a man acquires by the payment of bridewealth; these go far beyond the right to call on their labour, and this may be of little importance in some cases, but in pastoral societies their labour is of supreme importance. The necessity, as opposed to the mere advantage, of the children's contribution to the family subsistence, is one reason why pastoral peoples are so reluctant to send their children to school.

The division of labour

The development of technology consists essentially in the invention of tools and processes by means of which material goods can be produced in greater quantity and with less physical effort. Along with this goes greater and greater specialization, and a conspicuous aspect of this specialization, as we are familiar with it, is that the production of food is left to a small number of people, while the rest exchange for food the reward they get for their contribution to the total product of their society; this may consist in hewing coal, fixing in place some part of a motor-car, programming a computer, or even writing a book. So when we talk of societies of simple technology we are in effect saying societies in which there is little specialization. In such societies every household expects to provide for itself the essentials of food, clothing, and shelter. This applies even to royalty, and it certainly applies to ordinary folk who are skilled in particular crafts such as pottery or woodworking. None of these men or women is a full-time specialist; all follow their craft at times when they are free from work in the fields.

Adam Smith pictured the progressive division of labour in a rather simple way. At first, he said, human labour was directed wholly to the production of food. But there is a limit to what people can eat, and so a time came when men's stomachs were full and there was a surplus of food. This was available to exchange for other material goods, in which, he maintained, there are infinite possibilities of variety and for which there is an insatiable demand. So began the process we are familiar with, in which everyone lives by some specialized occupation and gets his necessities and whatever else he wants by exchanging with other specialists (not directly, of course, but through the medium of money). It has also been asserted that the division of societies by rank arises when there is a sufficient surplus of food to maintain full-time chiefs and priests who do not contribute any labour to food or other production; and this argument is supported by the fact that chiefs receive tribute from the produce of their subjects' fields and priests are rewarded for their offices.

But the question how to recognize a surplus is not easily answered. Populations which have not died out in successive famines have clearly had enough to live on; at what point do they pass from 'enough' to 'too much'? There *are* famines from time to time; does a 'surplus' mean more than the amount that should have been stored against famine? In fact the tribute that goes into a chief's granary is often distributed at a time when food is short; it does not always go to feed non-producers. One can calculate the excess of calories obtained from a given diet over those that went into producing the food. But this gives us no idea what the food-producers themselves regard as sufficiency or surplus. Individuals may exchange in times of plenty food that they reckon as surplus, and be sorry for it later. And as far back as we know, people have produced objects for decoration or display, as well as for religious purposes, whatever the deficiencies in their food supply.

So the division of labour in societies of simple technology is not a matter of the full-time practice of different special skills. For most purposes it rests on differences of age and sex. Children and old people cannot do heavy work; children, though, begin to be taught the work of farm and household almost as soon as they can walk. On the whole it is men who do the work that takes them away from the homestead; hunters and herdsmen are men. But West Africa knows women traders who travel long distances. Men are expected to have greater agility and are not hampered by carrying children on their backs. Men climb tall palm-trees for the fruit, or lop the branches off wild trees so that they can be burned on the ground to fertilize it for planting. Cooking is women's work. House-building can be divided in various ways. In Buganda women fetch grass for thatch and mix the mud for the walls, and men do the construction. Women may be thought too stupid for some activities, such as handling axes in New Guinea.

Specialists

But there is no society without individuals who have special skills in such crafts as weaving, pottery, or woodworking. Most of these craftsmen work in their 'spare time'—when there is no fieldwork or herding or hunting to be done, and other people would be making the rough objects that anyone can make, or just sitting around drinking beer and talking. They rarely accumulate stocks in the hope that somebody will want them, display them in front of their houses or hawk them around; mostly their products seem to be 'bespoke'. An unusual belief held by the Tonga of Zambia is that the skill of the craftsman is a gift from an ancestor who will be angry if he does not practise it; so he works all the time, but gives the objects he makes to his kinsmen.

In many African societies craftsmen were attached to royal courts, and worked to supply the rulers with especially fine products of their skill. This certainly encouraged the development of African art. Another factor encouraging specialization is the range of trading relations. Products of West Africa, notably gold dust and leather goods, were reaching the Mediterranean coast in Roman times, and after the Arabs entered North Africa and developed caravan routes across the Sahara, an extensive trade began, which eventually fired the imagination of Europeans with the idea of the immense wealth of this unknown region.

In this region the craftsmen were often organized in guilds, to give them the name applied to such associations in mediaeval Europe, and some had special privileges in virtue of their skill. The Ashanti goldsmiths, for example, were themselves allowed to wear ornaments of types that were otherwise made only for important chiefs. Often there were whole villages where one craft was practised, and indeed one can visit weavers' villages in Nigeria today. In cities the practitioners of each craft lived in their own quarter, again as in mediaeval Europe. The guilds have been described in some detail as they function in the kingdom of Nupe, in the north of Nigeria, by S. F. Nadel, the anthropologist who worked in that country in 1934–6.[4] Here the blacksmiths, brass-workers and silversmiths, glass-makers, bead-workers and weavers in any town were organized in guilds. Membership of a guild was in practice hereditary, as a son was expected to follow his father's trade. Each guild had a head, who bore a title indicating his office and was the spokesman for the members in dealing with the court; the king would place his orders through the guild-heads. In 1935 the king of Nupe built a new house and had all the nails and brackets in it made by the blacksmiths' guild, and rewarded the workers with a gift of food.

It is characteristic of many forms of production in small-scale societies that the craftsman is in some sense a magician, or, if he is not, his activity is subject to rules and precautions that we should call magical, and that he himself would describe in words that belong to the context of magic. We find the most striking examples in the south-west Pacific. The construction in the Trobriand Islands of a sea-going canoe is punctuated with the recitation of spells to make it fast, sea-worthy and a bringer of glory to its owner. In Tikopia rites are performed at the building of a canoe or the making of a fishing net; both may be formally placed under the protection of spiritual beings, and the technical process of making them is interrupted for offerings to be made to these, and invocations to them to make the objects efficient for their purpose. In Africa this kind of positive reinforcement of the technical activity by magic is less common, but some crafts, such as ironworking and pottery, may be surrounded by taboos and ritual precautions;

[4] *A Black Byzantium*, 1942.

for example, women are not allowed to come near a blacksmith at work.

Malinowski demonstrated conclusively that the performance of such activities must not be taken to show that 'savages' rely on mumbo-jumbo in their practical pursuits and have no understanding of technical principles. He showed that the people of the Trobriands understood very well how to make a canoe stable, and knew the properties of the different woods available to them for building, and that the delicate parts of the construction were done with the utmost care. He argued that the ritual of canoe-building gave the builders confidence in the successful outcome of their work. Firth, while agreeing with this, argues that ritual may in other ways be an obstacle to technical efficiency. It takes time that could otherwise be spent on finishing the job, and it may also deter people from experimenting with new methods, since failure is apt to be explained by shortcomings in the performance of the ritual and not by inadequacies in technique. But he also calls attention to an aspect of religious belief, in the particular case of canoe-building, which he sees as an incentive to steady work—namely the idea that the spirits to whom a canoe is dedicated are offended at having to see it in a dismantled condition.

Co-operation in production

I have been discussing specialist craftsmen as if they were always makers of objects for exchange. A specialist may also contribute his knowledge or his skill to some combined undertaking in which the materials used and the heavy work are supplied by others. In such an enterprise we might include among specialists the magician who recites his spells over the canoe. Its organization may be quite complex.

But before considering activities of this kind, which are exceptional in the lives of the people who engage in them, we should look at more humdrum ways of organizing a working team when more labour is needed than a single homestead can provide. The striking contrast between a subsistence and a market economy is that there is here no question of hiring labour in an impersonal manner by the offer of wages. Labour, like any service, should be rewarded, but the reward is not a contractual payment but the recognition of a social obligation.

The most common occasions of need for extra labour are the peak times of the agricultural year—preparation of the ground for planting, weeding, and harvest. In countries with a long dry season, the earth is baked until it is too hard to hoe. It cannot be broken up until the rains begin, and then the ground must be cleared and planted before it hardens again. Weeds grow up along with the crops, and fields anywhere must be weeded at least once. In the areas of high rainfall where rice is grown, there is no end to weeding.

In work of this kind neighbours help one another—a truism, since only people who live close together can join in work. But it is worth stating in order to make the contrast between neighbourhood and kinship. Kinship creates claims for help in trouble, but kinsmen are not necessarily neighbours nor available in the 'rush hours' of the farming year. In Africa work parties are rewarded mainly by beer at the end of the day. Once in Malawi I saw a man walk around calling out 'Who wants meat?' He was collecting a party of women to harvest his maize. Where people do not live in compact villages but in scattered homesteads, there may be a recognized 'neighbourhood' within which this mutual assistance is given. The Gusii of western Kenya used to have a name —*risaga*—for a working party, and the people who regularly combined in such a party were 'the men of the *risaga*'. Seven to ten homesteads would form a *risaga*; the average number of 'men of one *risaga*' (who of course included women) was forty. A *risaga* was generously rewarded with beer at the end of the day; but since the Gusii do not think it proper for women to drink beer in public, the men got a good deal more than the share their work had earned. But this was held to be a return to the men for supplying the work team.

More formal arrangements are made among the rice cultivators of Asia. They have been described by Derek Freeman[5] as he saw them in Borneo. There three or four families make an agreement to pool their labour and work on the fields of each in turn, a day at a time. A day's work on your neighbour's farm gives you a claim to a day's work by a member of his family on yours. If there are two women in your family and only one in his, only one of yours will join the work party on that neighbour's day. The other will stay at home and weed her own rice. But people try to join with families in which the numbers of workers are equal.

The Indian caste system provides the basis for a more permanent form of co-operation. An important element in this is that all the members of a village do not have equal claims to land. In the past it was normal for the land to be owned by members of one caste, the dominant caste as it is called. Nowadays it is possible for others to buy land, but there are still many landless villagers. Those who have no land earn a share of the produce, either by practising the craft appropriate to their caste, or by working in the fields as dependents of the landowner. F. G. Bailey[6] describes the operation of this system in Bisipara in Orissa. The land of this village was traditionally owned by members of the warrior caste, who thus controlled the rice supply for the whole village. The Brahmins served the village in the sense of performing rituals for it. Barbers, washermen, the temple custodian, the street sweepers, and herdsmen gave their labour in return for a share of the harvest with, in addition, special payments of rice for specific services. Outcastes—those whose touch is held to be polluting—worked on the land, attached as servants to different landowners who supplied them with food; this was a hereditary relationship. Although these relationships have been greatly modified where people can earn cash incomes from activities outside the village organization, this description remains largely true, and it illustrates the traditional working of the caste system.

The construction and use of canoes by the island peoples of the South Pacific, as they have been described by Firth and Malinowski, illustrate the way labour may be obtained,

[5] *Report on the Iban*, 2nd edn., 1970, pp. 234–8.
[6] *Caste and the Economic Frontier*, 1957.

and rewarded, for the performance of more complex tasks than those of food production. They also present us with an equivalent of the entrepreneur—the man who plans the operation and prepares for it in advance by accumulating the resources (capital?) that will be needed to carry it out. Canoe fishing, too, is an activity that calls for capital (the canoe), leadership, and labour (the crew), and some recognized rules for distributing the product.

Who are the labourers or the crew, and what do they expect to get out of it? Who is the employer? Is he a financier and if so in what sense? How does he become so? In Tikopia, Firth tells us, any head of a house may organize the building of a canoe, but it is mostly men of high rank who have their canoes consecrated to deities and ancestor spirits. Only a chief—here the head of a clan—can perform this consecration, and the 'sacred canoe' has to be periodically reconsecrated. This gives the chief control over it, not because of the economic contribution that he has made to its construction, but because of his monopoly of the indispensable ritual. Only the more elaborately built canoes necessary for deep-sea fishing are consecrated; in virtue of their dedication to the gods they are further elaborated with decoration which is not strictly required for technical efficiency.

The operation actually witnessed by Firth was the repair of a sacred canoe that had been originally built on the initiative of the Ariki (chief of) Kafika, who, therefore, was its owner. He secured the nucleus of his labour force by expressly inviting a few of his close kinsmen and neighbours; he also asked for the services of the expert craftsman in wood who would be responsible for the skilled work, and who was his sister's son. Other people turned up when they heard the work was going on.

A tree had to be cut down to make a new gunwale. The chief and his son did this. They did not make any return to the man on whose land they found it. Adverse comment was heard on this fact; nevertheless, they were able to treat the tree as a 'free good', and it was not by virtue of his command over the supply of wood that the chief could initiate this enterprise. The log was carried to the shore by a party of about twenty men whom the chief and his son asked to help them. These were not their clansmen, but all were either neighbours, matrilateral kinsmen or affines. They were rewarded with quantities of coconuts freshly plucked.

The expert carving work was done by a man of the Taumako clan, who owned an adze believed to have the magical property of killing borer beetles in any wood on which it is used. This man's brother had been the expert woodworker at the original building of the canoe. Four men worked under his direction to make a new gunwale. When it was to be fitted to the canoe about half a dozen men were needed to lift it up and hold it on the edge of the hull, but a good many more were gathered around, as many as twenty-six at one point, and they took turns at the work, while some went off to help in the cooking of food for the working party. The extra food needed for this large number was contributed by the affines of the chief, whose responsibility it was to cook it. All present, no matter how much or little work they had done, shared in the meal.

The rewards of labour

When the work was finished everyone who had helped in the building, except those who were close relatives of the chief, was given a basket of food to take away. The carving expert received a bundle of bark-cloth, and a present of food was sent to the chief of Taumako as 'owner' of the adze. One piece of bark-cloth was given to the man who had helped the chief to cut down the tree for the new gunwale, and a special present of food was sent to the owner of a brace-and-bit—one of the two on the island—which he had lent for boring holes to thread the lashings of creeper through.

The work, then, was rewarded partly by meals at the chief's expense and partly by presents in acknowledgement of specific contributions. But clearly it was not just for the sake of a meal that men gave their time to this in preference to other possible occupations. In Firth's view they were primarily influenced by non-material considerations: the obligations of kinship and neighbourliness, respect of commoners for the wishes of a chief, the prospect of later deriving advantage from the canoe as members of fishing expeditions, reinforced by the religious beliefs which made it necessary to keep a consecrated canoe in good condition. The obligations he refers to impose constraint, certainly, but yet the consciousness of having met one's obligation is a kind of satisfaction, even without the further satisfaction of 'earning' social approval. A man who has helped to build a canoe might have spent the time in some activity that brought him more material advantage, but he does not consider that he should receive a material reward commensurate with what he has missed.

The primitive entrepreneur

In the Trobriand Islands, as we learn from Malinowski, it is again the headman of a village or the chief of a cluster of villages who organizes the building of a sea-going canoe—who gathers the unskilled labourers together, engages the expert and rewards them all. He can expect his close kinsmen to work continuously till the construction is finished, but where a larger labour force is needed his whole village, and possibly men from outside, will be called upon. The rough shaping of the logs is a job for a small number of close kinsmen or neighbours, either of the expert builder or of the initiating headman. They get on with it in their spare time, and it may take them two to six months. Then comes the stage when a larger labour force is concentrated for a few days to build, caulk and paint the canoe and make the sail. After the launching a ceremonial distribution of food is held at which the workers receive their reward.

The object of sea voyages in the Trobriands and adjoining islands is the ceremonial exchange of valuables which will be described in the following chapter. Sometimes a combined voyage is made by all the canoes of a village under the leadership of one man. When such a fleet sets out, they land after the first short day's voyage, and the leader makes a ceremonial distribution of food to each of the canoe leaders in turn. This is in a sense an advance reward for their loyal companionship during the voyage. It puts them under an obligation, so that they do not feel able to turn back, however bad the weather or whatever disasters they may encounter.

Clearly the initiator of such enterprises must be able to dispose of considerable quantities of surplus food. The Trobriand chief obtains the pigs and yams that he needs from his kinsmen and affines; he is chief of a cluster of villages in virtue of his marriage alliances with these villages, and his brothers-in-law—that is, his wife's clansmen in these villages—have the obligation of supplying their sisters with garden produce. A monogamist gains little from this arrangement because he has to garden for his own sister, but a polygynist gains much. His own kinsmen contribute a share because they share in the prestige that he wins from his munificence. In other Melanesian societies men who seek to organize communal activities, such as the building or repair of a ceremonial house, rely entirely on their own energies and those of their kinsmen to accumulate the necessary food.

Malinowski, who interpreted the food gifts to chiefs from their affines as 'tribute', said the chief might be called the 'tribal banker'. This description might apply better to those African chiefs who collect tribute in virtue of their political position and use it to help needy subjects, sometimes in times of famine, distributing the grain that they have stored. Such a chief is banker in the sense that he keeps a store of resources which can be drawn upon. The Trobriand chief, or the 'big man' in Melanesian societies which do not recognize rank—who accumulates goods in order to reward the participants—is more like a financier. Indeed various writers describe such men as 'entrepreneurs' or 'managers'.

Clearly only a few men are in a position to 'finance' these large-scale undertakings. But such men do not form a separate social class of employers. There may be many men who can never be anything but labourers, but those who are in a position to organize large-scale enterprises do not consider that they should do no manual work themselves. For example, Firth observed that two sons of chiefs were among the party that carried the log down to the shore for the canoe-building. To take an example from a peasant economy where money is widely used, the Malay owner of a fishing boat goes out in it and fishes along with the rest of the crew. According to Herskovits, the king of Dahomey himself was not 'exempt from the command to participate in the common labour of farming',[7] and if this was not true of all African kings, certainly their wives often worked in the fields like other women.

In the more highly differentiated economy of Nupe, where, at the time of Nadel's study, all craft objects were sold for cash, we see people who are more like entrepreneurs in the western sense. In most crafts an extended family formed a working unit, the senior man buying the raw material and taking the payment. But in the case of blacksmiths, who used for some operations a larger work team than an extended family can supply, the guild head would advance money to any member of the guild to buy crude iron ore. When an order came from the court, which was always the largest customer, he distributed it among the workshops, and when payment was made he took more than half and distributed the rest. But unlike a modern entrepreneur he was himself a skilled craftsman; his share of the payment was as much a return for his skilled direction and advice to guild members as for the finance that he provided.

SUGGESTIONS FOR READING

Discussions of the economic aspects of life in societies of simple technology are to be found in both the expositions of anthropological theory for beginners by R. W. Firth, *Human Types* (2nd edn., 1958) and *Elements of Social Organization* (3rd edn., 1961). The same writer has published three detailed studies of the economics of simple societies: *Economics of the New Zealand Maori* (2nd. edn., 1959), *Primitive Polynesian Economy* (1939), about the Tikopia, and *Malay Fishermen: Their Peasant Economy* (1946).

Studies of the organization of production and exchange by anthropologists who are not economists include A. I. Richards, *Land, Labour and Diet in Northern Rhodesia* (1939), on the Bemba; M. Gluckman, *Economy of the Central Barotse Plain* (1941); G. Wagner, *The Bantu of North Kavirondo*, Vol II (1955); E. R. Leach, *Social and Economic Organization of the Rowanduz Kurds* (1940); C. D. Forde and R. C. Scott, *The Native Economies of Nigeria* (1946); L.

[7] M. J. Herskovits, *Dahomey*, 1938, Vol I, p. 30.

Pospisil, *Kapauku Papuan Economy* (1963). M. Douglas, *The Lele of the Kasai* (1963), deals with economic relationships in more detail than is usually found in a monograph describing all aspects of a society.

Craft specialization is discussed by S. F. Nadel in *A Black Byzantium* (1942), a study of the Nupe of Northern Nigeria; by E. Colson in 'Trade and Wealth among the Tonga' in P. J. Bohannan and G. Dalton (eds.), *Markets in Africa* (1962); and by Firth in *Primitive Polynesian Economy*.

The relation between the caste system in India and the division of labour is discussed in general terms in F. G. Bailey, 'Tribe and Caste in India' in *Contributions to Indian Sociology*, 1951, and illustrated by a field study in *Caste and the Economic Frontier* (1957).

The ritual of economic activity, and the relation between magical belief and empirical knowledge, is discussed by Malinowski with reference to canoe-building and sailing in *Argonauts of the Western Pacific* (1922) and with reference to agriculture in *Coral Gardens and their Magic* (1935). R. W. Firth makes critical comments on his theory in the essay 'Malinowski in Economic Anthropology' in the collection edited by him, *Man and Culture* (1957).

The most detailed analysis of the method by which labour is rewarded in a non-monetary economy is that made of Tikopia canoe-building by Firth in *Primitive Polynesian Economy*. His *Malay Fishermen*, an account of people who sell their fish for cash, describes the principles which they recognize in the distribution of the return.

The economy of food-gatherers is discussed in several essays in the collection *Man the Hunter* (eds. R. Lee and I. de Vore, 1968), and described for a pygmy tribe in the Congo in *Wayward Servants* (C. Turnbull, 1965).

CHAPTER 11   # The Exchange of Goods

Do people who have not a monetary system to enable them to calculate profit and loss in fact make such calculations? Do they ever ask themselves whether some way of spending time, or disposing of goods in their possession, is more worth while than an alternative? Some examples given in the previous chapter indicate that they do, and this is implied in the definition of 'primitive' economics given by R. F. Salisbury. Salisbury says he is studying 'those activities in which people . . . appear to organize their behaviour in terms of a rational calculation of the quantities of goods or services produced, exchanged or consumed, in such a way as to allocate scarce means to meet competing ends'.[1] In practice every anthropologist today assumes that he will find people asking such questions. What is interesting is the difference in the way they are answered between non-monetary and peasant societies on the one hand, and in-dustrial societies on the other.

The presence or absence of a commercial economy based on the universal acceptance of money as a medium of ex-change is the crucial factor here. Small-scale societies are small-scale because they lack means of long-distance com-munication, of which a common medium of exchange is one. Lacking this, they lack the means to conduct the kind of once-for-all transactions that we call buying and selling, transactions in which the parties need never meet, or if they do, it is only for a few minutes across a counter. They lack equally the means to conduct the 'single-strand' rela-tionship of wage-labourer and employer. All exchanges in non-monetary societies are between people whose relation-ships are continuing and 'many-stranded' or 'multiplex'. It

[1] R. F. Salisbury, *From Stone to Steel*, 1962, p. 4.

is of course also possible to argue that, because they do not
expect to conduct social relationships in this manner, they
do not *need* a common medium of exchange. Many small-
scale societies have strong views about the types of goods
which it is proper to exchange for one another, a topic to
be discussed in the following chapter.

Among exchanges which they conduct are the type the
economist thinks of first, in which each party has a surplus
of some commodity that the other lacks. Of course this is
not a matter of a *total* surplus such as Adam Smith postu-
lated. In the majority of cases such goods are bartered,
obviously not without some conception of a standard of
equivalence. But in many societies these exchanges are the
least important way of transferring goods, and certainly
they are the least interesting to social anthropologists. A
problem which has concerned them much more is that of
the kind of transfer in which the giver apparently 'doesn't
get anything'. *Is* this a rational way of disposing of one's
property? To answer this question one must know what the
giver does in fact get.

The exchange of gifts

The answer lies in the analysis of *gift exchange*. A theory of
the significance of gift-giving in simple societies was first
advanced by Durkheim's follower Marcel Mauss in his
Essai sur le Don.[2] Mauss used as his most telling examples
the *kula* sailing expeditions for the exchange of shell ornaments, which Malinowski had described in his study of the
Trobriand Islands, and the *potlatch* competitive distribu-
tions of property made by the Kwakiutl and neighbouring
tribes of British Columbia and Alaska, for which an important source is the texts collected by Boas. Since he wrote
his essay, anthropologists have studied many more systems
of gift exchange. They have also developed their understanding of the social significance of gifts for which no
direct return is made.

Most of the peoples who practise ceremonial gift exchange also engage in trade, and if it is necessary to make a

[2] First published 1924; an English translation by I. C. Cunnison published
1954 with the title *The Gift*.

long sea voyage in order to exchange gifts, they usually make the voyage an occasion for some barter deals. But they distinguish clearly between the two, and in a manner that would be readily understood in western society.

We often say that relatives should not engage in business transactions because they are bound to quarrel; some go further and say they won't have business dealings even with their friends. Implicit in this attitude is the recognition that in trade or business you are trying to make the best bargain you can, you are entitled to something you can legally claim, and if you don't get this you can either go to law with the person you think has cheated you or have nothing more to do with him, or both. But it is very difficult to make up your mind to have nothing more to do with your relations, or even to break off a friendship; and in small-scale societies it is all but impossible. From another point of view, it is hard to refuse credit to a kinsman and even harder to press him for payment.

Friends and relatives in western society expect to give and receive help when this is needed; they expect to give presents on appropriate occasions (birthdays, weddings, Christmas), and to offer one another hospitality. It would be unheard of to make a money repayment for such gifts, and most people would not dream of calculating what they were worth; but most people, nevertheless, have an idea that the balance between giver and receiver should be kept roughly equal.

Gift-giving in small-scale societies follows the same principles. You do not haggle, you accept what you are given with ceremonious politeness, gnashing your teeth in private if it is not what you expected, and it is left entirely to you to decide the appropriate return. Of course there *is* a general notion of the relative value of different objects, as there is a general awareness of what people will consider mean.

If we see gift-giving in western society in this light, if we realize that it is not a spontaneous expression of affection by the giver but a socially expected component of certain relationships, we shall be half-way to an understanding of its significance for peoples of simple technology. 'Material objects,' said Evans-Pritchard, 'are the chains along which social relationships run.'[3] Gifts are one way of maintaining social relationships in all societies, and in small-scale societies they are a particularly important way.

It is not only in small-scale societies that the objects given are usually in some way different from those of everyday use. In the western world people do not give, as serious presents, minor objects of household equipment; this would imply that the recipient was too poor to buy such things. Typically a gift is something that it might be considered extravagant to buy for oneself (even if it is returned in kind; there was once a family in which for years two brothers-in-law each gave the other a bottle of champagne for Christmas). Similarly in small-scale societies ceremonial gifts consist of highly-prized objects, and sometimes the only use of such objects, or so it seems at first, is as counters in the game of gift exchange. Characteristic of this game is the combination of social with economic considerations; recognition of the value of the goods exchanged is an essential part of it, but equally important is the social relationship that the exchange creates.

The kula

One of the most famous gift-exchange institutions is the *kula*, which was first described in detail by Malinowski,[4] and which appears to be similar in essentials to many other systems in Melanesia and Australia. In the Trobriand Islands, where Malinowski worked, every man who can forms partnerships for the exchange of shell ornaments with other men in his own and in other islands. These ornaments are of two kinds, necklaces of red shell and armlets of white shell. The exchange is not a single transaction in which both partners give and receive. When they meet, the one whose turn it is makes a gift; the return gift is made at their next meeting. If the partners are neighbours the two meetings may follow close on one another's heels. But

---

[3] E. E. Evans-Pritchard, *The Nuer*, 1940, p. 89.
[4] *Argonauts of the Western Pacific*, 1922.

the spectacular part of the exchange takes place when people travel by canoe to visit their partners in other islands. Exchanges are not made in all directions, but in a fixed order like a grand chain in a dance. Each man's overseas partners are in the islands on either side of his own, and each man receives necklaces from the partners on one side and armlets from those on the other. The most highly prized of these objects are named, and some are so highly valued that the history of the men who have possessed them, and their whereabouts at any given time, is known; a man who knows that one of these is on its way to his home is likely inwardly to be eagerly calculating his chance of getting it. But no one may retain possession of a *kula* object for long. For a little time he has it to boast of, and wear on ceremonial occasions; then it must go on to one of his partners.

Those who went on *kula* voyages did not take their gifts with them; they arrived empty-handed, offering only, by their presence, a reminder that a 'debt of honour' was due to them. Success in the *kula* was achieved, it was supposed, by using magic to soften up the partner and make him feel generous. The principle on which these 'delayed exchanges' were made was what has already been mentioned, that every gift should be the equivalent of that received, but that it was for the giver to calculate the equivalence. Although there was general agreement as to the relative value of different objects, there was no question of treating the inferior ones as 'small change'.

Clearly, in distributing their gifts, men were not influenced by magic, but by calculation, and this calculation must have been of two kinds—what gift would be most likely to elicit a prized countergift known to be on its way to one's partner's home, and whom one could least afford to offend. This is not a calculation of material return, but certainly it is a rational way of allocating resources.

The *kula* partner 'buys' glory; he also 'buys' friendship. His partners in distant islands are allies to whom he can look for protection in what would otherwise be hostile country; his partners at home are members of other lineages than his own, usually his affines, people from whom he is not in actual danger but on whose goodwill he cannot absolutely count.

Salisbury, writing of the Siane people of the New Guinea Highlands as he saw them in 1952, shows how they distinguish the exchange of valuables—pigs, shell ornaments, and bird of paradise plumes—between members of different autonomous groups from the transfer of less valued kinds of property between kinsmen and neighbours in the course of everyday life. The first kind of transaction is called *gimaiye*, the second *umaiye*. *Gimaiye* presentations are made on the types of occasion that are held to call for gift-giving in most societies of simple technology; at birth and marriage ceremonies, when peace is made after a homicide, as well as at the seasonal first-fruits rites. The gift is regarded as a transfer between descent groups, not between individuals; it is presented by the representative of one side and received with a formal speech of thanks by that of the other. The quantity given is carefully recorded; each valuable is represented by a bamboo chip, and when the return presentation is made the different objects are checked off by removing chips from the pile.

But within the descent group the accepted principle is that 'help'—*umaiye*—is given without any reckoning of scores. This is the context in which work parties are rewarded with food or a share of the crop harvested, and hospitality offered to casual visitors. In fact, approximate reciprocity is secured by the diffuse sanction of public opinion. Salisbury shows too that there is sometimes more calculation than the Siane will admit. They obtain salt—a rare commodity in the highlands of New Guinea—by 'help'—*umaiye*—from 'friends' or trading partners in the villages where it is produced. A party visits a salt-village taking with them pigs, which the hosts kill to entertain them, and when they leave the farewell present they take with them—a departing guest always gets a farewell present —consists of cakes of salt. The conventional description of this transaction is that they have been generously entertained on a friendly visit, but there is a pretty good idea that one pig ought to earn one cake of salt.

What Salisbury's account shows is that the type of exchange is determined primarily by the structural relationship between the parties. A formal *gimaiye* exchange could not be made between persons conceiving themselves as members of a group recognizing the obligation of *umaiye*; it is a way of creating and maintaining alliances between groups which without such exchanges would be strangers or enemies.

The potlatch

Just as the Trobriand *kula* is a particularly well studied example of an institution that is found over a very wide area of Melanesia, so the *potlatch* of the southern Kwakiutl of British Columbia is the most fully documented instance of an exchange system that is characteristic of four peoples of the American north-west, the Haida, Tlingit, Tsimshian, and Kwakiutl. But the documentation of the two systems illustrates the contrast between old and new theoretical assumptions and methods of fieldwork. Malinowski's 'functional' approach had as one of its principles that one should look for logical coherence and system in the behaviour one observed, and thus find a rationale for the institutions in question. Boas recorded what he saw and was told in most painstaking detail, but, since he believed that culture was a haphazard collection of traits, he did not look for coherence. His records tell more of what the Kwakiutl thought about the *potlatch* than what they actually did, and later anthropologists have had difficulty in picturing it as what Malinowski would have called a 'going concern'. However, a new reading of the data, based largely on the recollections of two Indians who had been active in *potlatching* in the past, enables us to see it in this way.

'*Potlach*' means 'give', and the principle that a gift deserves a counter-gift was important in this institution as in the *kula*. But it had a significance beyond that of linking pairs of individuals in a relation of friendship. A *potlach* was a public distribution of goods, made both to establish certain claims of the giver and to recognize the claims of the recipients. The Kwakiutl had an elaborate ranking system which placed every man in order according to his degree of closeness in descent to the remotest remembered ancestor. The line of eldest sons was senior, and provided the chiefs of the different descent groups. Chiefs had special ritual privileges—titles and the right to use songs, dances, carved masks, and so forth. But in order to demonstrate his claim to these—that is the claim to be a chief—a man had to give a *potlatch* at which he recalled the famous *potlaches* and other deeds of his ancestors, and made the distribution to his guests in strict order of rank. Thus he proved both that he commanded enough wealth (contributed by his descent group as a whole) to be able to give it away, and that he was properly informed about the accepted order of rank. As the Kwakiutl came to earn money and so acquire wealth from outside the system, lesser men began to *potlatch*, and now it became the rule that a man who had previously made a present to the giver should get a larger gift in return, even if this was out of proportion to his rank order. Rivals for a title or for precedence would assert their claim by trying to outdo each other in the amounts they distributed.

Another way in which the Kwakiutl used their property in a manner that might be considered 'uneconomic' was in what has been called the 'rivalry gesture'. Among their prized objects were large shield-shaped plaques of copper which—like the *kula* valuables—were used only in *potlatch* exchanges. The rivalry gesture consisted in publicly destroying such an object; this act committed an enemy to equal it or be humiliated. It put him in a worse position than the receiver of a gift who had later to make a return, since he received nothing. Such gestures might be made at a *potlatch*, where they got the maximum publicity, but they were not an integral part of the *potlatch* ceremony.

Nevertheless, they had in common with it the principle that material goods may be used deliberately and with calculation to attain non-material ends. The *potlatcher* 'buys' recognition of his status; the destroyer of a 'copper' 'buys' the humiliation of a rival. Both must certainly give much thought to the allocation of their resources.

As Mauss pointed out, one can find analogues of *kula* and

potlatch in many such societies. The Mandari of the upper Nile, who were not known to ethnographers in his day, illustrate the characteristic features of both. Mandari chiefs exchange valuables with their fellow chiefs, not in a fixed order as with the *kula*, nor with the same elaborate preparation; this is not necessary, as their journeys are made over dry land. These exchanges do not apparently create permanent partnerships or rivalries (the latter word was used by Jean Buxton, who studied these people) between pairs of chiefs.[5] A chief who has seen a fine weapon in another's house makes a formal visit to ask for it, bringing with him a band of retainers with presents of a more everyday kind—food and tobacco—to distribute in his rival's house. Later on a return visit is made to demand a return gift. It will be noticed that here the calculation of equivalence is not left to the giver. But the *potlatch* principle is operative in that he who refuses to give what is asked is shamed; he is said to be 'afraid' and is an object of ridicule. Another Mandari custom is for a band of youths to go to the home of a neighbouring chief and offer to honour him with a dance, for which they will expect to be rewarded with gifts—once bulls and spears, now bulls and money. This is not a challenge in the sense that the youths are in competition with the chief, but there is here the obligation to return a service which has not been solicited but cannot be refused without loss of prestige.

In Africa, as in many other parts of the world, the most conspicuous way in which social relationships are created by transfers of property is the payment which legitimizes marriage. This can be described as an exchange of goods for women; to Lévi-Strauss it is a substitute for an earlier direct exchange of women. But as the chapter on marriage has argued, it is certainly not the type of once-for-all transaction that we think of when we speak of a sale; on the contrary, it initiates a permanent relationship between the givers and receivers of the bridewealth. Other types of relationship rest on the exchange of cattle alone, and in that respect are analogous to the *kula*. The Turkana of northern Kenya establish, by gifts of cattle, friendships

[5] J. C. Buxton, *Chiefs and Strangers*, 1963, p. 75.

with individuals in remote parts of the country through which they wander with their herds.[6] On his home ground the partner in such an exchange is an ally and protector to his fellow. Here again there is no formal arrangement for making the return gift; it may be made at the initiative of the giver, or asked for by a partner who is in some urgent need, notably for bridewealth cattle. As the Turkana move about in small bands through their inhospitable country these transfers are made with the minimum of publicity, and there seems to be no sanction of shame or ridicule against the man who fails to make a gift when it is his turn; indeed sometimes it is necessary to refuse a partner because a close kinsman, whose claim is stronger, is also asking for help. Simply, if a gift remains too long unreciprocated, the friendship lapses.

These exchanges maintain partnerships between equals. In other cases a gift which cannot be repaid in kind creates a relationship of inequality, and in societies where political authority is not vested in recognized offices the deployment of superior wealth is one of the roads to leadership. A leader must have the qualities considered appropriate to the role, but he must also be in a position to put others under obligation to him. In this case he will not seek out persons on whom to confer gifts but will render help to those in need, and they, if they can make no material return, will become his 'henchmen', either in the full sense of being available to work for him when he needs them or in the narrower sense of simply giving him their support in public discussion.[7] Barth's account of the Pathans of Swat, quoted in the chapter on politics, shows how chiefs build up and maintain their following largely by the provision in the men's house of food which is a substantial part of the subsistence of poorer people. Some of them were famous for having distributed money also.

The procedure and values of gift exchange may operate also in peasant societies where value for exchange purposes

6 P. H. Gulliver, *The Family Herds*, 1955, pp. 224 ff.
7 See, for example, G. Wagner, 'The Bantu of North Kavirondo', in M. Fortes and E. E. Evans-Pritchard (eds.), *African Political Systems*, 1940, pp. 230 ff.

is regularly measured in money. The making of feasts—
that is, in effect, the distribution of food on a lavish scale
—to celebrate significant occasions in people's lives, notably
marriages, seems to be characteristic of all societies, and
'entertaining' without any such specific justification is
characteristic of many. In non-monetary economies the distribution of the food itself constitutes the economic aspect
of the feast; in industrialized societies this kind of distribution is an infinitesimal part of the giver's total economic
activity. But there is an intermediate stage where the continuing exchanges created by reciprocal feasting include
money as well as goods. When a Malay peasant in Kelantan
gives a feast the guests, most of them people who have previously entertained him, bring presents of money. The host
expects that these will amount to more than the outlay on
the feast; indeed, a man often gives a feast when he wants
to raise cash for some heavy item of expenditure such as
a new fishing net. Firth has described these feasts as a
means of calling in credit. Everyone who has earlier received a similar money contribution from the host is under
a social obligation to attend the feast and bring his gift. But
this procedure is quite different from pressing for the repayment of a loan. There is no legal obligation to return
the equivalent of what was originally received, or indeed to
return anything at all. The procedure is what would anywhere be associated with the making and returning of
gifts. Sometimes the host makes a loss on his outlay.

The ways of using property which have been described
might indeed suggest to a superficial observer a failure to
appreciate the value of material possessions. People whose
major preoccupation is accumulating vast stocks of blankets just to give away, people who keep 'open house', people
like the Swat chief who was said to come down to his men's
house with his shirt full of coins to hand out to whoever
was there, in western society would get the name of spend-
thrifts. A leading economist has called the *potlatch* a 'devi-
ation from the acquisitive behaviour of competition'.[8] But

[8] P. D. Samuelson, *Economics*, 1948, quoted R. W. Firth, *Capital, Saving
and Credit in Peasant Societies*, p. 22.

whatever may be said of the *potlatch*, there is nothing reckless about the long-term, elaborate preparations that are made for it; and other types of 'free' distribution are not reckless or irrational either. In this kind of transaction people 'buy', if one likes to use the word, honour and power; and though honour and power are not material goods, most men account them good. In societies of simple technology people allocate their resources among various possible ends on a different scale of priorities from that to which the western business world is accustomed, but they allocate them consciously and rationally. Firth has written in a discussion of gift exchange from the economist's point of view: 'It is possible to conceive of an economic system in which the items of productivity, of concern in maximization, are status tokens and symbolic ties.'[9] Of course, as he also makes clear, there is no actual economic system in which property is valued solely as a source of status, whether this is gained by possessing and displaying it or by giving it away. But this way of describing institutions of competitive gift exchange brings home the fact that they are not illustrations of inability to make economic calculations, but the very opposite.

In many societies more wealth circulates in transactions which are as much social and political as economic—payments of bridewealth and bloodwealth, gifts to create and maintain friendships and alliances, tribute to superior authorities—than in trade or barter where commodities are exchanged by a process of bargaining with overt calculations, however rough, of their relative value. But there are others in which barter is recognized and differentiated from gift exchange. The Trobriand Islanders have a word for it, *gimwali*. It may be conducted on various occasions. Makers of wooden objects, men from inland villages where there are more trees for their raw material, visit the coast and hawk them around for coconuts and fish. Sometimes coastal people visit these villages to look for some object they need. On *kula* voyages people barter such goods for the special-

9 R. W. Firth and B. S. Yamey (eds.), *Capital, Saving and Credit in Peasant Societies*, 1964, p. 26.

ities of the islands they visit, but a man must never conduct
a barter transaction with his own *kula* partner.

Markets

Although gift-giving has a larger place than market transactions—buying and selling, exchange with a view to a good
bargain—in the economy of societies of simple technology,
they are by no means lacking in markets in the concrete
sense; that is, appointed places where people meet to exchange goods. One could say that the beach where the *kula*
canoes land is a market-place for those members of the
crew who are not taking part in the ceremonial exchange.
And just as the *kula* exchange is a means of establishing
peaceful contact between peoples who without it would
take mutual enmity for granted, so is a market a place where
persons belonging to otherwise hostile groups can meet on
amicable terms. The political significance of the 'market
place' may be equal to its economic significance as a recognized point where goods can be exchanged.

Of course the fullest development of markets is found
where there is a great variety of goods to be exchanged, and
above all where traders come from long distances. In such
circumstances one finds what have been called 'solar systems'
of markets. The long-distance traders will bring their goods
to a large central one, and from these they will be conveyed
to 'satellite markets' which again form centres for a ring of
smaller ones. These last will be held in turn in a recognized
sequence which is sometimes called the 'market week', a
cycle of named days, not necessarily as many as seven. Such
market systems have been observed in regions as far apart as
central America, West Africa, and China.

A good description of such a system comes from the Konkomba of northern Ghana.[10] The Konkomba, like most of
their neighbours in this region, are an 'acephalous' people,
divided into small autonomous clans each claiming its own
territory where most of the members live. Each clan recognizes a cycle of six markets in its vicinity, all held at six-day
intervals and each on a different day; some clans call the

[10] D. Tait, *The Konkomba*, 1962.

days of their six-day week after these markets. The more important markets figure in the cycles of a larger number of tribes. Yendi is the principal one for the whole country and figures in nearly every cycle. Each of the other markets that form the Yendi people's cycle is the principal one in a cycle of smaller markets. Each market was traditionally under the control of the clan whose land it was, who collected dues and were responsible for keeping the peace. This was the duty of the market elder, who was also the custodian of the shrine associated with the market; a thief who was caught had to give a fowl to be sacrificed by the elder at this shrine. But in one market it was believed that undetected thieves would be attacked by a swarm of bees which live in the trees around the market-place.

A market-place is different from a shopping centre in that people do not go there merely to buy or sell. Chinese and Japanese merchants used to sit in tea-shops exchanging gossip and composing poetry; women in New Britain take yams for sale partly in the hope of meeting childhood friends from other villages; among the Tiv in northern Nigeria the concourse of people at a market-place provides the occasion for the elders to discuss disputes which are brought to them; among the Konkomba, and doubtless many other people, the market is a place where lovers can make assignations.

Readers may ask why, if the peoples of simple technology are so well able to plan the allocation of resources to their advantage, they have seemed so unwilling to adopt new methods that would increase their wealth. One answer, of course, is that some of them do. But most of these peoples hold very strongly to the view that wealth should not be too unevenly distributed. A chief is entitled by virtue of his office to be the wealthiest man in the land. But he is not expected by virtue of his wealth to lead a life of luxury; he should use it in lavish hospitality, in rewarding his subjects who work for him and in helping the needy. Ordinary folk should all be on much the same level, and one way of keeping them so—though of course not deliberately—is the rule that all a man's sons inherit equal shares of his property. Unless several generations go by with only one son in each—and this would not be regarded as good fortune—an Indian landowner cannot build up an estate. Cattle owners are kept equal by the circulation of bridewealth. Africans often believe that a farmer who outdoes his neighbours in the area he plants or the success of his crops must be a sorcerer. It is hard to tell how much this idea really deters men who want to make money, but it illustrates an attitude that is the very opposite of competitive acquisitiveness.

SUGGESTIONS FOR READING

A translation by I. C. Cunnison of M. Mauss's *Essai sur le Don* was published in 1954 with the title *The Gift*. For one of Mauss's type examples of gift exchange, the *kula*, we have the classic account by Malinowski in *Argonauts of the Western Pacific* (1922). The political aspects of gift exchange, which are touched on by Mauss, are developed in relation to the *kula* in J. P. Singh Uberoi, *Politics of the Kula Ring* (1962). For the other example, the *potlach*, an excellent account is given in P. Drucker and R. F. Heizer, *To Make My Name Good* (1967).

Gift exchange among the Maori is discussed in R. W. Firth, *Economics of the New Zealand Maori* (2nd edn., 1959). R. F. Salisbury, *From Stone to Steel* (1962), shows how the conceptions of gift exchange and of trade can be found together in a non-monetary economy.

Almost any modern ethnographic study has something to say about the way in which social relationships are created and maintained by the exchange of gifts. This is perhaps most clearly shown in accounts of peoples whose main wealth is in livestock. P. H. Gulliver, *The Family Herds* (1955), discusses in detail relationships between 'stock-associates'. M. Douglas in *The Lele of the Kasai* (1963) describes a society in which social relationships are maintained by gifts of raffia cloths.

The exchange, if it may be so called, of gifts for allegiance is the basis of political power in small-scale societies. This has been discussed in the chapter on politics. A study which goes in some detail into the economies of political competition is F. Barth, *Political Leadership among Swat Pathans* (1959).

The economic significance of feast-giving is discussed by R. W. Firth in his *Malay Fishermen: Their Peasant Economy* (1946), and mentioned in his introduction to R. W. Firth and B. S. Yamey (eds.), *Capital, Saving and Credit in Peasant Societies* (1964) and in his *Elements of Social Organization* (3rd edn., 1961), Chapter VI.

P. J. Bohannan and G. Dalton (eds.), *Markets in Africa* (1962), contains twenty-eight essays on markets in different parts of the African continent. T. S. Epstein has made a survey of the native market in Rabaul, New Britain, showing how prices are determined and how far social relationships inhibit economic calculation ('A Study of Rabaul Market', *Australian Journal of Agricultural Economics*, 1961). This is further developed in her *Capitalism, Primitive and Modern* (1968).

CHAPTER 12

Money

Economic concepts in non-monetary economies

ECONOMISTS define money in a very precise way, which fits the coin and, still more, the paper money and cheques, with which people do business in large-scale societies. When they find simple societies where some object that has no other use is taken in payment for goods or services, they begin to ask whether this is to be called 'primitive money'. The strings of shells that are used in New Guinea have often been so described, sometimes by anthropologists. But the economist usually finds that they do not fit the definition, and this becomes clear when European currency is introduced to the people who use the shells; it turns out that sometimes they will take shillings as an equivalent and sometimes not. A Tolai man in New Britain collects strings of shell-money which he winds into one big roll, and they are kept to be distributed at his funeral; it simply would not do if his heirs handed out bank-notes instead. But the essence of money is that you can exchange it for anything that can be exchanged at all; and so, if you wish, you can work out the value of a cow in terms of chickens, or anything else you fancy. As the American anthropologist, George Dalton, has pointed out, there is no need for such a universal medium of exchange unless the whole economy is geared to production for exchange.[1]

The reason why the introduction of a *money economy*—a phrase which means much more than a form of currency—has so greatly transformed the societies of simple technology is that they did not consider the possibility of reducing everything they exchanged to a single standard of value. Some commodities were appropriate in one kind of transaction, others in others. In any transaction people could tell whether they were getting a fair return or a good

[1] G. Dalton, 'Primitive Money', *American Anthropologist*, 1965, p. 44.

bargain, but the objects that belonged to one type of exchange were never measured against those belonging to another; there was no need to measure them.

Firth has described three 'spheres of exchange' in Tikopia.[2] People make and return gifts of food, they make a gift of food to acknowledge a service such as the loan of a canoe. In this 'sphere' food can be called the medium of payment. In the second sphere more highly prized objects, and the services of specialist craftsmen, are paid for in bark-cloths or in coils of sinnet cord. The third sphere includes canoes, shell fish-hooks for catching bonito and cylinders of the turmeric pigment that is used for decoration. These objects are normally the property of chiefs; sometimes they are destroyed when a chief dies, but sometimes another chief may acquire a canoe by giving a bonito-hook and a coil of cord to the heirs. The sinnet cord, then, moves in two spheres; nevertheless, most types of goods belong to one sphere only. As Firth puts it, 'It is impossible to express the value of a bonito-hook in terms of a quantity of food, since no such exchange is made and would be regarded by the Tikopia as fantastic.'[3]

Salisbury's economic study of the Siane refers similarly to what he calls three nexuses of exchange activity. The 'subsistence nexus' concerns the necessities of life, which kinsmen exchange in the form of loans or informal gifts—everything that Siane call 'help'. Objects that enter into this 'sphere' are what the Siane call 'nothing things'. The precious, but not practically useful, objects exchanged by descent groups on ceremonial occasions, to make or confirm an alliance, belong to the *gima* nexus; they alone are called 'things', and a close account is kept, not of values but of undivided 'things'. Then there is what Salisbury calls 'luxury exchange'. This kind of exchange is made between individual owners of goods that are not regarded as necessities and therefore are not subject to claims for 'help'; these the Siane call 'small things'. They include certain kinds of nuts, oil, tobacco, and salt. These objects are exchanged for one another and not for either food or valuables.

[2] *Primitive Polynesian Economy*, 2nd edn., 1965.
[3] ibid., p. 340.

The term applied to such an economy by Bohannan and other American anthropologists is *multicentric*. The Tiv system, as Bohannan describes it, has something in common with those of Tikopia and Siane. There is a subsistence sphere which includes all the foodstuffs produced from local resources, and houshold utensils, and most tools. People may exchange these goods in the form of 'help'—gifts that should be informally returned later—but in the old days they also bartered them in the many markets which operated all over Tiv country; nowadays, of course, they buy and sell for money in these markets.

Then there were goods that never went to market but were exchanged on ceremonial occasions, that is, to create or maintain social relationships. They included slaves and cattle, white cloths, and the metal rods that the Portuguese introduced into Africa as a measure of value for the slaves and other goods they traded in. Bohannan includes knowledge of magic among the 'goods' in this category, meaning by this that a magician or other ritual specialist is rewarded for his services by one or other of them. None of these objects ever came to market; nevertheless, Tiv can tell you how many cattle or brass rods a slave was worth, and how many rods or pieces of cloth a cow was worth.

In the third sphere the Tiv placed human beings, and these they exchanged in accordance with a marriage rule that required the descent group who received a wife to return a woman to the givers. Most anthropologists would probably treat an exchange of this kind as an example of gift and return gift, just as bridewealth payment is. The Tiv hold so strongly to the view that only a woman can be accepted in exchange for a woman that they regard a marriage with cattle payment as an inferor kind of transaction. (But it would seem that, by this standard, they do not count slaves as human beings at all.)

Another kind of special-purpose money comes from the Lele of the Kasai,[4] in the south-west of the former Belgian Congo, who dress themselves in aprons made from lengths

[4] See M. Douglas, 'Raffia Cloth Distribution in the Lele Economy', *Africa*, 1958, pp. 109–22.

of woven raffia sewn together. These are made by men and boys in the village, and they are used in the creation of social relationships—to conclude a marriage, at initiation into an age-set, to enter a cult association, in rewarding services such as those of diviners and healers, and in paying compensation for offences. They fulfil, that is to say, just the same functions as cattle do among pastoral peoples. In some obvious ways they come nearer to the economist's conception of money than cattle do; they do not multiply by generation, they do not have to be tended and fed. But although they do not die they do wear out, and pretty quickly if they are in constant use, and it takes some time to make new ones.

Raffia cloths—in this respect unlike cattle—are bartered in trade for goods made outside Lele country, and occasionally for the products of specialists inside it. But these latter transactions are rare, and are generally conducted between two people living some distance apart who have no kinship links. Most craftsmen supply their own kinsmen, and receive in return, whatever the object that they provide, one or two cloths which are thought of as an acknowledgement of a service rendered, a recognition of the kinship in virtue of which it is rendered, but not an equivalent in material value. The craftsman would demand a very much higher return from a stranger.

The supply of raffia cloths is limited, partly because today men have other demands on the time which they might give to weaving; in particular they have to earn cash to pay taxes. People keep a strict account of what is owed them, and pounce on a debtor whenever he appears to have gained possession of any cloths. Here, too, they will accept other commodities as the equivalent of cloths—axes, goats, camwood which is used for dyeing, and also francs.

American anthropologists, following the example of the economic historian Karl Polanyi, deal with all the arguments about 'primitive money' in a cavalier but quite satisfactory manner by proposing that objects such as these, which have some but not all the functions of money as the economist knows it, should be called 'special-purpose money', while that of a wholly monetized economy is 'general-purpose money'.

The *tambu* shell strings of New Britain might be called special-purpose money in the sense that although they are used in payment for other commodities, they are not 'a store of value'. For this to be so, somebody who acquired a string by selling, say, a pineapple, would keep it until he wanted to buy, say, a pumpkin. As was mentioned earlier, *tambu* are hoarded against the time of a funeral distribution, and a seller who was not interested in accumulating them for this purpose would accept cash in payment for whatever he had to sell.

Debt and credit

How far can the notions of debt, credit, and interest be applied to societies where there is no means of exactly calculating equivalences between different objects? It is easy to recognize the idea of a debt. Bridewealth payments in Africa are rarely completed before the couple set up house; sometimes cattle that are due may be left outstanding until they come in at a marriage of this couple's daughter. Blood-wealth payments have to be promised to bring a feud to an end, but they may not be actually handed over till long afterwards. This is true too of payments due in compensation in the Burmese highlands and doubtless in many other places. The strict accounting kept by the Lele of debts due to them has been mentioned. Each of their villages has an official whose duty it is to look after 'the things of the village' in the sense of remembering what is owed to it.

In the old days in Ghana a borrower might give the lender a woven cloth of the kind that used to be standard wear, and the lender would wear this until it was worn out. Here there is certainly the notion that a service deserves a return. But is there any calculation of the relative values of the object lent and that pledged? Is the pledge in fact a 'security', something which will eventually pass to the creditor if the debt is not paid? Is there any notion that the amount of the return should increase with the length of time before repayment?

Clearly this is not practicable where the exchange of loan and pledge is a once-for-all transaction. One could perhaps think of the wear and tear on a *kente* cloth, which increases with time if the recipient wears it, as analogous to interest; but there seems to have been no question of demanding another cloth if the first one was in tatters before a loan was repaid. Other West African attitudes are even more inconsistent with commercial views of credit and interest; where land is pledged, for example, it is sometimes regarded as a kind of sharp practice to redeem it earlier than the creditor expected.

A *kula* return gift, we know, is expected to be at least as good as, and preferably better than, the one received. We learn that a man who has been slow to make an adequate return is expected eventually to make his gift all the greater; and that in the meantime, if his partner calls on him—and, remember, he cannot choose the time of the visit—he will make some small gift as a sort of token. But this token gift must in its turn be repaid, so it can hardly be thought of as 'interest'. Can there be any calculation of the rate at which the value of the return to be made should increase with time? This hardly seems possible, the more so if we assume, with *kula* as with *potlatch*, that the value of a gift expresses the giver's estimate of the value of the receiver. Men apportion their precious objects according to the store they set on friendship with different individuals.

One or two anthropologists have, nevertheless, written of New Guinea shell-money in exchange as if it involved the principle of borrowing at interest. The first of these was W. E. Armstrong, who spent two months on Rossel Island, and in 1928 published an account of the system he found there. He maintained that it was possible to work out a recognized rate of interest which increased with the length of time before a loan was repaid. But his data are so incomplete that it is difficult to judge what actually happened, and nobody has gone back to Rossel Island to see. L. Pospisil, with much fuller information, makes the same assertion about the Kapauku Papuans of West Irian, but what he says can be equally well interpreted in terms of the familiar gift exchange. In such a system the rule that you should make a larger return the longer you delay might be thought to express the idea that you should indemnify your partner for making him wait, but one can hardly interpret the extra repayment as a compensation for the loss of alternative investment opportunities.

Capital

Is there capital in non-monetary societies, and if so, how is it identified? Thurnwald, thinking of capital as what produces interest, said the capital goods of non-western societies were their crops and livestock. Firth prefers to think of capital as resources directed to productive ends, and shows that people with very limited technical knowledge such as the Tikopia can have a considerable range of these—'nets, fishing lines, canoes, adzes, digging sticks and coconut-grating stools'.[5] The materials used in making canoes can also be classed as capital. But he continues his argument by pointing out that the same goods may be 'consumption' goods at one time and 'production' goods at another, because articles not directly used in production can be used to reward labour. The mats used to sleep on, the bark-cloth used for clothing, and food, may all be used in this way.

In such an economy, as he points out, there is little need for a credit system, since people 'raise capital' by diverting to the purpose of future production goods that they would otherwise have used themselves.

Salisbury holds that the equivalent of capital in non-monetary societies is 'a stock of goods, present before a productive act is performed, used in production and "immobilized" from direct consumption while the act is in progress'.[6] Income is that part of the addition to the stock of goods created by this act of production which is distributed and consumed. This definition includes among 'goods' natural resources as well as manufactured goods, and also skill and knowledge. Salisbury includes among capital goods *umaiye* valuables, tools, axes, digging sticks, needles of bone, and also houses and clothing, trees, gardens, and stocks of fibre to make cord (these latter count as 'raw materials' or

---

[5] R. W. Firth, *Primitive Polynesian Economy*, 1939, p. 237.
[6] *From Stone to Steel*, p. 122.

'half-finished goods'). He measures the value of these goods in terms of labour cost, arguing that time is for the Siane the only resource that can be used for competing ends. Labour given to assist in A's enterprise is repaid by assistance in B's; no one asks whether A is a more productive worker than B. They do not keep a strict account of the number of hours worked either, but it is assumed that a man who helps in a co-operative enterprise gives the whole day to it whenever he turns up.

Firth has suggested that in discussing these questions it is convenient to include 'peasant' as well as 'primitive' socie-tis in the field of inquiry.[7] This makes it possible to examine data from societies which make a limited use of money, and from the rural sector of countries such as India, Mexico, and China. By a 'peasant' society he means 'a socio-economic system of small-scale producers with a relatively simple non-industrial technology'. Such a society is assumed to be part of a wider whole, dependent on a city from which comes political authority and in which goods are marketed.

According to the economist's definition of capital, it con-sists in goods and services which are not devoted to im-mediate consumption but used to increase the goods available for consumption in the future. Capital is not just hoarded goods; it is goods destined to be used in this way. It can be said to include resources of technical knowledge and skill as well as material goods. The social anthropologist —like the economist—needs to know why and when goods are withheld from immediate consumption. Firth shows how the form that capital takes in non-monetary or only partially monetized societies may be something that the economist would not suspect. For example, when a Tikopia chief lays a taboo on the consumption of particular food-stuffs in order that they shall be plentiful when the time comes for an important ceremony, he is using the unhar-vested yams or the unpicked coconuts as capital. The same might be said of the stock of blankets that the Kwakiutl chief must accumulate before a *potlatch*.

7 R. W. Firth and B. Yamey (eds.), *Capital, Saving and Credit in Peasant Societies*, 1964, p. 17.

A western economist would call the *potlatch* or the Trobriand funeral distribution 'conspicuous consumption', as he would lavish entertainment by a businessman. We draw the line in a different place because, as Firth points out, it is possible in our economy to use resources to increase production on such a large scale that the benefits the businessman gets from entertaining are hardly worth including in calculations of the return on investment.

Some peasant societies, such as the Malays, have words to distinguish capital from income. The Tikopia have no such words, but their use of terms for 'valuables' and for 'return gifts', and the way in which they discuss the relation of return to service or to initial gift, imply, in Firth's view, the same kind of calculation as we make when considering the return on an investment.

The withholding of goods from present consumption may be a prelude to an activity that most of us would not regard as economic—to a large-scale religious ceremony such as the one which the Tikopia call 'the work of the gods'. But this ceremony is wholly bound up with the belief that the gods of the different descent groups look after the productivity of the principal foodstuffs, one being responsible for each; and, if people seriously believe that this is at all times under the control of supernatural beings—as opposed to invoking them occasionally in times of unusually severe weather—this might almost be thought of as part of the system of economic activities. It has been observed already that enterprises of a more obviously economic character, such as the building or repair of a canoe, are punctuated with ritual performances, and the food which is accumulated for such an enterprise is used in part to make offerings to the appropriate deities (which of course are mainly consumed by humans).

Can the affines of the canoe entrepreneur, who bring the firewood and raw food for the feast that rewards the workers, be thought of as making an investment? In Tikopia terms, it is their obligation to do this because they are married to his sisters and daughters, and when the canoe is sea-worthy they will not have any priority in the right to use it. But there will be other occasions when each of them is in a position to call on his own affines for the same kind of contribution. There is here no direct 'return on investment'; rather, the total network of mutual obligation ensures a rough balance between services and contributions given and received.

Livestock may be thought of as capital, or at any rate as savings. A Japanese peasant may buy a buffalo when he has surplus cash so as to sell it when he may later be in need of cash. Fredrik Barth writes in this way of the Basseri of southern Iran, who own herds of sheep and goats and meet their cash needs by selling butter, wool, and hides. He calculates that the capital necessary to make a family independent is a herd of sixty sheep or goats. The Basseri herds are regarded as capital partly because the owner of animals in excess of the indispensable minimum can give some time to other activities than the management of the herd; the man trains horses, hunts, and attends political discussions, his wife and daughters make rugs (not to sell but to add to the family's comfort). But income in this sense does not increase in a simple ratio with capital in this sense. If the herd is too large for the owner to look after himself he hires a herdsman. As in all societies, the herdsman is not as careful of the animals as their owner would be, and, as in many societies, herdsmen steal animals from time to time; hence, the more herdsmen a man employs, the less proportionately he gains from his larger flocks. But it is possible to invest the income earned from the sale of the butter, hides, and wool in the purchase of land, and this can be used in part to grow the grain which would otherwise have to be bought for cash, and in part to rent out to other cultivators.

Barth makes it explicit that the reservation of lambs—which might be eaten—for the replacement of stock is a form of saving. He shows also how an economic choice has to be made between milking sheep and letting the lambs have the milk; if other circumstances are favourable for their health, the risk of depriving them of milk is less. Obviously there is need for considerable exercise of judgment here. 'The management of pastoral capital requires a constant awareness of savings and investment policy; it breeds an attitude of continual and thrifty concern for the herd in its practitioners.' Yet hospitality, with the dissipation of resources that this implies, is also valued. As so often, the question an individual must answer is where to draw the line between thrift and meanness.

It was remarked earlier that awkwardness can arise if people embark on commercial dealings with kinsmen. This is equally true of village neighbours, who see one another every day and who expect to be on friendly terms, to ask and receive small favours of which no strict account is kept. The pressures to give easy credit on a man setting up a store in his own village are apt to be so great that he cannot make a success of his business. This is one reason why storekeepers and traders in peasant societies are so often ousiders to the community where they operate.

Debt among peasants

Interest-bearing loans of the kind that any economist would recognize are found among the hill villages of Orissa alongside what might be called 'friendly' loans of rice between harvests. Wealthy landowners finance petty traders, such as women who buy paddy (unhusked rice), husk it and sell it. Larger loans are incurred by people who have to meet unforeseen calls on their resources—social requirements such as a funeral, or economic ones such as the loss of a buffalo in the ploughing season. Security for such loans is given either in land which the creditor cultivates or jewellery which his wife can wear. If they are not repaid by the time agreed upon he takes possession of the land or sells the jewellery.

Firth distinguishes between 'social' and purely economic loans. The simplest form of the latter is the loan of a tool or a household utensil. No question of interest arises here; it is taken for granted that services cancel out. Lender and borrower know each other, and some time in the future their roles may be reversed. People who borrow and do not return presently find that their neighbours will not lend. These are short-term loans, as is the borrowing of grain from neighbours to be repaid at harvest—often by a larger quantity, say three bundles for two.

Long-term loans in non-monetary societies usually take the form of pledging land. But in peasant societies, producing for sale as well as for subsistence, long-term cash loans are common, and many of these are of the social kind.

Development authorities have often been concerned about the debts incurred in peasant societies for the sake of 'unproductive' expenditure on ceremonies (particularly weddings). In southern India an attempt was once made to organize Better Living Societies, the members of which would agree to cut down this kind of expense so as to have more money for such things as clothes and schooling. The people who joined would have taken the same kind of decision as somebody who has been associating with people better off than himself and concludes that he cannot afford to keep up with them. But most of us want to keep level with the Joneses, whichever section of Joneses we aspire to belong to, and in most peasant societies this is done precisely by celebrating family events on the appropriate scale. Thus, just as a Kwakiutl chief 'buys' prestige in the *potlatch*, a farmer in Orissa can be said to 'invest' in social status when he borrows rice for his father's funeral; it may of course lead to his having later to sell a piece of his land, but it is not likely that he does not foresee this; he simply accepts the expectation of his fellows that he will bury his father in the appropriate style.

Such loans may be investments on the part of the creditor, but they are not capital investment in the sense that they increase production. The extent to which they are or are not purely economic transactions depends largely on the nature of the social relationship between debtor and creditor, in other words whether they are fellow-villagers, whether the creditor is an alien tradesman living in the community or someone right outside it. The sanctions for the repayment of a debt within the community are primarily social. A persistent defaulter loses esteem, and sometimes people may believe that the creditor can employ sorcery against him.

The outsider is more likely to rely on the purely economic sanction of refusing further credit. He can make his own judgments on the financial status of his customers, and in doing so is not held to be disregarding the norms of many-stranded relationships. But he too is unable in practice to operate with the detached impersonality of a bank manager towards a too large overdraft. He has to keep his customers, and allowing credit is the only way to do this. Anthropologists[8] have described the relationship between storekeepers (usually Chinese) and their Indian customers in Mauritius, or their Dyak customers in Sarawak, or their Chinese fishermen customers in Hong Kong. Here we are dealing with peasant societies which have come to regard certain cash needs as indispensable. Indians in Mauritius live on the wages they earn in sugar plantations; they do not grow food. Nor do the 'boat-people' of Hong Kong. The peasants of Sarawak (and elsewhere in South-East Asia) grow their own rice, but they expect to buy tea and sugar, and kerosene for lamps, if nothing more. It is for these daily expenses that they require credit. They make very small purchases at any one time, and pay at the end of the month. But they never clear off all they owe; a certain amount is left outstanding, and there may be a tacit agreement as to the amount. Burton Benedict has described this a 'a kind of capital investment which the shopkeeper makes in his customer in return for which he secures his custom'.[9] As time goes on he builds up a personal relationship with his clients, of a different kind, certainly, from those based simply on kinship or neighbourliness, but nevertheless a relationship of interdependence. To cut off credit in Mauritius, where there is no subsistence production, can amount to reducing a family to destitution; in order to avoid being driven to this, the storekeeper must limit his customers to a number that he can keep his eye on. This is one reason why in so many peasant societies there are large numbers of storekeepers, all

[8] See, for example, B. E. Ward, 'Cash or Credit crops?' in *Economic Development and Cultural Change*, 1960, pp. 148–63, and B. Benedict, 'Capital, Saving and Credit among Mauritian Indians', in Firth and Yamey, op. cit., pp. 330–46.

[9] Firth and Yamey, op. cit., p. 342.

apparently stocking the same goods, though another is that most of them have themselves very little capital.

This chapter has been explicitly concerned with small-scale societies where people make money transactions as well as those that operate without money. One reason is that so few of the latter are available for study; another is that economists are more interested in what anthropologists can tell them about societies where people have got used to money than about the few where they have not. This is one of the fields in which social anthropologists have been most anxious to offer information that can be helpful to practical men, and the practical economists are concerned with economic growth. What the anthropologist can offer is a reminder that, on the one hand, people everywhere lay out resources to attain social as well as purely material advantages, and that, on the other, people whose technology does not allow them to amass great material possessions are well aware of the choices open to them in the use of what resources they have.

SUGGESTIONS FOR READING

Armstrong's data on Rossel Island were published in his *Rossel Island Money* (1928). They have been discussed by Lorraine Barić in an essay in *Capital, Saving and Credit in Peasant Societies* (1964) edited by R. W. Firth and B. S. Yamey; also by R. W. Firth in an article on 'The Place of Malinowski in the history of Economic Anthropology' (1965) in *Man and Culture*, edited by R. W. Firth, and by George Dalton in an article 'Primitive Money', in the *American Anthropologist* for 1965. P. Einzig (not an anthropologist) in his book, *Primitive Money* (1949), discusses all the different objects which in different places can be thought of as media of exchange.

The question how far the concept of capital is applicable to a non-monetary economy has been discussed by R. W. Firth in *Economics of the New Zealand Maori* (2nd edn., 1959), *Primitive Polynesian Economy* (1939), and by R. F. Salisbury, *From Stone to Steel* (1962). L. Pospisil, *Kapauku Papuan Economy* (1963), has a chapter on money, savings, and investment.

Firth and Yamey's *Capital, Savings and Credit* contains fourteen essays on societies in which production is directed partly to subsistence needs and partly to the market. Firth's *Malay Fishermen: Their Peasant Economy* (1946) is a detailed field study of one such society.

The place of the middleman in such societies, both as an indispensable link in communications and as a source of credit, is discussed by B. E. Ward, 'Cash or Credit Crops?', in *Economic Development and Cultural Change*, 1960. J. K. T'ien, *The Chinese of Sarawak* (1953), is an ethnographic account of a trading community.

CHAPTER 13   What Is
Religion?

RELIGION differs from the other aspects of social life that
have been discussed so far, because it is concerned with
systems of belief as well as systems of relationship and action,
and because its systems of action are themselves directed towards entities the existence of which is not open to observation. At every point in his work the anthropologist is
asking 'What do people think?' as well as 'What do they
do?' But in most fields of social behaviour ideas are nor-
mative; they are concerned with what ought to be done and
the reasons why it ought to be done. Religious thinking,
although in one sense it is the type of thinking about what
ought to be done, also includes concern with what is and
why it is—with the nature of the universe and man's place
in it, what the nineteenth-century anthropologists, along
with most theologians, called the 'great mysteries'.

It is only in very recent times that people have gained a
confident mastery of the world around them through the
understanding of its processes that we call science. Two
results of this mastery can be seen in the industrialized
world today. In the first place, its society is largely secular-
ized, in that many people take little interest in religious
practices and some deny the validity of religious belief altogether; and in the second, religion is held to be concerned
primarily with moral values and hardly at all with attempts
to secure God's help in practical ventures. Some anthropologists have suggested that members of their profession who
are not religious believers are debarred from understanding
the religion of the people among whom they work; but one
might ask whether many religious believers can put themselves imaginatively in the state of mind of people who
really think that if they don't go to church the rain will
never fall again, their wives will have no children, and all
the cattle will die. Yet this is the significance, for most small-

scale societies, of the obligation to perform periodic religious ceremonies. It is partly because so many westerners live in towns and think of rain as a nuisance and cattle as a source of steak that this kind of attitude is so alien to them.

In all societies of simple technology, people believe that the process of nature and the success of human endeavour are under the control of entities outside the range of everyday experience, whose intervention can change the course of events. The word that is generally used to describe such entities is 'supernatural'. A number of anthropologists have pointed out that the people among whom they have worked do not make the distinction that we do between the natural and the supernatural.[1] Some writers meet this criticism by substituting such words as 'ultra-human', or 'non-empirical'; but many are content with the more ordinary usage, and it has certainly never been a cause of misunderstanding.

Religion as a system of beliefs

Religion consists of beliefs and practices. Anthropologists have always agreed on the importance of the practices, but their treatment of the beliefs has been very different at different times. In the nineteenth century the beliefs were thought to have existed first as naïve interpretations of experience, and the religion to have been built on them. Then came a phase in which practices were treated as all-important, and beliefs were held to have arisen to justify practice. Today, although we have not returned to the nineteenth-century interpretation of religion as the product of fallacious reasoning, we do recognize that every society has its 'world-view', and that in the societies which have no tradition of experimental science this is formulated in the shape of religious dogma.

Durkheim was the first writer on primitive religion to be an avowed unbeliever, and so to treat all beliefs on a level as far as their truth or falsehood was concerned. Tylor and Frazer, though not partisans of particular theological views (Tylor was a Quaker), did hold that some beliefs were truer than others and therefore also superior, more 'ad-

[1] See, for example, E. E. Evans-Pritchard, *Witchcraft, Oracles and Magic among the Azande*, 1937, and S. F. Nadel, *Nupe Religion*, 1954.

vanced'. With them begins the attempt to divide types of behaviour directed towards supernatural entities and forces into the religious and the magical. This might be called a popular classification, in the sense that in their day, as to-day, people who were confident that religion was true were equally confident that magic was false. Tylor and Frazer were interested too in the question why the religious beliefs of small-scale societies took the forms they did; for them this question did not have to be asked, as it did for Durkheim, about all religions.

Most of the previous chapters have been concerned with the ways in which social purposes are attained with very limited techniques—how one can have government without an official apparatus, or law without police, or economics without money—and it would not be unreasonable to say that they have illustrated rudimentary forms of the institutions discussed. Anthropologists have been much interested in rudimentary forms of religion, but since religious practices are not closely correlated with levels of technology, they have usually judged what is rudimentary by other criteria. For Tylor and Frazer the criterion was intellectual: the more fallacious the ideas on which it rested, the more rudimentary the religion must be. Durkheim took a different line when he said categorically that totemism in its Australian form must be the original form of all religion because the *techniques* of the Australian aborigines are the most rudimentary that we know of. All his predecessors thought of religion as an idea which at some point dawned on simple minds.

Tylor, opposing those who sought to evaluate primitive religions in terms of their approximation to those that we can study in written records, and insisted on such criteria as the belief in a supreme being or the performance of actions recognizable as worship, offered as a 'minimum definition' 'the belief in spiritual beings'. Of course people who direct ritual actions towards such beings must believe that they exist, but for Tylor the *belief* was more important than the actions. He constantly referred to the ideas he was writing about as 'doctrines.' He introduced the word 'animism' to cover all forms of belief in spiritual beings, and divided these into two main classes—the 'doctrine of souls', the idea that human beings have souls which survive their death, and the 'doctrine of spirits', the idea that other spiritual (personalized) beings exist. These beliefs, he held, must have arisen from certain universal human experiences. When a person dies, something seems to leave his body; and, short of death, people can be observed in conditions of unconsciousness, in trances or asleep. People dream that they see other people, and that they themselves are in strange places. All these experiences can be explained if one supposes that inside the body there is a soul which can leave it, temporarily or permanently, and go elsewhere. The idea of survival of the soul gives rise to the cult of the dead, particularly in the form of ancestor-worship, which Tylor saw as the typical expression of animism. The 'childlike philosophy' which ascribes to the objects of the environment the same kind of reactions as the observer experiences in himself peoples the non-human world with spirits. 'Spirits are simply personified causes.'[2] To Tylor these views were, of course, delusions, but if all they did was to give people misleading explanations he regarded them with tolerance. But magic he described as 'one of the most pernicious delusions that ever vexed mankind'.[3] Magic, he held, arose from the idea that 'association in thought must involve similar connections in reality'. This led people to suppose that they could foretell the future, and also injure one another by the use of means which experimental tests would show could not be efficacious. Tylor did not consider magic in the context of religion, but in a quite different part of his book on *Primitive Culture*, where he was illustrating his theory of 'survivals'; magic to him was a pseudo-science which had become obsolete with the development of genuine science, but had left its traces in superstitious practices of various kinds.

Frazer too thought of magic as a pseudo-science. He developed further the explanation of magical beliefs in terms of the association of ideas, and indeed elaborated the

[2] E. B. Tylor, *Primitive Culture*, 4th edn., 1903, Vol. ii, p. 100.
[3] op. cit., Vol. i, p. 112.

principles of the pseudo-science. Its theories, he held, were two. The theory of homœopathic magic was that objects which have common characteristics affect one another, so that you can produce an effect on one of them by imitating this effect with the other; the classic example is sticking pins into an image of somebody you dislike. The theory of contagious magic is that you can affect the health or life of a person by doing something to a part of him—his hair or nail-clippings, or even his footprints. Although the examples I have given are magical methods of harming others, Frazer also considered methods of beneficent magic. He elaborated his theory by reference to a vast number of examples taken from Greek and Latin writers, as well as ethnographic works and the information given by missionaries and others with whom he corresponded. The fallacy in his interpretation of magical belief as a theory supposedly applicable to nature in general is, as was originally pointed out by Malinowski, that people who thought that like objects were affecting one another all the time would never have been able to make sense of the everyday world at all.

Unlike Tylor, Frazer linked magic with religion; also unlike Tylor, he held that magical beliefs preceded religious ones. One might say that he was more interested than Tylor in the 'applied' aspect of the 'bastard science', as he called it. As Frazer reconstructed the inaccessible past, man looked for a way to control his environment, and thought these principles were the answer. But when they failed to give results, he concluded that there must be a personified being somewhere who had to be propitiated; thus was religion born.

Some writers rejected Tylor's definition on the ground that there are peoples who do not believe in spirits but yet have ideas that should be called religious. Codrington, a missionary who spent many years in Melanesia, reported the existence there of a belief in an impersonal power called *mana* which could be both beneficent and dangerous, and which was not necessarily the attribute of spiritual beings, but could be found in inanimate objects. R. R. Marett, who argued that the mainspring of religion was an emotional and not an intellectual response to the world of experience, described this belief as pre-animistic.

The idea of *mana* comes very close to one of the types of 'beliefs in spiritual beings' that Tylor enumerated. This is *fetishism*, or the worship of material objects supposed to have inherent power. The word comes from a word meaning 'charm' which was used by early Portuguese travellers to describe such objects in West Africa. At the fertility shrines in Yakö villages in Nigeria, offerings are made to a variety of objects.[4] Evans-Pritchard describes little bundles of sticks, believed to be able to injure a person's enemies, to which their Nuer owners make offerings of food and tobacco.[5] Ganda sorcerers were supposed to have animals' horns, filled with substances of various kinds, to which they made offerings. Fetishism comes within Tylor's definition of religion, since the objects to which the offerings are made are supposed to 'contain' some kind of spirit, though not a personalized being.

Another candidate for recognition as the first form of religion is the belief in a supreme god. Whereas in the nineteenth century this was held to be the mark of a highly developed religion, in the early twentieth an Austrian missionary, Pater Schmidt, who taught anthropology in the University of Vienna, advanced the view that it was intuitively held by all men in their 'natural' state, but became overlaid or forgotten as humanity degenerated. His evidence came from the Nilotes of the southern Sudan, in whose religion such a divinity has a more prominent place than is usual in small-scale societies.

But the most famous of all the rivals to animism was totemism, a name originally taken from a North American Indian word and later applied very widely. Something more will have to be said about the confusion that has surrounded this word, but for the moment what is important is that Durkheim used Australian totemism to illustrate his theory of religion, arguing that since the Australians had the most elementary social organization that we know of, theirs must have been the most elementary religion. It will

---

[4] D. Forde, *Yakö Studies*, 1964, pp. 263 ff.
[5] E. E. Evans-Pritchard, *Nuer Religion*, 1956, pp. 100 ff.

be noticed that here the question is not so much what is the simplest form of religion, but what religous ideas are found among the simplest people.

Australian totemism can be briefly described as the belief that descent groups are linked with animal species in such a way that the members of one species protect the members of one descent group, and they in return not only refrain from killing or eating animals of the species but perform periodic rituals to make its numbers increase and, on these occasions, do ritually eat their own totem species. It is this last feature that distinguishes Australian totemism from the innumerable other ways of associating descent groups and natural species which are found all over the world. Durkheim argued, in opposition to Tylor, that this religion—and, he added, many others—had no cult of the dead, and that totem animals were not endowed by their worshippers with personality but with the kind of impersonal power that the Melanesians call *mana*; other words for this which have made their way into anthropology are the American Indian *wakan* and *orenda*.

An American writer of the early twenties remarked cynically that every anthropologist nominated for the most primitive form of religion that of the people he had worked among himself. It must be remembered too that beliefs such as the idea of *mana* are not actually found in isolation, but side by side with beliefs in spirits and also with those which have commonly been called totemic.

Totemism

Earlier writers on primitive religion interpreted totemism as the worship of animals. Australian totemic rituals could possibly be so described, as might perhaps the custom among some North American Indians whereby, after ritual preparations, a young man seeks a dream which will reveal to him that some animal is to be his 'guardian spirit'. But here, at the very outset, we come up against the difficulty that has beset all attempts to define totemism.

If something called totemism really is one of the basic social institutions it ought to be possible to identify its essence (i.e. define it) in such a way that this can be recognized in all the different forms that it takes. But this has simply proved to be impracticable. The word has sometimes been used as the technical name for a supposed special association, involving ritual behaviour, between certain animal species and certain social groups. But the North American Indian guardian spirit does not belong to a social group; it belongs to the individual who has seen it in a dream. In general it is true that members of a group associated in this way with an animal species refrain from killing or eating the animal; this rule is a ritual prohibition, but it would be stretching language to call it animal *worship*. In the great majority of cases the groups associated with animal species are descent groups, but this is not always so; in parts of Australia women have common totems. The great majority of the descent groups associated with animal species are exogamous, but not all exogamous groups have totems. Also, as has been mentioned, a few unilineal descent groups which do have totems do not strictly impose exogamy.

To many writers the association of totemism with exogamy was the most important fact about it. Frazer wrote four vast volumes on this subject, and the entry under 'Totemism' in the *Encyclopaedia Britannica* for 1929 remarks that 'where totemism is not associated with exogamy it is not difficult to suppose that exogamy has been lost'. Attempts were made to find in beliefs about the totem animal reasons for the rule against marriage within the group. The belief, again common but by no means universal, that the original ancestor of the descent group had actually been an animal of the totem species, inspired Freud with the theory of his *Totem and Taboo,* published in 1913, the year after Durkheim's *Elementary Forms of the Religious Life.* Freud saw in the ritual of the Australian aborigines a symbolic expression of the Oedipus complex, the unconscious desire of the human male to kill his father and mate with his mother. As Freud reconstructed the social life of what we should perhaps call pre-social days, humans roamed about in hordes, a word which has been much used to describe the roaming bands of Australian aborigines. The leader of the horde retained for himself all the women in it, so that all the other men—his sons—had to look for mates outside. Eventually, the sons rose up in revolt, killed and ate the father; but, overcome with guilt, they could not bring themselves to profit by their victory, and so they imposed upon themselves the rule of exogamy. This is the event commemorated in the annual eating of the totem animal, which as has been pointed out, is a rite found nowhere in the world outside Australia. An anthropologist today, accustomed to looking for and finding descent and marriage rules documented by genealogical records, will find it difficult to picture the actual kinship constitution of the Freudian horde.

Nowadays the structural consequences of exogamy can be quite adequately discussed without any mention of the 'totemic avoidances' characteristic of exogamous groups. Moreover, theories to explain these which depend on supposed relationships between sentient beings break down as soon as it is realized that some descent groups are called after, and 'respect' or 'avoid', inanimate objects, so that within the same society some people have animal totems while others do not.

Durkheim had pointed out that the totem is the emblem of the group called by its name. Lévi-Strauss[6] has punctured the theorizing about the relationship between totemism and exogamy (in any case now rather old-fashioned) by remarking that if descent groups are to remain distinct and identifiable long enough to deserve names and make use of emblems, there must be marriage rules of such a nature as to keep them distinct. Hence, where you find totemism you should expect to find exogamy.

In the same context Lévi-Strauss has remarked, as did Radcliffe-Brown before him,[7] that the identification of human beings with plants and animals takes many forms, of which totemism is only one, and that this is a subject worthy of study in itself. In fact the discussion of totemism by British social anthropologists during the last forty years has been largely concerned with the reasons why natural species

[6] *Le Totémisme Aujourd'hui*, 1962, p. 15.
[7] 'The Sociological Theory of Totemism', in *Structure and Function in Primitive Society*, 1952, p. 126.

—and particular species among particular peoples—have been selected as totems.

Durkheim said animals and plants were suitable emblems because they could be shown pictorially in ritual. But many Australian tribes never make pictures of their totems. Radcliffe-Brown argued that people develop ritual attitudes—not necessarily totemic—towards objects in their environment which have practical importance for them, particularly, of course, as food. But as detailed ethnographic studies accumulate, it becomes increasingly clear that species selected as totems are often of very little economic interest. Fortes has remarked that no characteristic can be found which is common to all the creatures treated with ritual respect by the Tallensi (and also by a great many other peoples in the interior of West Africa). They are not a class either in the zoological, the economic or the magical sense.[8] He shows, however, that they are not arbitrarily chosen badges but have something in common with what they symbolize. Not all of them, in fact, are associated with lineages. Those which are thought of as 'creatures of the earth' must not be killed because they are associated with the shrines of the earth. Those which are associated with lineages are mostly carnivorous animals, who are feared as the ancestors are feared and whose vitality makes them symbols of immortality.

The latest of the writers on totemism, Lévi-Strauss, sees this emphasis on symbolism as a great advance in the understanding of the subject, but himself carries it further in a direction which makes totemism an intellectual rather than a religious phenomenon. His own interpretation develops further the argument of Radcliffe-Brown's Huxley Lecture, *The Comparative Method in Social Anthropology,* which has been referred to in another context.[9] Radcliffe-Brown was there concerned with a much wider field of phenomena than totemism, although one of his themes was the striking fact that two very similar kinds of birds have totemic associations with major divisions of society in places as far apart

[8] M. Fortes, *The Dynamics of Clanship among the Tallensi*, 1945, pp. 141–2.
[9] See p. 50.

as Australia and the north-west coast of America. The fundamental principle of social structure with which he was there concerned was the coupling in certain contexts of groups which in other contexts are thought to be opposed; Eaglehawk and Crow are both birds, but they are birds with sharply contrasted characteristics. Many other examples of 'complementary opposition' can be found, and totemism, with its animal analogies, is only one of a much wider class of phenomena. Lévi-Strauss goes beyond this, and argues that the important thing about totemism is precisely that it is a way of recognizing differences as such; it is the most elementary way of classifying the objects of experience. 'At last,' he writes, 'we realize that totems are chosen not because they are "good for eating" but because they are "good for thinking".'[10]

Religion as a social fact

More interesting than the question what is the most primitive religion—a question that does not much interest the social anthropologist of today—is how people have distinguished the religious from the secular on the one hand and the magical on the other. The earlier writers had been concerned primarily with belief, with what people thought there was in the universe in addition to the objects of direct experience. Another way of looking at religion was proposed by Robertson Smith, who interested himself in the contemporary life of Arab society for the light it could throw on the Old Testament. His conclusion was that where there are no sacred writings and learned men to expound them, the due performance of ritual is considered to be much more important than adherence to orthodox belief. People are not asked whether they adhere to all the tenets of their religion; what matters is that they should not neglect the ritual actions that it prescribes. This view, with which most social anthropologists would agree, contributed much to the theory of religion that Durkheim was to put forward in his *Elementary Forms of the Religious Life*.

Durkheim was also influenced by his teacher, Fustel de

10 op. cit., p. 128.

Coulanges, who had argued in *The Ancient City* that the religion of the Greeks and Romans developed on parallel lines with their social organization. First every family worshipped its own ancestors, and then, as larger populations came together in cities, cults arose which transcended the divisions based on descent and united all citizens in common ritual. This could be taken today as a description of the contrast in Africa between the religions of societies based on segmentary lineage systems and of those organized as states. The Yakö system, with its colleges of lineage priests as the source of leadership for the whole village, might have seemed to Coulanges the perfect illustration of the transition.

Durkheim, as has been mentioned,[11] based all his studies of social institutions on the principle that the social can be explained only in terms of the social. In other words, one should not look for the explanation of social institutions in the impulses of individuals, since in every existing society the institutions are part of the world in which the individual finds himself; he has to take them as given, and they are in fact created by the necessity which man, as a social animal, is under to live according to an ordered system of rules. Hence Durkheim rejected interpretations of religion as an answer to speculation about the mysteries of the universe, and concentrated on the relation between religious activities—that is ritual—and other social institutions.

Interpretations of religious attitudes must differ according as the interpreter does or does not himself believe that they are directed towards something that really exists. If he does, he will consider that all religions—or the belief systems which he allows to be such—are attempts, some more successful than others, to grasp the nature of this reality. If he does not, he will hold, with Durkheim, that they are metaphorical ways of expressing aspects of human experience. Both sides would agree, however, that religion is a matter of metaphors, and that the metaphors themselves must necessarily be drawn from human experience.

To Durkheim religion was a metaphor for society itself—

[11] See p. 26.

or, it might be more accurate to say, for the indispensable conditions of life in society. Various writers have called attention to the misunderstandings that have arisen from thinking he meant his readers to regard society as itself a kind of personalized being—though certainly he sometimes wrote as if he did.[12]

Durkheim argued that the religious believer is not asking how to think, but how to act, and that what he derives from his religion is the necessary strength for right actions. Stated so, this view would certainly be accepted by the modern believer who sees religion as a moral guide and not an explanatory theory. In simple societies, says Durkheim, this is precisely the function of ritual, even where the ritual is not attached to any explicit assertion of moral codes; because, he says, the ritual itself is a heightened expression of the interdependence of men living in a society. He describes this as their dependence *on* society, and writes of the demands that society makes on them. This is where he slips into the personification of society. And, he continues, if the ritual is directed towards a personified being, this can be none other than the society itself. The phrase 'God is society', in which this argument is summed up, does not (I think) actually occur in the pages of his long book; but it does not misrepresent his argument. If at first this seems astonishing, we should remember that when theologians seek to describe the attributes of God, they enumerate qualities that are admired in relationships between men—what else could they do? The necessity of representing divinity in human terms is one theme of a recent study of the religion of a Nilotic people, Godfrey Lienhardt's book on the Dinka, *Divinity and Experience* (1961).

It is important to realize that Durkheim did not suggest that people *consciously* asserted their dependence on society in the symbolic activities of ritual. What we learn from Durkheim, and might perhaps learn more easily from Fustel de Coulanges, though we read him less, is that religious symbols are often attached to social groups, so that when one is studying the structure of a society one must ask what groups form ritual units, and when one is studying

[12] See, for example, J. H. M. Beattie, *Other Cultures*, 1964, p. 221.

ritual one must ask in what ways the status of particular persons or groups is reflected in the ritual roles assigned to them. Paradoxically, in view of Durkheim's dismissal of the cult of the dead as unimportant, many of the most interesting answers will be found in the field of ancestor-worship. But students of religion today think there are many more questions to be asked besides the question of its relation with the social structure—questions of the symbolism used in religious rites and in talking about religion, and also questions about religious beliefs as intellectual systems.

In offering a definition which would distinguish the religious from other aspects of social life, Durkheim took the view that particular *kinds* of belief were not important. He bade the inquirer look for something which he asserted would everywhere be found—the existence of a realm of objects and practices recognized to be different from the objects and practices of everyday life. This was the realm of the *sacred*, and religion was what concerned the sacred.

This conception of the sacred gives Durkheim his definition of religion—'a unified system of beliefs and practices relative to sacred things, that is to say things set apart and forbidden—beliefs and practices which unite into one single moral community called a church all those who adhere to them.' Durkheim's view that there can be no religion without a church is an integral part of his interpretation of religion as a way of reasserting the importance of membership of social groups; it may at first have seemed surprising when applied to the small-scale societies, but every social anthropologist would accept it today.

Religion and magic

It is on this criterion that Durkheim based his distinction between magic and religion. Magic, he said, has no church; it is performed by individuals for the benefit of other individuals. Moreover, while religion is a social force maintaining in the participants in ritual the sentiments that they must have if they are to accept the constraints that society imposes, magic is anti-social; it is practised by individuals to gain their private ends. Like Tylor, Durkheim paid more attention to harmful than to beneficent magic, and neither of these writers considered the type of magic performed on behalf of the community which was described so fully by Malinowski in his work on the Trobriands.

Whereas Durkheim excluded magic from the field of the sacred altogether, Malinowski held that it had more in common with religion than with the world of everyday which we manage by our common-sense knowledge of the properties of the objects we use. Malinowski denied that either magic or religion grew out of speculation, and really implied that, outside the field in which man knows from practical experience what to do next, he does not ask questions. Magic and religion, he held, both arise from emotional needs; they are man's way of facing the situations that he cannot control. Magic supplements technique, as when it is invoked to make a canoe sail faster; or it deals with problems for which there is no appropriate technique, as when a young man uses it to make his girl kind to him. Magic, then, is directed to specific ends. Religion, in contrast, provides, in the religious act, its own ends; it gives man reassurance in facing the uncontrollable universe. Malinowski saw the origin of religion in the need to overcome the threat of disruption which is presented to a society when any of its members dies. When Malinowski said that the religious rite fulfilled its purpose by the feelings that it generated, he was not so far from Durkheim, though he was thinking primarily of feelings of confidence and hope, and Durkheim of feelings of social responsibility. For Malinowski religion met what he called the 'integrative needs' of man in society, but again, though Durkheim might have *said* just that, he would have *meant* something very different. Malinowski fully recognized the need for what Durkheim called 'collective representations', commonly held beliefs the effect of which was to justify and so uphold the existing social order, but to him the essential significance of religion was that it gave man courage to face the world, and in particular the inevitability of death.

Most anthropologists have thought it was an advance to see magic and religion as belonging to a single complex of phenomena, where earlier writers, each for a different reason, had treated magic as something of an inferior order. But it has never proved possible to sort out the ritual activities of a society into Malinowski's two categories. What are we to call the action of a Christian who wards off evil by making the sign of the cross, or prays for rain, or even that our most gracious sovereign should always walk in God's ways? These words and actions are surely directed to specific ends. Individual believers may pray for benefits to themselves which may well not be conducive to the general good; if they do so, they are behaving in the anti-social way that Durkheim said was typical of the magician. It is quite possible that people whose religion condemns magic resort more to private appeals to God, but the making of sacrifices by people seeking relief from specific misfortunes, particularly sickness, is common in many parts of the world, and most people would think it a distortion of language to say this was magical and not religious.

The efficacy of magic may be thought to depend essentially upon the correct treatment of the substances used (including words spoken over them) independently of assistance from any supernatural being. But many magical spells recite the names of ancestors, and some explicitly call upon them. Does this not bring them very close to prayer?

E. R. Leach,[13] observing that Durkheim excluded magic from the field of religion while Malinowski included it, sought to transcend this opposition by offering a new definition not of magic or religion, but of ritual. Before this, anthropologists had generally meant by ritual a formal stereotyped sequence of acts performed in a religious or magical context. Christians, with Durkheim, would speak of the ritual of their liturgy, but might deny that magical practices were ritual; Malinowski, on the other hand, reiterated that the essential elements in all magic were the *rite*, the spell and the condition of the performer. Stereotyped practices not concerned, or not primarily, with religion were commonly called ceremonial.[14] Thus the Queen's coronation would be called a ritual, but her open-

[13] *Political Systems of Highland Burma*, 1954, pp. 10–16.
[14] Though some dictionaries would say that they too could be called ritual.

ing of parliament (although prayers are said) would be regarded as a ceremonial. Implicit in the use of these words is the assumption that neither rites nor ceremonies can have any practical (technological) effect. Leach and others have found a difficulty in this classification. Whereas the anthropologist, with his scientific training, knows that none of these activities can have effects on anything except the minds of the participants, the participants may not make the same distinction; they may believe, for example, that the magic makes the canoe swift in precisely the same way that the use of the right wood makes it buoyant. All human activities, Leach further said, even those which Durkheim would have unhesitatingly classed as 'secular' or 'profane', include elements that do not contribute anything to their practical success; and are not expected to by the performers. These non-essential frills are added to the technical activity because 'this is the way *we* do it'; they are assertions by the performers of their membership in a social group defined by a common culture. Magic, it would seem implicit in his argument, is a technical activity to the extent that those who practise it think it is. All non-technical activities are ways of expressing the social status of the performer, and to all these activities he gives the name of ritual. It is impossible, he argues, to divide *activities* into those which are technical and those which are ritual. These words describe aspects of all activities, one or other of which may be more pronounced in different cases. He *then* equates the opposition of ritual and technique with Durkheim's opposition of sacred and profane.

But Durkheim's argument stands or falls on the definition of 'sacred' as 'set apart', and of religion as being concerned with what is set apart. If the sacred can never be separated from the profane, it is impossible to talk about it in Durkheimian language at all, and if Leach is taken to say that the sacred cannot be *distinguished* from the profane, the word as ordinarily used loses all meaning. This is not the same thing as to say that certain peoples do not make the distinction. Moreover, Leach's argument, interesting as it is, does not purport to offer a definition of *religion*. Later in the book in which he propounds it, he discusses a sacrifice to spirits. From all the actions performed in the course of the sacrifice he singles out the technical—killing, cooking and eating animals—and *that part of the ritual* which asserts that the ranking of spirits corresponds to that of their worshippers, and implicitly assumes that what makes the sacrifice religious is that it is directed towards spirits. He admits the existence of a host of other non-technical actions, but he does not describe those.

The field, then, that Leach is defining is much wider than that of religion, and at the same time he does not allow that religion falls wholly within it. Moreover, he is *defining* ritual, not *explaining* it; he is simply saying, 'This is what I think it would be useful to call ritual.' Although most anthropologists have not found his definition useful, the assertion that he has said *religion* 'makes statements about social structure' is off the mark.[15]

The problem of definition raised by Leach has been further discussed by his Cambridge colleague J. R. Goody.[16] Goody finds that the Durkheimian distinction between religion as social and magic as individual behaviour cannot always, or perhaps ever, be made. It is true that we have been accustomed to describe as magical the rites that are performed in private, without a congregation. But in the sense that beliefs in the efficacy of magic in any society are 'collective representations', common to all members of the society, magic too could be said to have its congregation— and, one might add, the beliefs associated with the rites which have been called magical and those which have been called religious often form a whole, and never contradict one another. Goody argues that the types of activity which Durkheim saw as essentially religious—those that gather people together and induce in them a feeling of solidarity— are not necessarily religious at all but ceremonial. Mass

---

[15] R. F. Horton, 'A Definition of Religion and its Uses', *Journal of the Royal Anthropological Institutes*, 1960, p. 202.
[16] 'Religion and Ritual: The Definitional Problem', *British Journal of Sociology*, 1961.

ceremonials include not only the Australian totemic rituals but the explicitly non-religious Bastille Day celebrations in France.

Durkheim did not attempt to establish any category of objects that would be universally regarded as sacred; on the contrary he said that what was sacred depended on the particular religion, and could vary infinitely. This approach to the data made it impossible for him to exclude from the category of the sacred objects which are 'set apart and forbidden' because they are thought to be sources of pollution; and, as Goody says, why should not *any* opposition that is recognized in a society—say that of 'day' and 'night'—be interpretated as an opposition of sacred and profane? Goody could not find among the Lo Dagaa of northern Ghana any recognized opposition of sacred and profane.

Leach's distinction between technique and ritual is based on the proposition that ritual does not *do* things, it *says* things—a point already made by Talcott Parsons and by Radcliffe-Brown.[17] But *what* does it say? Leach answered the question by saying it indicates status and status relationships. But most anthropologists who have made a close study of ritual think this is the least part of what it says. How then are we to decide what it is saying? Monica Wilson in her exhaustive account of Nyakyusa ritual quoted the words of informants whenever she could, but she could not have given a coherent interpretation of its symbolism without adding something of her own. Radcliffe-Brown went so far as to indicate that the interpretation *must* come from the observer, and this is the view taken by Turner in reference to Ndembu symbolism.[18]

With this view Goody agrees, and he adds that, since we cannot find among the peoples we study any principle universally recognized by them which delimits the field of religion, we must make our own. This, he remarks, is

[17] T. Parsons, *The Structure of Social Action*, 1937; A. R. Radcliffe-Brown, *Structure and Function in Primitive Society*, 1952.
[18] V. W. Turner, 'Symbols in Ndembu Ritual', in M. Gluckman (ed.), *Closed Systems and Open Minds*, 1964.

no more than we have done in the fields of economics, politics and law. In fact Leach's distinction between the technical and the ritual—between acts that we, as observers with some knowledge of scientific principles, can see produce the ends they aim at and those which do not—though it is not the same as Durkheim's distinction between sacred and profane, is the one that all anthropologists have made in distinguishing the magico-religious from the field of everyday life. As we see it, there is an aspect of life in which people seek to attain ends that are either not attainable by any human action or not attainable by the means they are using. They purport to be calling in aid beings or forces which *we* consider to be outside the course of nature as we understand it, and so call 'supernatural'. To this field of activity belong both the religious and the magical.

Goody rejects theories which lay stress on the emotional attitudes of the actors in magical or religious rituals. He and others have pointed out that these rituals are often performed in a very matter-of-fact way. Nevertheless those who have sought to interpret the symbolism of ritual argue that it does express (among other things) the deeply felt desires and feelings of those who practise it. In Beattie's view its expressive character is as important as whatever is believed to be its practical effect.[19]

As for the difference between religion and magic, ordinary people have a general idea that they know what it is, and this general idea is correct. It might be epitomized as the difference between *communicating* with beings and *manipulating* forces. Where the idea of communication dominates, the activity is primarily religious; where the idea of manipulation dominates, the activity is primarily magical. Though it is difficult to conceive of communication with forces, there are certainly many attempts at manipulating beings.

One could put this in another way by saying that it is precisely *through* communication that one manipulates personalized beings. Beattie would say that men have to personify the objects of their religious interest so as to feel

[19] See J. H. M. Beattie, *Other Cultures*, 1964, Chapters 12 and 13.

that they are communicating with them. R. F. Horton goes further, and sees a large part of religious activity as an attempt to persuade or control these personified beings in just the same way as one would a human being: for example, constraining them by a sacrifice to make a return gift. Of course you cannot see the deity's reaction to your approach as you can that of a human being; so the best you can do, if the answer does not come at once, is to repeat the same approach and hope it will be more effective next time. This is why approaches to deities become stereotyped (ritualized).[20] Accordingly Horton proposes to call religion 'an extension of the field of people's social relationships beyond the confines of human society'. This is an explanatory description of religion, not a definition which would indicate how religion is to be distinguished from that which is not religion. If it is conceived as describing everything that can be called religious, we must conclude that Horton regards magic as something that can be distinguished from religion by the criterion that the magician is not trying to conduct transactions with personified beings; and in fact the whole of Horton's argument in this context is about 'gods'.

SUGGESTIONS FOR READING

The classic studies of primitive religion are E. B. Tylor, *Primitive Culture* (3rd edition 1891), Chapters XI–XVIII, J. G. Frazer, *The Golden Bough* (abridged edition, paperback 1957) and E. Durkheim, *Elementary Forms of the Religious Life* (translated by Joseph Ward Swain, 1954). All these books are long, but Durkheim's is manageable; the translation is not always reliable, and those who can read it in French are advised to do so. C. Lévi-Strauss, *Totemism To-day* (translation by R. Needham, 1962), conveniently summarizes the history of his subject.

Malinowski's theory of religion and his distinction between religion and magic are expounded in his essay on the subject in the collection of his works entitled *Magic, Science and Religion* (1948). E. R. Leach advances his definition of ritual in the introductory chapter of his *Political Systems of Highland Burma* (1954). A useful discussion of the validity of distinctions between magic and religion can be found in R. W. Firth, *Human Types* (2nd edition 1956), Chapter VI. R. F. Horton's article, 'A Definition of Religion and

[20] Horton, loc. cit.

its Uses', was published in the *Journal of the Royal Anthropological Institute* for 1960. J. R. Goody, 'Religion and Ritual: The Definitional Problem', *British Journal of Sociology*, 1961, discusses the same question. The question whether early religious thinking is or is not similar to the reasoning of scientists is argued by J. H. M. Beattie, 'Ritual and Social Change' in *Man*, 1966, and R. F. Horton and R. Finnegan eds., *Modes of Thought*, is largely devoted to this subject.

CHAPTER 14 ## Religion and Society

ARGUMENTS about what is to be called magic and what is to be called religion are no more than a clearing of the ground for a discussion of the place of religion in social life. Except in a rather general way in the context of Durkheim's theory, the relation between religion and morality has so far hardly been mentioned Nothing has been said on the question of occasions for religious ritual, and very little on the way in which a religion provides its adherents with a coherent view of the world.

The occasions that are thought to call for ritual, for seeking contact with the supernatural (or the ultra-human or the non-empirical, or spiritual beings or just 'the gods'), are remarkably similar in all societies.

Evans-Pritchard introduces his discussion of the meaning of sacrifice among the Nuer by a division of occasions for sacrifice into two types, 'confirmatory' and 'piacular', and this division would hold good for ritual in general, whether or not it includes a sacrifice in the sense of killing an animal;[1] a great deal of ritual includes symbolic giving of some kind, as Horton has remarked. A distinction must be made between the terms *ritual,* used as a noun and implying a complex of actions engaging a number of people, and *ritual behaviour,* describing individual actions of a ritual nature, among which Leach would include wearing a ring to show that you are married, and most anthropologists would include the observance of 'totemic' avoidances.

Some rites, Evans-Pritchard says,[2] are concerned with changes of social status and the interaction of social groups; these are the ones to which Durkheim directed his atten-

---

[1] Or of 'destroying something', as the wider definition of sacrifice given by Hubert and Mauss has it (H. Hubert and M. Mauss, *Sacrifice, its Nature and Function*, trans. W. D. Halls, 1964).

[2] *Nuer Religion*, 1956, p. 272.

tion. Others are 'concerned rather with the moral and physical welfare of the individual'; these are the ones that people have in mind when they reject Durkheim's interpretation of religion as inadequate.

The occasions for rites of the first type, which Evans-Pritchard calls 'confirmatory', are remarkably similar all over the world. In western society the large number of people whose adherence to their religion is merely nominal nevertheless set store by the performance of ritual on three occasions, all concerned with changes of status—at birth when a new person enters society, at marriage and at death when a person leaves it. Such people, we may suppose, are not greatly concerned with the spiritual effects of these rites; yet the fact must reflect a general feeling that these events ought to be in some way sacralized.

'Rites de passage'

The first writer to consider the social significance of 'confirmatory' ritual was Van Gennep the Frenchman, who contributed to the language of social anthropology the term *rites de passage*. There is a certain difficulty in choosing an apt English rendering of this term, since in speech 'rites' may be confused with 'rights' and 'rites of passage' to be taken to refer to something legal (although this is the title of the English translation of Van Gennep's book).[3] A better phrase is Beattie's 'transition rituals',[4] but many people say 'life-crisis rituals', thereby limiting themselves to a narrower field than that covered by Van Gennep. Some of us simply say 'passage rituals'.

Van Gennep in fact argued that in simple societies *every* change that could be thought of as a passage from one state to another was ritualized—changes in the phases of the moon or in the seasons, as well as changes in the social status of individuals, the movement of a community to a new village, the entry of a couple into a new house, or even entering or leaving any house. For example, he mentions the pre-Islamic Arab custom that everyone who entered or

[3] A. van Gennep, *Les Rites de Passage*, 1909, translated by M. Vizedom and G. Caffee, 1960.
[4] *Other Cultures*, p. 211.

left a house touched the image of the household god as he passed the door. Social anthropologists today find his theories more interesting where they bear on the sacralization of changes in social status. Van Gennep pointed out that a human being does not become a member of his society merely by being born; he has to be formally accepted into it, and this is done by a public naming of the infant or a presentation of him to his parents' kin. The attainment of social adulthood is marked by ritual, as are marriage and death, and one of the effects of mortuary ritual is to establish the status of the dead person as an ancestor. All such changes, said Van Gennep, can be interpreted as 'goings out' and 'comings in'—not just 'passages' but rather 'passings through'.

The person whose status is to be changed is first removed from everyday contact by a *rite of separation,* which places him in the realm of the sacred in Durkheim's sense of the word. Examples are the ritual departure from an African village of a band of boys or girls to the place outside it where they are to spend the period of their initiation, or the placing of a bride in the hut where she will spend a period of seclusion, either before she goes to her husband, or at her husband's home before she takes up the household duties of a wife. This is followed by a transitional period when the person going through the ritual has left one status behind but has not yet entered on the other. The rites at this stage Van Gennep calls *marginal,* but he also uses of them the French word *liminaire* which drives his metaphor home. *Liminaire* means 'of the threshold'; Van Gennep imagines somebody actually on the doorstep, neither in nor out. Then comes a *rite of aggregation* in which the new status is formally confirmed—or one should rather say created, since status is a matter of social recognition and not of any act or condition of an individual. The three stages have also been called in English translation rites of separation, segregation and integration. Van Gennep was careful to point out that the sacralization of the change of status is never the *sole* purpose of the rites which surround it. They usually include elements directed to the person's success in his new status; for example, marriage rites are concerned with fertility, the ritual of birth with the safety and health of the infant and his fortunate progress through life.

The symbolism of transition rituals is often that of rebirth; in some initiation rites the boys are said to be swallowed by some mysterious creature and born anew from its belly. Their mothers may believe that they literally die and are reborn; especially since, in those initiations which include a long period of subjection to physical hardship, they sometimes actually die. Often they go through a door, as the Nyakyusa chiefs and headmen used to do when they entered together on their offices, at a ceremony which was actually called the 'coming out' because this was thought of as the most significant part of it; or as the Kikuyu boys at initiation used to pass under an arch made of banana stems.

In addition to transition rites which solemnize the entry of individuals on a new status, confirmatory rites may be performed on behalf of a whole community. These are usually annual, and Van Gennep could have brought them into his category of transition rites by emphasizing their timing at the passage from one year to another. Certainly some annual rites are of this kind, such as those of southern Ghana, where the evils of the past are ritually thrown into the sea and a new year begins with a clean record. But although many people reckon a new year from the time when the crops are harvested, this is not the major significance of such rites. They are concerned rather with the continued satisfactory working of both the natural and the social order. These are the rites that Durkheim saw as containing the essence of religion.

The reason why changes in social status should be surrounded with ritual has been discussed by Gluckman and Fortes.[5] Gluckman's theory has something in common with his explanation of the processes of African law. He reminds us again that in a small-scale society relationships are 'multiplex'; the roles of father, headman, priest and so on are all played in relation to the same people. Hence failure in any one role is likely to affect other relationships

[5] M. Gluckman (ed.), *Essays in the Ritual of Social Relations*, 1962.

than those logically involved in that particular role,[6] and so—this seems to be the argument—is more serious in its consequences than it would be in a society where roles are segregated, so that a highly unsuccessful father can be a very successful university don. Ritual, as we should all agree, is attached to matters that people take very seriously; in small-scale societies people attach great importance to the correct playing of roles. Ritual, Gluckman adds, segregates one role from the *intrusion* of other roles: quoting the famous ethnographer Junod, he instances the ritual of preparation for hunting among the Tsonga, and explains this as due to the separation of the hunter from his normal milieu and activities as cultivator.

A role, as Fortes reminds us, is not something the actor *becomes,* just as a stage actor does not turn into a mediaeval prince whose father has been murdered whenever he is engaged to play Hamlet. Society confers or allots roles, it instructs the actors in them, all the time through the diffuse sanction of public comment, and in a concentrated form through the rituals of change of status. But these rituals are not just—indeed they are hardly at all—processes of technical instruction; their overt purpose, as well as their effect, in the view of Fortes, is to stress the moral aspect of the role, the obligations towards his fellows which the actor undertakes by assuming it, even if the status that he is entering is an ascribed one so that he has no choice. Referring specifically to the installation rites of kings and chiefs, but as part of an argument concerned with all transition ritual, he says their aim is 'that the bonds of office that bind the holder to those for whom he holds it may be irrefragably forged.'[7] Moreover, rites of the annual type, in addition to their concern with the harvest and the recurrence of good harvests in the future, often include reminders to the holders of political office of the obligations which it entails. Perhaps the most striking example is the new year ceremony of the Swazi, with its simulation of rebellion against

<hr>

[6] This is a more sophisticated way of describing what Malinowski used to call 'the functional interrelationship of institutions'.

[7] *Essays on the Ritual of Social Relations,* pp. 70–1.

the king and his triumph over it.[8] Fortes cites also the Great Festivals of the Tallensi, the series of rites that extend throughout the dry season, from one harvest to the next sowing, during which, as a part of a very complex ritual, the mythical origins of the complementary offices of chief and earth-priest are recalled. 'So the ceremonial cycle confirms annually the occupation of each office and thus re-imposes on its holder his duties and capacities.'[9] It also reminds each one how indispensable to the community is the existence of his office and the due performance of its responsibilities, by assigning to each a part in the ritual drama that only he can perform.

Fortes extends his generalizations beyond the field of publicly performed ritual into that of taboo, or ritual prohibition, and here makes an observation which bears on the discussion of 'totemic' avoidances. Every time a person has occasion to remember that a certain food is forbidden him on account of his clan membership or—an unusual taboo that is found among the Tallensi—because he is a first-born son, he is reminded of his duties as a member of his clan or as the first-born son of his father.

Ritual and social structure

Fortes' argument shows how the understanding of the relation between religion and society has advanced along the path first opened by Durkheim to the recognition that religion does more—and also perhaps less—than create a general awareness, in circumstances of heightened emotion, of the dependence of every individual on life in an ordered society. Close observation of the confirmatory rites of small-scale societies has shown how much they emphasize the interdependence of different divisions in a society by distributing ritual tasks among them. This can be seen both in societies which consist of autonomous lineages and in those which recognize a supreme head. The Tallensi Great Festivals, which have just been mentioned, are a classic example of this type. The People of Taleland are divided into *real* Talis, who claim to be the descendants of the first inhabi-

---

[8] H. Kuper, *An African Aristocracy*, 1947.
[9] *Essays on the Ritual of Social Relations*, p. 25.

tants, and Namoos descended from more recent immigrants. The heads of Tale lineages are priests of the earth; they alone can sacrifice to it and so secure that the crops may flourish and people in general prosper. The heads of Namoo lineages are chiefs, and what is more significant in the ritual context, they alone have the magic of rainmaking, which they claim to have brought with them from their home in the north. The Great Festivals consist of rites performed alternately by Namoos and Talis, each accompanied by dancing, in which the celebrants take part while persons belonging to the other section look on. At key points in the rites there are formal encounters between the senior chief and the senior earth-priest, each pronouncing the blessings on the whole community that his ritual office empowers him to give. As Fortes puts it, the 'rituals vividly insulate each group from the other, while at the same time uniting them in common responsibility for the welfare of the country'.[10]

While these festivals are being held, quarrelling is not permitted. This does not signify by any means that the goodwill—or the Durkheimian emotional awareness of social interdependence—which they engender purges men's hearts of anger and hatred. What it does mean is that disputes cannot be openly pursued, and those which are already public must be brought to an end before the ceremonies can be performed. Disputes of this kind are concerned with contested claims, and must be settled by the surrender of one party's case or by some form of compromise. The imminence of the ceremonies, the performance of which is believed by everyone to be absolutely indispensable to their welfare and even survival, makes settlement urgent; this is how, in practical terms, they reinforce the solidarity which their ritual symbolizes.

The elaborate ritual of Tikopia known as 'the work of the gods' again illustrates how religion imposes the obligation of co-operation for the general welfare on sections of a society which are autonomous in the conduct of everyday affairs. Each of the four Tikopia chiefs—in the days before their conversion to Christianity—was held to be ritually

[10] 'Ritual Festivals and Social Cohesion in the Hinterland of the Gold Coast', *American Anthropologist*, 1936, p. 602.

responsible for one of the principal foodstuffs.

Accession rites in Africa illustrate the distribution of ritual responsibilities among the recognized divisions of the community. The territory of the Shilluk of the Upper Nile is divided into eleven sections, each having at its head the headman of the lineage which is dominant there. The Shilluk recognize a 'divine king', the *reth*, who through the ritual performed at his accession becomes the incarnation of the founder of the nation, the demi-god Nyikang. His kingdom is thought of as consisting of two halves with his capital in the middle, and the most dramatic element of the installation rites is a mock battle between them, fought on the banks of a watercourse that is supposed to mark the mid-point of the kingdom. In this battle the king's army is defeated, but only by an army bearing the image of Nyikang, who thus conquers him before entering into him. Each of the hundred settlements into which Shillukland is divided, and each of the principal clans, is responsible for providing some specific object to be used in the ritual. Special ritual roles are played by the royal lineage, by those branches of it which have lost the right to provide a king, and by his hereditary bodyguard.

Among the Alur of western Uganda the heads of the five senior clans go through the accession rites along with a new chief, and each of them has its peculiar ritual task. Men from one carry the new chief on their shoulders to visit his ancestor shrines; another clan rekindle the fires that were quenched on the death of the previous chief; and so on. A Ganda king's accession rites included the taking of life, believed mystically to strengthen the new king and through him his people; and some clans had the responsibility of providing victims. But even these duties were a matter of pride, in that they emphasized the status of the clans who were thus bound to the kingship.

The annual confirmatory rite of the Swazi—the *incwala,* or first-fruits festival—is one of the most elaborate that we know of, and has been performed in quite recent years. It includes an enactment of the triumph of the king over his enemies, in which the political structure of the nation is clearly symbolized by the parts allotted to persons of dif-

ferent status. At the height of the ritual a division is made
between the faithful subjects of the king, his agnates (who
might become his rivals) and foreigners who do not owe
allegiance to him; these two last categories are ordered
away before the king appears in triumph, encircled by his
army.

Piacular rituals

Piacular[11] rituals, Evans-Pritchard's second category, are, he
says, 'performed in situations of danger . . . often thought
of as being brought about by some fault', and in them
'ideas of propitiation and expiation are prominent.'[12] Since
they are concerned with 'the moral and physical welfare of
the individual' it is in them above all that one sees the
connection between religion and morality.

It has been asserted that in some primitive religions
there is no such connection. This statement can mean that
the gods are not good, as Euripides said about the gods of
Greek religion, that they do not set an example to men of
obedience to the moral rule that men accept. Certainly
there are gods whose principal attribute is power, and some
who are admired for having over-reached their adversaries.
But it may be that in societies where the gods are seen in
this light, it is not supposed that men should try to please
the gods by imitating them. Religion may also be thought
to be divorced from morality where its emphasis is on pleasing the gods by correct ritual rather than by right conduct.

But it must be rare indeed to find a small-scale society in
which men's fortunes are not held to depend in some way
on their moral conduct—in which, in other words, humanly
uncontrollable events are not supposed to be directed by
personalized beings who share human ideas of justice.
Where there is very little recognition of impersonal causa-
tion, men must believe that these beings are in principle
on their side; otherwise life would be impossible.

The beings to whom they appeal, in situations where they
are helpless, *must* help them unless there is some reason

---

[11] This word was introduced into our literature by Durkheim.
[12] 'The Meaning of Sacrifice among the Nuer', *Journal of the Royal
Anthropological Institute*, 1954, p. 21.

why they do not deserve help, and though reasons are sometimes found in the inadequate performance of ritual, they
are found at least as often in failures to respect social obligations. In other words, the universe is thought of as a moral
order within which people are not punished unless they
deserve to be.

Piacular ritual, therefore, must be considered in the context of the possible explanations that may be offered when
a person suffers misfortune, and particularly the misfortune
that befalls everyone at some time, sickness. People who fall
sick in societies where there is no scientific medicine may go
to 'doctors' with knowledge of herbal remedies, but in the
many cases that do not respond to these they turn from
treatment of their bodies to examination of their con-
sciences. They ask whom they have offended and to whom
they must make reparation.

Spirit-mediums and diviners

For the answer they must go to someone who has access to
the necessary information; that is to say, a person who can
somehow make contact with beings outside the reach of
ordinary faculties. Such persons are always specialists who
have learnt their profession. They are of two main types,
which may be called *spirit-mediums* and *diviners*. As these
terms are most commonly used, a spirit-medium purports
to speak, in a condition of trance or dissociation, with the
voice of some non-human being who knows the answers to
people's questions. A diviner, while remaining his normal
self, manipulates objects which are supposed to give the
answer without his intervention.

In Africa practitioners of both these kinds are popularly
called witch-doctors. The word is used in a classic on this
subject, Evans-Prichard's *Witchcraft, Oracles, and Magic
among the Azande* (1937). The name 'witch-doctor', simply
because it includes the word 'witch', is popularly supposed
to imply something sinister, and its use is associated with the
belief that the specialists to whom Africans go in trouble are
themselves witches and are objects of terror. 'The dreaded
witch-doctor' is a phrase to be found in many writings.
Hence the word is better avoided by people who wish to

avoid misconceptions. The role of spirit-medium or diviner is indispensable in the societies in which such people operate, and is thought of as a socially beneficent one.

In the sense of the word used by classical scholars an oracle is an utterance, so that it should be the spirit medium who gives oracles. But most anthropologists use the word 'oracle' to describe the objects used in divination. There are innumerable such objects. One of the simplest is the Lugbara 'rubbing-stick'. This is a 'do-it-yourself' oracle which anyone can use. While someone rubs a twist of grass against a millet stalk, the names of people, living or dead, who may have caused the sickness are spoken. When the grass sticks, this is held to indicate that the right name has been mentioned. This is only one of a number of methods of divination that Lugbara use; if they are doubtful about the answer it gives, or dissatisfied with it, they seek confirmation by trying a different one. The Ndembu of Zambia use more complicated methods. One, in principle typical of modes of divination in many places, is to put a number of objects in a basket and toss them in the air. The diviner reads the answer in the way they fall.

Divination and mediumship cannot always be clearly distinguished. Ndembu diviners, for example, although they operate by asking questions of the objects in the basket and not by going into trances, believe that their skill has been conferred upon them by a spirit in the same way as that of spirit-mediums.

It is an interesting fact that the activities of diviner or spirit-medium are often taken up by people who are debarred from advancement in the secular field. In some societies they are professions for women. Among the Lugbara, where the position of lineage elder must be held by a son of the previous elder's first wife, a son of a junior wife has no hope of ever attaining to it. He cannot succeed his half-brother, and he is too close to him to break away and head his own descent group. Such men may seek reputation as the manipulators of oracles; they succeed if their oracle gets a name for giving answers that satisfy the consultants.

Spirit-mediums must have a special type of personality. They must be able readily to fall into a condition of dissociation and speak as though with a voice entering them from outside; they commonly find their vocation after a period of disturbance which a psychiatrist would probably call a mental illness. This disturbed state is usually taken as a sign that a spirit wishes to enlist the person in his service. But it is of some significance that we do not often hear of persons who hold positions of authority being 'possessed' in this way. Perhaps such people may sometimes experience the same kind of disturbance, but it would be very inconvenient to interpret it in a manner which ascribed to them a role quite inconsistent with their existing one.

Diviners do not claim, as western fortune-tellers do, to know all about their clients by occult means, so that it would be useless to try to discredit a diviner by showing that he could not do this. Of course a shrewd man will be able to impress strangers by drawing intelligent inferences from their appearance and behaviour, but this is a matter of professional manner rather than of diagnosis. The people who consult him usually offer him a fairly narrow range of possibilities from which his instrument 'chooses'. Although Turner[13] says of the Ndembu that some diviners have been in danger of their lives after giving unpopular answers, this seems to be exceptional. Any answer is likely to be unpopular with someone, but it is often possible to try another diviner or another method if you don't like the first one. A wholly unexpected answer is unknown.

The reason for this is obvious. When a man falls sick and cannot recover, he searches his conscience. He may find there a number of actions that could have offended spirits of different kinds; or he may find none, in which case he looks for an enemy who wishes him harm. But the system of ideas that links religion with morality is such that it would be meaningless to look for the explanation of sickness in some circumstances of which the victim and his neighbours were not aware.

The basis of this system of ideas is the conviction that suffering should be deserved, that the beings on whose protection man relies should not withdraw it without good

[13] V. W. Turner, *Ndembu Divination*, Rhodes-Livingstone Papers no. 31, 1961, p. 14.

cause. Good cause means, in general, what it would mean in the case of a human authority; breaking the rules which it is that person's responsibility to maintain. This is one of the ways in which religion can be thought of as an extension of social relationships beyond the human sphere.

In most African societies the spirits of the ancestors are believed to be concerned with the behaviour of their living descendants, and to visit with sickness those who disregard the obligations of kinship. Sometimes ancestors in different kin relationships (from the point of view of an individual) may be thought to be interested in different aspects of conduct. The dead are also thought sometimes to be angered by the forgetfulness of living persons who neglect to make offerings to them. 'Hunger has conquered us,' the Lugbara ancestors are supposed to say, 'our children give us nothing to eat.' Once the offended ancestor has been identified, a sacrifice is made; this is the piacular rite, which should make peace so that the sufferer can be restored to health. Lugbara, in this respect rather exceptional, do not make the sacrifice until they have seen the cure; they just 'show' a beast to the spirits, thereby earmarking it for sacrifice at the appropriate time. This is indeed treating gods like more inaccessible humans.

But what happens if no offending spirit can be identified or if, which is much more likely, the victim and his close kin refuse to accept his sickness as a merited punishment? People in general are aware that not all suffering is deserved. Some instances, therefore, must be due to evil influences and not to good ones, to beings who are not chastising the sufferer to teach him a lesson but simply seeking to do him harm. These beings are conceived as human; it is they who figure in the mythology of many peoples as witches.[14] This is why witchcraft must be considered as an element of religious belief and not as something separate from it.

---

[14] Anthropologists do not make the distinction found in English folklore between witches and warlocks (or wizards). The special kinds of sexual depravity associated with English (and Scots and American) witches in the seventeenth century are not ascribed to witches in the contemporary world.

Witchcraft

The first detailed study of witchcraft was made by Evans-Pritchard in 1926–30 among the Zande of the Sudan-Congo border. He found there a belief that has since proved to be very widespread in Africa. This is the notion that witchcraft is an actual substance present in some people's bodies, which can operate even without their volition. If this were all, one would have to say that witchcraft was neutral, simply a way of personifying accident. But Zande believe that once a person finds he has this power—as he does when a diviner identifies him as the cause of someone's illness— he soon begins to use it deliberately to harm people he does not like.

People who imagine witchcraft in this way distinguish between witches and sorcerers; the latter are believed to use material substances to harm their fellows, and men (or women) who claim the knowledge of such substances can generally be employed to use them on behalf of others. Where this distinction is made it is usually supposed that sorcery can sometimes be justified—for example, in order to punish an unknown thief who, because he is not known, cannot be brought to justice. In the Trobriand Islands it was thought that the chiefs, whose prestige rested largely on their supposed powers of magic to control the weather, employed sorcerers to punish their enemies, and this was not regarded as wrong.

Anthropologists have tried in their writing to follow the Zande distinction between witches, relying on their inherent powers, and sorcerers using 'medicines', as their materials are nearly always called in ethnographic literature, but there are societies to which it cannot be easily applied. Some peoples do not make a sharp distinction, but hold that there are different kinds of people using 'medicines', who in many respects can be distinguished as witches and sorcerers are.

The fundamental reason for the belief in witches is far more important than the imaginary characacteristics ascribed to them by particular people, interesting though these may be. It is the necessity of accounting for undeserved misfortune where it is not recognized that misfortune can come by chance. Evans-Pritchard in his analysis of Zande belief emphasized the fact that it is an entirely logical way of explaining events. Of course the Zande knows that if a tree falls on you the blow will kill you, but he still asks 'Why should it have fallen on *me*?'

The answer must be, 'It was your fault,' or 'It was not your fault.' Either the misfortune was brought on the victim by one of the supernatural guardians of the moral order, or it was caused by some force subversive of the moral order, the principle of evil. So there must always be, somewhere in the cosmogony, a force that is wholly evil, a personified being whose actions can never be justified. In the majority of African societies this is the witch, defined as the Zande define witches; but in some it is a person using medicines, whom the Zande, with a good many anthropologists, would call a sorcerer.

Evans-Pritchard's study of Zande witchcraft was concerned with it largely as a system of beliefs. He showed that on its own terms it was perfectly rational, supplying causal explanations of events that would otherwise have to be unexplained, and, along with the explanations, a practical recourse without which men would be helpless in situations of crisis. He showed how some aspect of the belief system could be invoked to account for any situation. He also discussed the question of the honesty of the diviners and the credulity of their clients. A feature of Zande, as of many other African, cultures is that the specialists who are consulted in case of sickness purport to remove from the patient's body objects put in it by witches, and supposed to be the physical cause of the trouble. Obviously they cannot do this unless they bring the objects with them, and this is enough in the eyes of many Europeans to brand them as charlatans exploiting a credulous population. One point to note here is that their function in providing an explanation of the sickness is far more important than this supposedly curative action. Even more significant is the reflection that people cannot do without a recourse of some kind in difficulties for which they know no technical solution. As Evans-Pritchard has shown, they may be sceptical about the genuineness of particular practitioners, but everyone believes there are genuine ones somewhere; in time of real trouble they could have no hope without this belief.

In most societies where people believe in witches there is a rich store of ideas about what they look like and how they behave. The essence of the belief is that there is no empirical way of detecting a witch's activities. Nevertheless there are many ideas about the nature of their invisible antics. What is important about these ideas is the symbolism through which they are expressed. This is always the symbolism of the anti-social. Night, when secret evil can be done, is the time for witchcraft, and night creatures are associated with witches, as are venomous creatures such as snakes. They are associated with deformity and with the wild country, the bush, outside the village area that man has civilized. They are pictured as performing acts that outrage the decencies, such as dancing naked, or excreting on the smooth ground in front of the homestead. There is also generally an idea of the kind of human being who is likely to be a witch—a morose, unsociable, grumbling person, who eats alone but complains that his neighbours do not offer him food.

In such beliefs are crystallized a society's picture of all that it most abhors, and what it prizes is asserted by this assertion of the opposite. Ideas of the typical witch-personality form part of the system of social control; again, they provide an anti-image, an epitome of what those who deserve the esteem of their fellows should not be. Sometimes, as among the Nyakyusa, children are taught not to act in any way that may provoke resentment, lest they anger a witch. For it is a characteristic of witch beliefs that they can be used to justify any suspicion of witchcraft. Witches exercise their powers, as Iago did his more material ones, from 'motiveless malignity'; all the same, if you provoke one it increases your risk of finding yourself a victim. Believers in witchcraft are not concerned that their ideas on the subject should form a logical whole, least of all at the time when they are applying the belief to concrete cases.

The typical concrete case is that of sickness; other mis-

fortunes are ascribed to witchcraft, but most attempts to
identify a witch are made when somebody is sick. It is significant that the generalized image of the witch is not then
called in aid; nobody asks if a mysterious person accompanied by a cobra has been seen lurking around the victim's
homestead. If there are people with a reputation as witches,
their names are not canvassed. People ask who has a griev-
ance against the sick man.

Accusations of witchcraft, then, are a way of pursuing
quarrels, though it would be too much to say that they
were deliberately used in this way. A number of anthropologists recently have paid special attention to the
direction that accusations take, and have found that in any
given society there is a characteristic context for such
accusations. They are typically made between persons who,
according to the rules of the society, should be on friendly
terms, but who are in fact at odds. Situations of strain are
brought to a head by accusations of witchcraft, and sometimes such an accusation can be held, when nothing else
would, to justify the termination of the relationship.

A particularly interesting example is provided by the
Lugbara.[15] These people believe, as some others do, that the
anger of humans at the wrongdoings of others can inspire
the ancestral ghosts to punish the wrongdoers. They believe
too that the envy of humans at the success of others can
bring harm to the envied; this is their conception of witchcraft. They use the same word (*ole*) for both these feelings.
It is a duty of the elder of a lineage to invoke the intervention of ghosts against members of the lineage who transgress
the rules of lineage amity and respect for seniors, and if one
of his juniors falls sick he will claim to have done so. But as
lineage elders grow old in years their authority inevitably
grows less, and they find themselves constantly driven to
invoke the ghosts. The time comes when a branch of the
lineage wants to assert its autonomy; the way to do this is
to claim that the elder has no authority over it. If he causes
sickness where he has no authority to do so, he is practising
witchcraft. Thus *the same action* is or is not witchcraft
according to the attitude of the people looking at it; it is

15 J. F. M. Middleton, *Lugbara Religion*, 1960.

those who are seeking to establish their own position as independent elders who make the accusation of witchcraft. Where such ideas are current it would be impossible to think of witches as a separate class of people, and for the Lugbara the sorcerer, not the witch, is the type of evil

Among the matrilineal peoples of Zambia and Malawi, also, the fission of a descent group is commonly precipitated by an accusation of witchcraft against the headman. The Yao of Malawi and Ndembu of Zambia do not sharply distinguish sorcery from witchcraft; this would be hard to do where the person to be accused is one who up to that point has been the leader and cherisher of the village. These peoples do not have the elaborate ideology of the Lugbara. One simply observes with them that when a section of the small village community is anxious to secede, sickness among the members of that section is apt to be ascribed to the witchcraft of the headman. Anthropologists have noted that, in the ecological conditions of Central Africa, it is difficult for a community to find subsistence if it increases beyond a certain size, so that a time must come round periodically when a village is due for a split. But so strong is the conviction that the descent group ought to keep together that no section could move away just because it wanted to. Only the belief that they are victims of an unpardonable wrong can justify the division. It is not suggested, however, that the witchcraft accusations are consciously fabricated to meet the occasion.

Accusations of witchcraft against named persons are not equally common in all societies. In some they are the stock in trade of the chiefs' courts; in others people ascribe their misfortunes to unknown witches, but hesitate to invite the enmity of a real man by an accusation. One must distinguish too between formal accusations, made in cold blood and on the basis of divination, and name-calling in the heat of a quarrel. But even this latter kind of accusation, not perhaps seriously meant, may have its characteristic context. Lienhardt observed among the Dinka that the people who accused each other in this way were usually in a competitive relationship with a third person, as co-wives are to their common husband, a relationship in which no rule establishes that one is superior, and so by definition in the right in a disputed matter, and in which there are favours to be distributed.

Since witchcraft is conceived as the embodiment of evil, it is not surprising that attempts should sometimes be made to rid a community of witches once and for all. Such attempts are occasionally institutionalized. The Nupe in the north of Nigeria, for example, had a cult association whose sole function was to detect and denounce witches. The masked dancers of the cult would visit a town or village where the women—the Nupe believed that all witches were women—would be assembled at the dancing place. The dance went on all day; every now and then the dancers would stop and swoop on a woman. The person so accused might pay a fine, but if she could not she was put to death. The possibilities for extortion by such an organization are obvious, and under British rule it was suppressed. But when the Nupe discussed the subject with Nadel ten or fifteen years later, they did not regard its disappearance as an unmixed gain; they felt uncomfortably that they had no protection against witches.[16]

Individuals offering such protection have appeared from time to time under colonial rule, and some writers have suggested that their appearance is a symptom of the increase in anxiety resulting from all the new problems that the attempt to modernize Africa has created for the unsophisticated. It is also argued that the proliferation of these witch-finding cults is a response to the specific anxiety created when colonial authorities refused to allow the courts to try people on charges of witchcraft. We cannot really be certain that no such movements ever arose before the colonial days, although they could never have spread over wide areas in the way that modern communications make possible.

There is no denying that persons claiming to have means of detecting witches, and of either destroying or curing them, meet with immense success in Africa today. They have much in common with Christian revivalists, and their message to the witches to repent and thus escape the other-

[16] S. F. Nadel, *Nupe Religion*, 1954, pp. 194 ff.

wise fatal consequences of their wickedness has no counterpart in the traditional religions, in which one makes good a
specific wrong done to man or deity by a specific act of
atonement. The detection of witches is often an element in
the kind of religious movement that is called *millenary*, or
occasionally *chiliastic*, according as you prefer the Latin or
the Greek word for 'a thousand'.

Millenary cults

This word links the breakaway Christian sects in Africa
today, the cults that have appeared in so many parts of the
South Pacific through the present century, and some older
ones among North American Indians, to a long history that
goes back to the Middle Ages. This is the history of Christians impatient for the arrival of heaven on earth, who at
different times persuaded themselves that its coming was
imminent, and that only those who knew this and prepared
appropriately for the event would be saved. The year 1000,
as it approached, was thought by many people to be the date,
and it was also believed that the reign of God on earth
would last for a thousand years—hence the description of
such beliefs as millenary, which, as purists point out, is not
a strictly accurate use of the word.

The essence of these beliefs is that a perfect state of the
world, free from any of the evils that are part of the human
lot, is about to be brought into existence by some miraculous event. The event itself depends upon the performance
of the appropriate rituals, and when it comes those who
have performed them will enjoy the perfect world, while
people who, by refusing to do so, have delayed its coming
will be destroyed. Such beliefs are more likely to be found
among the adherents of religions which look forward to a
state of perfection in the future, as do Judaism, Christianity,
and Islam in their different ways. In most small-scale societies people see the Golden Age as a past state of affairs, lost
through some action of man and never to be restored. But
a few have the 'millennial dream'. Some of the Amerindians
of Brazil believe in the existence here and now of a 'Land
without Evil', and people have sometimes embarked on
long migrations in search of it. The people of Biak Island,

off the north-west coast of New Guinea, also have a myth—apparently indigenous—promising the return of a hero who lived long ago, and with it the disappearance of sickness, death, old age, and the need for hard work. Often the Golden Age is held to include the return to life of those who are already dead, and if people consider that oppression by those more powerful than they are is one of the evils from which they suffer, their ideal world is bound to be one without the oppressors. The myth is activated when a prophet appears with a message that the time is at hand.

When we are dealing with societies without written records we cannot tell what circumstances may have prompted people to suppose the promise was on the point of being fulfilled. The cases that have come to the notice of anthropologists have all been in territories under colonial rule, and in them the destruction of the oppressors has bulked large in the dream. It has been argued too that the millenary movements of the Middle Ages arose among the dispossessed, and particularly among people who had no recognized secular means of asserting their claims and pursuing their interests. This is the argument of Norman Cohn (not an anthropologist), who notes that many such movements drew their followers from the immigrant workers in the new towns that were growing up from the eleventh to the thirteenth centuries in northern France, the Low Countries, and along the Rhine.[17] It has been pointed out that some millenary movements have arisen among people who were neither poor nor oppressed. This shows that there may be more than one reason for people to feel impatient with the existing state of affairs, and powerless to alter it by secular means. It remain true that a sense of oppression has very often been an element in these movements.

One of the most famous was the Ghost Dance of the Indians of the western plains of the United States, so called because it looked to the return of the dead, and because the means of bringing this about was thought to be dancing for days on end in a manner prescribed by the prophet. The millennium envisaged here was a return to the state of affairs before the coming of the white man—an idealized

[17] N. Cohn, *The Pursuit of the Millenniun*, 1957.

state of affairs in which hunting was always successful, there was no quarrelling and no witchcraft. American anthropologists called this backward-looking movement 'nativistic', and for a time the word was used as a general term to describe all religious movements in which 'natives' made symbolic statements about the kind of world they would like to see. But the Ghost Dance seems to have been pretty well unique in its idealization of the past. Most contemporary millenary movements aim at getting a better share of the future—that is to say, of the products of machine technology. Most of them, too, seek to adapt Christian doctrine and ritual to their own aspirations. So they are often called 'syncretistic'—'mixing together'.

A type of movement that has attracted much attention from anthropologists is the 'cargo cult' which has appeared in so many forms in the South Pacific. The essence of the 'cargo cult' is the belief that when the millennium comes the ancestors will bring with them vast quantities of the imported goods to which all Europeans appear to have unlimited access, while they are out of reach of native cash incomes. Sometimes the leaders of a 'cargo' movement have attempted to set up their own political authorities; sometimes they have been content to believe that when the day comes the last shall be first, the world turned upside down, and black superior to white.

African movements of this kind have been less fully studied by British anthropologists, though there is a good deal of literature on what have been called 'prophet' movements in the Congo area under both French and Belgian rule. In these movements political aspirations have been much more clearly expressed, as they were in the Chilembwe rising of 1915 in Nyasaland (Malawi). The French sociologist Georges Balandier has described them as 'total reactions to the colonial situation'[18]—what might be called in English protest movements. Balandier holds that political protest takes this form at a time when there is no chance of successful rebellion, an argument which brings him close to the mediaevalist's argument just mentioned. Cohn has remarked, however, that mediaeval millenary movements

[18] G. Balandier, *The Sociology of Black Africa*, 1970 p. 485.

often appeared at a time when a secular revolt was actually going on. It is true of the movements observed during the colonial era that their leaders have often purported to put their trust in God alone, and to reject the use of force against their fellow men. Those in authority have not often believed them. Since they have usually considered that those in authority are evil, they have frequently resisted orders— for example, public health measures—and made it necessary for the authorities to take forcible action against them, and sometimes this has led to a direct confrontation of force. While these words were being written the press was reporting daily the numbers killed by the Lumpa sect of the prophetess Alice Lenshina in Zambia; it seems that they were not willing to wait for the act of God which would destroy the unbelievers. (It has also been reported that the unbelievers attacked them first.)

If we say, with Beattie, that the essence of religion is the symbolic statement of strongly felt desires, we can see how these desires can sometimes reach a pitch of intensity beyond what orthodox, established religious systems provide for. Orthodox systems, as Durkheim pointed out, support the social order—by justifying it if not by ritualizing it. Heretical sects may come in time to be orthodox religions, but if they do they abandon their millenary ideals.

Myth

The myths of millenary religions have been mentioned in passing. This was an anticipation of the discussion of *myth* as an important element in religion.

In ordinary usage the word myth may be used of any statement that the speaker supposes to be untrue. The statements that the anthropologist calls myths are certainly untrue. They describe events that a scientifically trained person knows could not have happened, and indeed events that the tellers of the myths do not expect to happen again; they belong to a distant 'age of miracles', when things were different.

But what is important about myth in the context of religion, as Malinowski insisted, is not simply that it is a story of miraculous happenings. In his view it was a mistake to regard myth either as garbled history or as garbled science. The essence of myth, he declared, was as a *charter*. The myth is the story of the first doing of some act that is still repeated in ritual, or that validates some claim in social relations. It lays down 'the effective precedent of a glorified past for repetitive actions in the present'.[19] Stories of the coming of the first ancestor of a royal line, bringing with him the arts of civilization, of the miracles of the first ancestor of a ritual authority, or the first man to use a type of magic, are myths because they validate the claims of their descendants to exercise political or spiritual authority, or to have a monopoly in the practice of the magic. Myth is associated with ritual when the ritual re-enacts the happenings recounted in the myth. All the stories that tell how some object became the totem of a descent group are 'charters' for the ritual behaviour enjoined towards the totem object.

In this theory, then, myth has little or no relation to cosmology. It is not an attempt to explain the universe, or how things came to be; it explains why what is done today is the right thing to do. Leach[20] develops this attitude further when he says it is absurd to ask questions about the statements made in myth as if they formed part of a body of theoretical knowledge that could be elaborated. A myth, he argues, is simply the verbal part of a ritual. If a Kachin tells you that the rite you are observing is a sacrifice to beings called *nats*, you accept that this is all there is to be said. You may gather from the ritual itself that some *nats* are more important than others, but it would be absurd to ask questions about the appearance and mode of life of *nats*, and Kachins could not answer such questions.

Malinowski distinguished between myth, legend, and fairy-tale. Legends, he said, were told and believed as if they were history, although the aim of the teller was usually to support the claims of some group to which he belonged; but they did not contain any element of the miraculous, nor were they regarded as sacred. Fairy-tales were full of miraculous happenings, but had no connection with ritual;

[19] B. Malinowski, *Sex, Culture and Myth*, 1963, p. 251.
[20] *Political Systems of Highland Burma*, 1954, p. 14.

they were pure entertainment, and nobody supposed they were true. Myth was 'a statement of a higher and a more important truth, of a primeval reality, which is still regarded as the pattern and foundation of primitive life'.[21]

Firth has remarked that the tales told in small-scale societies cannot always be clearly divided into types in this way. In Tikopia it is not always easy to separate sacred stories —myths—from profane ones. In a sacred story 'the words, or the characters in the tale, or the act of telling in itself, are regarded as having some force of power or some meaningful virtue of their own.'[22] Some tales are clearly sacred, in that they are concerned with powerful spirits, and it is dangerous to tell them in any other than the correct way. But the same spirits occur in entertainment stories such as Malinowski would have called fairy-tales.

But just as with the arguments about the way to distinguish religion from magic, there is little difficulty about recognizing what kind of story has most of the characteristics of myth. Sacredness and a close connection with ritual are characteristics of myth, which in any given story may be combined with characteristics of legend or fairy-tale as Malinowski defined them.

But some stories which most of us would call myths have no very close connection with ritual, and some have little connection with social structure either. For examples of myths unconnected with ritual one might go to the rich mythology of the Shilluk.[23] Some of it does tell how the demi-god, Nyikang, was born and came to Shillukland, and this is closely asociated with the political and ritual claims of the Shilluk king in whom he is believed to be incarnated, and with the ritual performed at a new king's accession. But other stories are what Malinowski would have called legends; they tell how the Shilluk and their neighbours arrived in the countries where they live, and what adventures they met on their way. Attempts have been made to recon-

---

[21] *Sex, Culture and Myth*, p. 305.
[22] R. W. Firth, *History and Traditions of Tikopia*, 1961, p. 8.
[23] R. G. Lienhardt, 'The Shilluk of the Upper Nile', in D. Forde (ed.), *African Worlds*, 1954.

struct from such sources the history of the migration of peoples in the upper Nile valley. These tales, though they are not associated with or re-enacted in ritual, do provide a 'charter' for the whole *status quo*. They give, as the myth of Genesis does, the assurance that the world of experience is divinely ordered; they support the view of the world held by most peoples whose traditions do not record dramatic changes, that it has always been and should always remain as they know it.

Malinowski rejected the view that myths were a kind of allegorical description of the world of nature—the sun, moon, and stars, the movement of the seasons. Nobody now supposes that the personages of myth personify these entities and processes. But not all myths are charters for specific actions. They do answer questions. It has been said that science answers 'how' questions while it is left for religion to answer 'why' questions. Most peoples have myths to answer the universal 'why' questions—why must we die, what has happened to the Land without Evil? Such myths tell how death came into the world, and how earth was separated from heaven, because somebody (usually a woman) disobeyed a divine instruction, usually a morally neutral command which was often disobeyed not through defiance but through mere carelessness.

Since Malinowski's day we are all agreed that myths are much more than attempts to satisfy objective curiosity about the world of experience. But some anthropologists today would hold that they do have this aspect, and that it has been too readily ignored by those who lay the emphasis on the relation between myth and social action. People do want the world to make sense, it is argued; they seek for unifying principles of some kind beneath the diversity of experience. It is not only sophisticated scientists who try to impose this kind of order on the world. R. F. Horton[24] has compared the religious ideas of African societies with the 'theoretical models' of the western scientist. In making such a model the scientist uses some fact of common experience as an analogy for the process he is trying to explain. Hor-

[24] 'Ritual Man in Africa', *Africa*, 1964, pp. 85–103.

ton points out that his model must be a system, a set of phenomena in an ordered relationship, since it is assumed that there is a system in the phenomena he is using it to explain. Western scientists find their models among things; African cosmologists find theirs among people. Horton remarks that in societies that have changed little over long periods of time, and, he might have added, do not think they change at all, the relationships among people are readily taken as a model of an ordered system. He offers another explanation for the difficulty of discussing with Kachins the characteristics of their *nats*.[25] When, he says, people use the idea of a personified being as a model to explain the uncontrollable forces of nature, they need only ascribe to him such qualities of a man as are necessary for the analogy—human motives, and power like that of man, only greater. This is the reason why, as Leach remarks, the Kachins do not consider where *nats* live, though many other peoples might, or whether they have legs.

One cannot leave the subject of myth without referring to the work of Lévi-Strauss, who by 1968 had published three volumes of a projected four on *Mythologiques*. It is to myth that Lévi-Strauss now looks for evidence of the fundamental structures of human thought that it has been his life's work to identify. It is hard to summarize his theory in a paragraph. In this context its most important aspect is the idea that the basic subjects of myth are ambiguities or 'contradictions'. According to Lévi-Strauss, it is a universal characteristic of human thinking to categorize the world of our experience into pairs of opposites. Some of these are 'given', and nobody would question their universality: hot/cold, above/below, right/left, for example. Even with these simple pairs examples may be found which do not fall clearly on one or other side of the line; myth is concerned with more troubling ambiguities. The distinction between nature and culture is one: man is an animal, part of nature, but by possessing culture he is apart from the rest of nature. Myths in which animals behave like humans refer to this ambiguity. Then there are the 'contradictions'

[25] See p. 255.

between reality and the world as we should wish it to be. People hate to die, but they must. They should not commit incest, but they wish to. Children should obey and respect their parents, but society cannot go on unless they destroy them (that is, replace them and succeed to their authority). To Lévi-Strauss it is not the story itself, but the underlying structure, to be perceived by the analysis and comparison of many versions of the same myth and then of the myths of different peoples, that is important. This is a wholly different approach from that of the social anthropologists, who take the details of a particular myth in the context of the people who tell it, and ask how they form a charter for the social order of that particular society. Myth analysis can almost be said to have become an industry, particularly among French-speaking anthropologists. In England Leach has tried it, with results about which some have been sceptical. He himself maintains that it often brings us new insights which illumine other ethnographic facts.

SUGGESTIONS FOR READING

A critical survey of theories of sacrifice is given in E. E. Evans-Pritchard, *Nuer Religion* (1956), Chapter XI.

The English translation of Van Gennep's *Les Rites de Passage* was published in 1960, with the title *The Rites of Passage*. An evaluation of the significance of this book in the light of current anthropological theory is given by M. Gluckman in his editorial introduction to the collection *Essays on the Ritual of Social Relations* (1962). The latter book contains a valuable essay by Fortes, 'Ritual and Office in Tribal Society'.

One of the most detailed ethnographic studies of ritual made in recent years, which discusses both its social context and its symbolism, is that of Monica Wilson in the two books, *Rituals of Kinship among the Nyakyusa* (1957) and *Communal Rituals of the Nyakyusa* (1959). V. W. Turner's writings on the symbolism of religious ritual include *Ndembu Divination* (1961), *The Forest of Symbols* (1967), *Drums of Affliction* (1969), and *The Ritual Process* (1969).

For accounts of rituals referred to in this chapter, see Tallensi, M. Fortes, 'Ritual Festivals and Social Cohesion in the Hinterland of the Gold Coast', *American Anthropologist*, 1936; Tikopia, R. W. Firth, *The Work of the Gods in Tikopia* (1940); Shilluk, E. E. Evans-Pritchard, *The Divine Kingship of the Shilluk* (1948); Alur, A. W. Southall, *Alur Society* (1956); Nyoro, J. H. M. Beattie, 'Rituals of Nyoro Kingship', *Africa*, 1959; Swazi, H. Kuper, *An African Aristocracy* (1947), and M. Gluckman, *Rituals of Rebellion* (1952).

J. F. M. Middleton, *Lugbara Religion* (1960), discusses the relation between secular and religious authority. J. R. Goody, *Death, Property and the Ancestors* (1962), analyses mortuary ritual as a *rite de passage*, showing how this entails the separation of the dead person from his property and other rights and the distribution of these. M. Fortes, *Oedipus and Job in West African Religion* (1959), discusses the relation between religious ideas and lineage authority.

Studies of religion which are concerned more with belief systems than with the connection between religion and social structure are E. E. Evans-Pritchard, *Nuer Religion* (1956), and R. G. Lienhardt, *Divinity and Experience* (1961), a study of the religion of the Dinka. *African Worlds*, edited by D. Forde (1954), is a collection of essays on the religious beliefs of different African peoples; one of the contributors, J. J. Maquet, discusses the difference between the qualities attributed to the Ruanda god and those which his worshippers admire in their fellows.

Witchcraft has attracted the attention of anthropologists since the publication of E. E. Evans-Pritchard's *Witchcraft, Oracles and Magic among the Azande* in 1937. This book is concerned primarily with ideas about witchcraft as an explanation of misfortune and the means of combating it, and showed for the first time how these ideas form a coherent and—on their own premises—reasonable system. M. Wilson, *Good Company* (1951), first showed the place of witchcraft beliefs in a system of moral ideas.

The most recent writings on witchcraft trace the typical direction of accusation in different societies and relate these to the sources of tension and hostility inherent in certain social relationships. This approach was initiated by an article of S. F. Nadel, 'Witchcraft in Four African Societies' (*American Anthropologist*, 1955). It is one of the themes of Middleton's *Lugbara Religion*. The most substantial study of this kind is V. W. Turner, *Schism and Continuity in an African Society* (1957). A collection of essays edited by J. F. M. Middleton and E. Winter, *Witchcraft and Sorcery in East Africa* (1963), discusses the subject from various points of view.

P. M. Worsley, *The Trumpet Shall Sound* (1957), gives a comprehensive account of the millenary movements of the present century in the South Pacific. Much of the writing on comparable movements in Africa is in French; there is a detailed study of the Kimbanguist and Matswanist movements in the former French and Belgian Congo in G. Balandier, *The Sociology of Black Africa* (1970). An account in English of the rise of the Kimbanguist movement has been written by a Swedish missionary, E. Anderson, *Messianic Popular Movements in the Lower Congo* (1958).

Malinowski's theory of myth is expounded in his *Myth in Primitive Psychology* (1926), reprinted in the collection edited by R. Redfield, *Magic, Science and Religion* (1948), and discussed by R. W. Firth, *History and Traditions of Tikopia* (1961). E. R. Leach, *Political Systems of Highland Burma* (1954), has a few pages on the

subject (pp. 13–14). The article by R. F. Horton referred to in the
chapter is 'Ritual Man in Africa', *Africa*, 1964. There is a succinct,
if not altogether easy, statement of Lévi-Strauss's theory of myth in
E. R. Leach, *Lévi-Strauss* (1970), one of the Fontana Modern Masters
series.

CHAPTER 15

Related Subjects I: Social Change

THE subject of social change falls into a different category from the topics so far discussed. Most of this book has been taken up with descriptions of the kind of institutions we should expect to find in societies of simple technology, and the assumption has been made that such institutions had been for some considerable time as they were found to be when anthropologists observed and described them. This is a reasonable assumption, since people living in small-scale societies usually see their own institutions having 'always been' what their mythical first ancestor made them. Of course they cannot in fact have 'always been' the same, since human institutions must have come into existence gradually, but it is permissible to suppose that they changed only very slowly over long periods of time. Twentieth-century anthropologists, looking back to the records of explorers of the eighteenth or earlier centuries, find, where these are specific enough to be useful, that they refer to institutions which still exist, or at least did so within living memory. One might say it is precisely because they have changed so little that the societies of simple technology are still small in scale.

The nineteenth-century anthropologists, as has been mentioned, believed that these societies had already experienced dramatic changes in the unrecorded past, and it was in reaction against the tendency to interpret existing institutions as meaningless survivals of previous conditions for which we have no evidence that Malinowski insisted on looking at a culture (as he called it) as a 'going concern' in which every usage has a meaning here and now. This precept has indeed been fruitful in practice; and when anthropologists are given the opportunity, they try to inculcate it in people who go to small-scale societies with the aim of promoting various kinds of social change.[1]

Malinowski's functional theory was developed from the metaphor used by Spencer and Durkheim, comparing the place of institutions in the life of society with that of organs in the life of a body. It started from a position that all students of society today would accept—that for any social order to exist there must be certain institutions regulating the fundamental human relationships, and that though these may take very different forms, they fulfil the same functions everywhere. He also insisted on the close interconnection of the different institutions, and the bearing of this on colonial policies aimed at the eradication of 'uncivilized' practices. It should be noted that when Malinowski wrote of social change he was always thinking of the changes that have been created by the external pressure of colonial rule; he was rightly not interested in unsupported conjectures about the past, but he was almost equally uninterested in what historical evidence could tell us. He rightly pointed out that a change deliberately introduced at one point might have repercussions elsewhere which the framers of policy did not expect—though, he maintained, an adequate study of the society concerned would have taught them what to expect. A standard example of the unexpected repercussion was the prohibition of war expeditions in New Guinea. This made it unnecessary to build sea-going canoes, and therefore unnecessary to produce food to supply the canoe-builders; so people ceased to produce a surplus of food.

We still urge welfare workers and community development agents to be aware of the vested interests that their schemes may injure and the readjustments, outside the technical field of the schemes themselves, that their adoption may necessitate. In doing this we are using Malinowski's principle of the interdependence of institutions, though we do not go as far as he was apt to do, and argue that all attempts to improve the conditions of small-scale societies are liable to do more harm than good. This attitude was an expression of his own disgust with machine

[1] See the following chapter.

civilization rather than a logical consequence of his theory of society.

It is true that when, as he sometimes did, he argued not only that all customs have significance for the people who practise them, but that their function was always indispensable to the society in which they were found, he was in effect maintaining that all social change must be for the worse, and it might seem to follow—though he never actually said so—that no institution could ever have been changed by the action of the people to whose social system it belonged.

Perhaps this is what has led a number of writers to assert that functionalist theories 'cannot account for change'. But even if this is true of the exaggerations of Malinowski's theory, it is not so of more sober functionalisms, or even of his own in its earlier stages. One can say that a certain outfit of institutions is indispensable to any society, and yet observe that particular institutions have disadvantages in particular situations. One can think it important to understand why people value their own customs, and yet see that they might be better able to attain ends that they themselves desire if they modified or abandoned some of these customs. One can recognize with Durkheim and Radcliffe-Brown that social order is maintained by the adverse reaction of a majority of people to actions that break the rules, and yet be aware that, as breaches grow more common, the adverse reaction becomes weaker. Students of society must recognize the strong conservative elements on which social order rests, but it does not follow that they themselves must always be on the side of conservatism (they do, however, recognize that revolutions are much less common than some might hope).

There is, of course, a sense in which the study of social change is nothing more nor less than the study of history. The early writers of 'conjectural history', when they sought to trace the development of social institutions, were pursuing a worthy aim; and it is one that some modern historians would like to see pursued in a more sophisticated way as the centre of their teaching. They do not seek to penetrate the unrecorded past; after all, the historian's profession rests on the evaluation of documents. But one of them has recently advocated an emphasis in history which comes very close to that of studies in social anthropology. This is what the Professor of Modern History at Cambridge, J. H. Plumb, wrote in *Encounter* for June 1971:

For me the present world has an ever-deepening need to be conscious of the process of time because it is witnessing the close of an epoch that began roughly ten thousand years ago: the end indeed of societies based primarily on agriculture and craftsmanship, in which towns were rarely more than centres for the organizing and servicing of these activities, or of religion and government. ... Of course, within these millennia societies differed greatly in complexity, in extent of power, in achievement and in sophistication. And yet there are basic similarities, whether we compare Tang China with the France of Louis XIV or the Peru of the Incas. In general the same social institutions are common to them all—family, organized religion, warrior castes, an elite of bureaucrats, more often than not a semi-divine authority. And between the literate societies there are many resemblances in ideology; a symbolization of natural forces that clearly links the rituals of the agrarian year or reflects the family structure; often this is combined with a religion of personal salvation and hope. Often the present is sanctified by an interpretation of the past. Men of authority possess the genealogies which confirm their power; and the history of their societies is theirs.

Professor Plumb draws his examples from literate societies of wider scale, and at a higher level of technical attainment and political complexity, than those that are amenable to the characteristic methods of the anthropologist. Yet we must surely recognize in his description all that we from our point of view see as typical of *our contemporary* pre-industrial world. Only the bureaucrats are missing from ours—and we can find them in some of the studies now being made of India, China and the Islamic world.

He goes on:

This world of peasant craftsman, merchant, priest and warrior began to crumble in the nineteenth century and collapse in the twentieth, so creating acute problems in the social institutions which were so appropriate for a less complex world—the family, organized religion, class structure etc. ... Many ills which publicists lay at the doors of modern society are the results of the conflict between two almost incompatible methods of human organization, one with long, long historical roots going back some ten thousand years, the other scarcely yet born.

Anthropologists have to take most of those ten thousand years for granted for lack of records. But the process that we study at close quarters and in detail is precisely the confrontation of different types of organization of society to which Professor Plumb refers. We in our fieldwork can actually see it going on. Historians are becoming more and more interested in the type of records that throw light on this process in the past, and what they find illuminates changes on a large scale. Anthropologists, by narrowing their field, can trace out the direct effects of individual choices.

If then the most important problem for the historian, as some sociologists hold it to be the most important problem for them, is the response of human society to industrialization, the social anthropologist need not be distressed by the criticism that we have not sufficiently probed into the knowable past of the societies we study. We are following out the most important *knowable* process of social change in the world's history; and we have been doing so ever since the International African Institute and the Rhodes–Livingstone Institute were founded between the two world wars with the express aim of studying 'the changing African'.

There have, however, been some striking differences in the point of view from which we have evaluated the changes we study. It is hardly possible to take a wholly detached view of a process in which we are all involved. The industrialization of the Third World is a major issue of world politics today; at the time when British anthropologists began to study the process it was a matter of the policies to be pursued in colonial territories for which we as British citizens had responsibility. Our attitude at that time was influenced in part by the conception of trusteeship enshrined in the Covenant of the League of Nations, but we rejected the idea that 'trusteeship' meant the imposition of alien institutions on people who cherished their own. When we looked at the process of industrialization in Africa—and in the Pacific too, though less work was being done there— what we saw was the denuded village with its menfolk absent earning the cash income on which their families had come to depend. We believed in the preservation of village life, and held that it should always be possible to find some source of income that would make the migration of labourers unnecessary. We did not foresee a world in which this would become the pattern of life for peasant societies in Europe as well as Africa. Nor did we see that something as fundamental as the structure of the family would be altered, even within the village, when its members began to look outwards for cash incomes and no longer inwards for mutual aid in producing their own subsistence.

In part this was an appropriate attitude for a period of economic depression; very little development seemed to be in prospect, and what there had been seemed to have done more harm than good—deprived people of one way of life without enabling them to benefit from the other. After the Second World War, however, attitudes changed. The earlier view could now be characterized as an attempt by the trustee to prevent the ward from growing up. Economic growth became the prime desideratum, as a remedy for poverty, hunger, and ill-health, and a basis for the independence that the colonial peoples had begun to demand. Along with this has gone a shift of interest from the rural areas to the rapidly expanding towns; anthropologists have become more interested in the kind of society that is developing there and how immigrants to them combine the attitudes of 'townsmen' and 'tribesmen'. On the whole, today's students of social change take it for granted as inevitable and are more apt to ask why it is incomplete than to deplore it.

What are we studying?

Certainly the study of social change is a historical one; it is a matter of tracing a process over time. The comparison that Professor Plumb has drawn between 'the world we have lost' and the one we live in is only a beginning. The anthropologist must ask *how* the change is brought about, and he must know where to look for his answers. Just *what* is it that is changing? Ideas on the study of social change have developed along with ideas on the subject-matter of anthropology in general.

There was a stage at which the process to be studied was conceived as a contact of *cultures,* in which elements of one were adopted or rejected by the other. Theories were propounded about aspects of culture that were or were not resistant to change, and about the kind of relationship between two cultures most likely to lead to 'acculturation'. Such theories do not attract much notice nowadays, as we see essentially the same process of change going on wherever we look. Moreover, 'cultures' are ways of behaving, not people. Does it mean anything to talk of relationships between such entities?

Malinowski, though he still saw the process of change in terms of the contact of cultures, criticized the idea that their elements were 'mechanically pitchforked like bundles of hay' from one to the other; the metaphor was actually first used by his pupil Fortes. Insisting, as he always did, that the units to be studied were institutions and not isolated objects or usages, he argued further that the institutions reacted upon each other and produced something which could not be broken down into traits contributed by one or other. British anthropologists found it more profitable to follow out the development of institutions than to pursue the diffusion of cultural traits, but as we recognize the domination of machine technology as the major historical fact of our era, we find the theory of the mutual influence of institutions less helpful.

Fortes[2] brought the wind of common sense into the discussion by observing that it is peoples and not customs who react to contact. This statement can perhaps be taken to epitomize the movement away from the earlier focus on change in customs to today's interest in change in social relationships.

Malinowski began by deploring the wanton interference of rulers claiming a higher civilization with institutions which he pictured as ideally well adapted to the needs of the peoples who had evolved them; but after he had travelled in southern Africa he changed his position, and argued, as liberals there were arguing, that the African had the worst of both worlds as long as he was offered only those

[2] L. P. Mair (ed.), *Methods of Study of Culture Contact,* 1938, p. 62.

aspects of European culture that made him useful to Europeans.

This was the theme of Godfrey and Monica Wilson in their *Analysis of Social Change,* first published in 1945. They were concerned with the conflicts that had been created by the incursion of Europe into Africa. They used the word 'conflict' in a number of different senses. Sometimes it meant the resentment of Africans when Europeans forbade them to do things that they considered perfectly right and proper, such as brewing beer or accusing people of witchcraft. Sometimes it meant competition for scarce resources, notably as a result of the alienation of land to Europeans. Sometimes it meant a direct and open conflict of interests. Following Radcliffe-Brown, they argued that social forces tended towards equilibrium, a word which, as he used it, meant little more than his other favourite word 'euphoria' —a state of affairs with which most people are content. They saw in southern Africa a condition of 'radical opposition'—'a struggle between nascent and opposing structures about which shall prevail'. A concept which they first introduced, and which most anthropologists today find valuable, is that of scale. Societies of simple technology are small in scale because of the limits that their technology sets to communication; mechanical invention has made the scale of social relationships world-wide.

In the Wilsons' terms, the scale of material relations had increased in southern Africa out of proportion to that of religious (some might prefer the word 'moral') relations; Africans were welcomed as servants but not as competitors. The whole world, they further argued, was suffering from the same kind of unevenness; and since equilibrium was necessary to society, it must go on changing until this was restored. Well, we have seen many changes in the past twenty-five years, but few of us would say that equilibrium *in the Wilsons' sense* had been attained. Yet the world persists, with some degree of order in it. Were they advocating revolution? They did not say so.

They have been severely handled by Edmund Leach, who ascribes to them the view that the products of 'culture contact' were 'somehow fundamentally immoral and "destruc-

tive of law, logic and convention" '.[3] In summarizing the
sentence to which he refers, Leach misquotes it. The argument in fact is that 'intolerable oppositions . . . threaten,
unless some change is quickly made, to destroy law, logic
and convention'.[4] Certainly the Wilsons held that the situation which Europe has created in Africa is of this kind,
and most polemics against colonialism take the same line,
if in less esoteric language. Many people consider that the
course of recent history has benefited the peoples of the
temperate zones relatively to the rest. Is this to argue that
social change is in itself something to be deplored? I think
not.

Leach's contention, however, is that change is not deplor-
able but is in the nature of society. In illustration he offers
the Kachins of upper Burma, where, for as far back as their
history is recorded, groups of villages have oscillated between accepting the hegemony of a chief and claiming to be
independent each under its own headman. This story has
been compared by Gluckman with that of the expansion and
contraction of African kingdoms in the centuries of wars
and conquests that preceded European penetration. From
it Leach draws the conclusion that it is nonsense to say any
society is ever in equilibrium; all are in process of constant
change. Gluckman draws the opposite conclusion: that both
examples illustrate a moving equilibrium such as one sees in
the swing of a pendulum.

Leach recognizes, as we all must, that the year or two that
an anthropologist spends in the society he is studying is not
long enough for him to observe any appreciable change; we
have to describe it, he says, *as if* it were static. One might use
a different metaphor and say that you cannot look closely
at anything unless you hold it still. The anthropologist may
see the structure of a society as consisting of the rules that
the majority of its members profess to obey. If these rules
were absolutely precise, and if they were always obeyed,
there could be no change. But the reality that he can observe, even in the course of a year or two, is not like that;
there are ambiguities in the rules and there are areas where

[3] E. R. Leach, *Political Systems of Highland Burma*, 1954, p. 284.
[4] *The Analysis of Social Change*, p. 183.

choice is free. It is through these loopholes that men pursue their ambitions, and both Gluckman and Leach, in different ways, look to the manipulation of these ambiguities for the source of social change. Leach explains how the Kachins assert that the rules of succession to the office of chief are quite simple; but there is room for most subtle arguments as to whether a given individual's claim is valid in terms of the rules.

Gluckman discusses the ambiguities in social systems from a point of view which, though superficially different from Leach's, has actually a good deal in common with it. Social systems, he asserts, are not inherently consistent. They are 'systematized'—he would seem to mean made to work— by the *inconsistent* actions of individuals, who align themselves now with one group, now with another, according to the situation in which they find themselves. Writing of the Zulu in South Africa, he says a trade unionist can ally himself with fellow workers, an action which at home in Zululand could imply banding with enemies of his chief, because the two situations, of the work-place and the reserve, are separate; he is never faced in the same situation with a choice between the two allegiances. Again, Zulu who have something to gain by accommodation with the White authorities may choose this course while condemning it in their fellows. The well-recognized inconsistency between Christian and business ethics, which need not prevent a successful businessman from being a churchwarden, is an instance of the same kind.

Leach cites his examples to show how a social system may change while the people involved in it, and the anthropologist looking at it, suppose that everyone is obeying the traditional rules. Leach *explains* the changes that he describes in terms of the pursuit of their interests by ambitious men. For Gluckman the major factor in setting change afoot has been the establishment of European rule, and explanations following on this are simply explanations of resistance or accommodation. His theory of 'situational selection' shows why, or at least to what extent, it has been possible to create the new South African society without continuous recourse to direct force; he would reject those American interpreta-

tions of history which see the whole colonial period as one
of smouldering African resistance.

Equilibrium

Like Leach, Gluckman makes much of the concept of
equilibrium, but unlike Leach he thinks equilibrium is not
an anthropologist's will-o'-the-wisp, but a reality. The word
has certainly been bandied about as much as any in the controversies of anthropologists, but it is by no means easy to
know what they mean by it. We hear a good deal about the
'equilibrium model'. If a model is a construction in which
two or three variables are isolated, and each in turn is
manipulated so as to see how this affects the others, there is
no connection between models and talking about equilibrium. In fact the use of the word is no more than a metaphor. And one of the difficulties in its use is that very few
anthropologists have a grounding in the physical sciences of
a kind to enable them to be clear about what the metaphor
is. Leach is one of those who have; I have to admit that I
am not.

Most anthropologists use the word 'balance' as freely as,
or more so than, they use 'equilibrium'. This is a more
everyday word and does not imply very great precision. Certainly if it is meant literally it should refer to equal weights
in the two pans of a scale, or to a see-saw with a child sitting
on each end. Take off one weight or one child; the other
side dips as far as it can go, and could logically, one supposes, go on dipping for ever. Neither social stability nor
social change can be described in such a metaphor.

The notion of balance was first used extensively by Fortes
and Evans-Pritchard in 1940 in their introduction to
African Political Systems, and an oblique reference in
Leach's *Political Systems of Highland Burma* suggests that
he may have had that book in mind. The idea of 'checks and
balances' in modern constitutions, notably the American,
was of course familiar to students of politics and history long
before that. Fortes and Evans-Pritchard refer to *forces*,
not weights—'the forces that maintain the supremacy of
the paramount ruler . . . opposed by the forces that act as a
check on his power'; but also to 'a balance between conflict-

ing tendencies and between divergent interests', 'between different parts of the administrative organization', 'between central authority and regional autonomy'.[5] Thus they seem to have in mind at one time the pursuit of sectional interests, certainly a matter of dynamic forces, and at another the accepted institutional arrangements which they see as limiting the power of the supreme authority, something more suggestive of dead weights. Later they write of 'a balance between power and authority on the one side and obligation and responsibility on the other'. These abstractions, not all of the same category, are balanced within a single role, that of ruler.

Gluckman (with Spencer in mind?) describes the equilibrium of a system as 'the interdependence of its parts', but does not indicate how he identifies the different parts. We seem here to have a notion of a number of weights (or forces), a change in the strength of one of which influences the distribution of strength among them all. Gluckman interprets the history of Zululand as a succession of 'equilibria'. Each is reached after a brief disturbed period and then maintained for a considerable time; that is to say, the factors that were going to produce the new situation gradually built up until some crucial event led to a very rapid change. One is reminded of the Marxist theory that at a critical moment a quantitative change—the sum of a great number of small changes—becomes a qualitative one, and from that point society is differently organized. Equilibrium, as the concept is used here, is clearly not a condition in which weights or forces are so nicely balanced that nothing can move; it is rather a word for a period during which change is not very marked. A society in this condition is one that an anthropologist can look at, as Leach says we all must, *as if* it was in equilibrium.

When Gluckman reaches the time at which he himself is writing (1940), he remarks that 'the threat of force remains one of the dominant factors in Zululand equilibrium'.[6] Some might find it hard to see anything readily discernible as a

---

[5] *African Political Systems*, 1940, p. 11.

[6] *Analysis of a social situation in modern Zululand*, reprinted as Rhodes–Livingstone Paper 28, 1958.

balance between rulers and ruled at this period of history, when attempts at forcible protest against the existing system have been most successfully crushed. But if 'equilibrium' simply equals 'stability', one must admit that the kind of system in which the Wilsons saw an intolerable *dis*-equilibrium has proved remarkably stable so far.

Beattie, writing of another centralized political system, that of the Nyoro in Uganda, asserts that it would have been inappropriate to describe it in terms of balanced opposition.[7] Yet one of his central themes is the ideal of reciprocity in services between the tribute paid by subjects and the largesse expected of chiefs, and another is the limitation that is imposed on the king's power by the need to share it with territorial chiefs. Gluckman would certainly have seen this in terms of an equilibrium.

The fact is that there is no precision in the way this metaphor has been used. The statement that most of the time the relationship between the factors which maintain established institutions and those which oppose them is such as to prevent chaos or violent change, is a truism; and nobody seriously argues that societies can be found in such a delicate state of perfect balance that any modification must destroy them. The real opposition is between the students of society who follow the American sociologist Talcott Parsons and hold that all social processes are a matter of gradual adaptation to changing conditions, and the Marxists who maintain that social change is the working out of conflicts which are inherent in every society. The latter have used an imaginary ideal of equilibrium as a stalking-horse; but this issue could be discussed without any recourse to the word.

The direction of change

In the discussion of non-literate, non-monetary societies we have seen already how, as centralized political power is built up, a new organizing principle complements and gradually replaces that of kinship. Kinship continues to be the basis of claims to property, but people now turn to an authority outside the kin group to defend their claims; and, as has

[7] J. H. M. Beattie, *The Nyoro State*, 1971, p. 245.

just been mentioned, they can look to the favour of political superiors as well as, or in preference to, affines in seeking to build up their fortunes. When they enter the field of large-scale commerce, they come to depend economically on relationships outside the kin group. If they are farmers they may still seek to keep their sons with them as a working team; but the new significant relationship will be that with the buyer of the crop. If they enter the commercial world as labourers, they form a relationship with an employer, and at the same time become part of a quite new social group, the employees of that particular business with its sub-divisions into workers at particular grades and possibly its wider extension into a trade union. Here kinship and family are of no significance at all, and wage employment often separates the worker physically from his family if he has to go to a town at a distance from his home. New institutions arise to undertake activities that used to be left to the extended family. Schools undertake the teaching of a new technical skill indispensable in the new society—for this is what writing is; only after it is taken for granted can one begin to ask whether education should be 'general' or 'technical'. Hospitals take the responsibility for the sick that used to be the business of the family head seeking advice from the diviner.

Thus people become more independent of kinship ties and readier to disregard these where they are irksome. Anthropologists have often noticed how in non-monetary societies the desire to have fuller control of one's share of the lineage patrimony conflicts with the ideal that lineage unity should be maintained through the generations. A strong incentive to seek independence is inequality in fortune. Inequalities may develop even among cattle people living at a very low material standard; one man's cattle find good pasture and are able to resist a disease that decimates another's; one man is raided, another has more daughters than sons and builds up his stock from the bridewealth he receives. The fortunate ones do not readily recognize the obligation to share outside a very narrow circle.

These are reasons why the nuclear family should supersede the extended family as the basic kin group. Quite often lineage organization disappears altogether, and, in so far as people choose to live near their kin, these may be any kin. When there is no longer any lineage patrimony, lineage membership has no significance. Along with the disappearance of the lineage there often goes a loss of interest in the formalities of marriage which were necessary to establish lineage membership. This has sometimes been interpreted as a rejection of sexual restraints and of family responsibility in general. But this is to assume that couples who do not go through marriage rites must all be engaged in casual liaisons, which is by no means the case. The Ngoni of Zambia, for example, have a word for what they call a 'poorly fixed marriage', a union, set up without formalities, that they do not think will last. But if it does last, as often happens, then people stop saying it is 'poorly fixed' and just call it a marriage. In the West Indies a high percentage of children are illegitimate in the sense that their parents were not married when they were born. But a study in British Guiana showed that most children grew up in families, in the sense that at the time when their mother was occupied in caring for them she was able to depend on a man for their subsistence (not always their father).

This leads one to ask what is the significance of legal fatherhood established by marriage. The answer that has seemed to follow from recent studies is that the legal bond is not important as a guarantee of the economic support of the mother and her children; on the one hand, the laws of some countries require a father to maintain his children even though he is not married to their mother, and on the other, an unmarried couple may often live as a domestic family. The crucial question is whether the status of the children depends upon their legal relationship to their father. This is so where the social structure is based on patrilineal descent; and is so in complex highly stratified societies where a child grows up in the social class of its father and he, if he rises to a higher one, will take his own children with him. In the Caribbean, and in some South African cities, there is no lineage system, and for the class of unskilled labourers there is little hope of social mobility. For them, therefore, the legal aspects of marriage are of little significance.

Wage-earning and commercial production of cash crops have similar effects on lineage obligations. Both, by offering outside sources of income, create inequalities among people who by tradition are sharers in a common patrimony. In India, the principle of the joint family system is that brothers work together on their father's land, pooling the produce, which the father administers for the common benefit of the group. A system of this kind cannot work without some friction at the best of times. Fathers may be accused of favouritism, brothers of shirking their fair share of work; one component household may think it has a claim for special consideration that others will not accept. When some of the members begin to earn incomes from wages, as happens more often in Indian than in African villages, they are most unwilling to contribute these to the common stock, and they assert their independence by demanding an early division of the joint estate.

The introduction of cash crops in Africa has similarly led to the assertion by individuals of independent control of their share of lineage resources. The most significant consequence here has been a change in attitudes towards lineage control of land. Land has a cash value where it can be a source of cash income, and people who see the advantage to be gained by leasing or selling it become impatient of traditional obligations to consult their fellow rightholders before disposing of it. Usually some people begin to deal in land while others still cherish the ideal that lineage land should never pass out of lineage hands.

As economic activities become commercialized people form direct relationships outside the small-scale society, relationships of buyer and seller. The significant changes occur when the resources of the small-scale society become commodities in demand in the wider world. They may be supplied by independent villagers, as is cocoa in Ghana or rice in Malaysia; or production may be organized in plantations drawing their labour force from a distance. If the resources to be developed are minerals, production must be organized on a large scale for technical reasons.

Wage labour on plantations and mines draws people into new communities in which they are separated from their close kin and regrouped partly by choice and partly by the action of superior authority. Mine managers and township officials tell men where they are to live and with whom they are to form work gangs. They also build up new associations of their own. At work they form trade unions; in leisure activities one finds organizations of the people living in a single street, as well as associations of people with some common background other than that of place of origin, notably 'Old Boys' of the few secondary schools. Studies made on the African Copper Belt show how people align themselves for some purpose in accordance with their new interests, for others in accordance with older loyalties. Protests against the policies of employers or urban authorities are made by associations representing all those whom they affect; but within such bodies there may be rivalry between people of different ethnic backgrounds, and the choice of representatives may well be thought of as a contest between tribes. One of the leisure-time amusements is to watch dancing teams who sing songs praising their own tribe and ridiculing others.

It is in connection with urban populations that the term 'detribalization' became popular in discussions about Africa. It referred to the removal of the urban dweller from his home environment, with the assumption that the move released him from all the restraints on conduct among which he had grown up. This assumption was characteristic of rather naïve and not altogether unbiased observers. Some of these were people opposed to any influence that led Africans to reject the domination of Europeans, including education among those influences. Many were idealists of the kind who all through recorded history have praised the simple virtues of the countryside and deplored the corruption of the city. If they had been more fully aware that there are problems of social and moral welfare for new immigrants to cities in all parts of the world, they would not have sought an explanation for them in 'detribalization'.

However, there is still a question whether the word can be held to describe a process, as distinct from making a moral judgement on a state of affairs. It could refer to the abandonment of village rules of conduct and usages, without the implication that this implied the abandonment of *all* rules. Obviously some village ways have to be abandoned in the city—the leisurely time-table set by the sun, for example. Others, such as the gathering of friends to drink beer, are sometimes forbidden. Others are deliberately rejected, as when Africans on the Copper Belt resented the idea that law cases should be judged by elders brought in from the villages where it was held that tribal law was better known. But does this mean that these rules have been rejected for ever? Is this a process of 'acculturation', the substitution of new 'culture traits' for traditional ones?

Gluckman prefers to this interpretation, and to Malinowski's picture of the appearance of hybrid institutions, his theory already mentioned of 'situational selection'. If the immigrant worker learns, as he must, to follow city ways, this is a matter of choosing the behaviour that the situation demands; at home in the village he will choose differently, though no doubt he will never behave exactly as he would if he had never left it.

It has been remarked also that people may deliberately seek to maintain village standards, as far as may be, when they are in the cities. This entails associating exclusively with others from the common village background, and it is perhaps only possible for people who are able fairly often to go back to the village. In these circumstances the sanctions of adverse comment on departures from village norms are at a maximum. This is the situation of some Xhosa working in the South African city of East London, which draws most of its workers from a rural hinterland close at hand.

The extension of political relationships is one of the most striking social changes of the present century. Small political units, of the kind described earlier in this book, were brought under the rule of colonial powers which needed to control wide areas in order to have security for economic development; and the end of colonial rule has not restored their autonomy. On the contrary, the units created by the colonial powers have become independent, each under a single government with a civil service organization established by the former rulers and a constitution based on that of some older nation. They find themselves, then, with a political structure consisting of offices which must be filled, and a set of rules laying down the way to fill them and the limits of the power that they confer. The colonial power withdraws, and the hoisting of the national flag is like the blowing of the whistle to begin the new game. The game is played in some respects differently from that on which it purports to be modelled; in particular it has quickly diverged from the kind which is thought in the West to be typical of parliamentary democracy.

Some anthropologists have sought to explain this by referring to the traditional values of the peoples concerned. They observe that the political sytems of small-scale societies do not usually make provision for recurrent contests for leadership, still less for the organization of groups expressly dedicated to the aim of wresting power from those who hold it. English writers have remarked that the languages spoken in their former colonies contain no word for 'opposition' other than that for 'enemy'. (It should not be a matter for surprise that they cannot directly translate 'opposition' in its parliamentary sense when the other great English-speaking democracy, the United States, does not use the word.) It is certainly true that the political systems of the newly independent states are unlike anything of which their own past history can show examples. But it would be a mistake to assume that they are trying to find their way through the game by looking to the past for examples, even though they may sometimes say they are.

The interpretation suggested here is one which would lay the emphasis on the new relationships in which the new politicians find themselves. These are relationships for which rules have not yet crystallized. Social rules are a matter of the expectations attached to roles, and in these new political systems people in general have hardly made up their minds what to expect. Nevertheless, it is doubtful whether many of them expect ministers and civil servants to behave like old-fashioned chiefs and their retainers; or whether members of the National Assembly of Tanzania really see themselves as reproducing the conclave of the village elders under a tree with which, it is true, Dr. Nyerere has compared them.

Rather, they have set themselves aims that imply the deliberate adoption of new ways of conducting the business of the community. They are as well aware as any outside observer that the relationships of ruler and ruled are not those of the old days. When they condemn 'tribalism' they mean precisely those relationships of allegiance to a descendant of the first ancestor, his authority sanctioned by religious belief, which now divide the peoples that they lead. The authority they exercise is legitimized by the popular acclaim that elections have come to symbolize. Certainly it is often maintained by methods that the west considers undemocratic, but these methods are not rooted in tribal tradition. In many cases they have been learnt, or simply taken over, from colonial régimes. They are commonly justified by the need to move rapidly away from the traditional past.

One can see some negative reasons why it has proved difficult to play the democratic game as idealists in the West hoped it would be played. One can say that there is *no* tradition requiring the peaceful resolution of struggles for power, precisely because the contenders for power belong to units which have no tradition of peaceful co-operation. But one cannot stop there. One must ask where such traditions have come from in the societies that cherish them. The most satisfying answers have come from historians, political theorists, and sociologists rather than from anthropologists. They have to be sought by asking what the large-scale societies have got that is not characteristic of the small-scale ones, not by starting from the small-scale ones with the assumption that their past must determine their future. The question what leads governments to accept restraints on the exercise of their power is simply not one to be answered from the small-scale societies alone, even though, when we examine their own political systems, we can inquire what restraints are built into them. We can assume that nobody who holds power gladly relinquishes or refrains from exercising it. Then we have to ask how expectations have been built up that make it possible for the subjects of governments to demand 'human rights and fundamental freedoms', and what social pressures operate in support of these expectations.

Some illuminating answers have been given by the American sociologist E. A. Shils.[8] He points out that in the new states the ruling élite consists of the people who have chosen to reject traditional values and seek deliberately to modernize their society, but the majority of the population have not yet entered into many of the relationships characteristic of the industrialized world; this is even truer perhaps of India than of the new African states. This majority may entertain the traditional expectations of the role of ruler, but the new rulers are not interested in satisfying these. The people who are acquainted with the theory of democracy are so few that they are either in the government or in exile; in other words, those who wish to offer critical opposition are too few to insist on being heard.

It is too much to ask the rulers to play a role that limits their freedom of action when that role is not well defined in the public mind. The kind of discussion that would define it is one that too few people in the new states are equipped to carry on. Authority is kept within bounds not by definitions in legal instruments, but by the readiness of the subjects to protest when the bounds are overstepped. In the old small-scale states tradition provided various means short of rebellion, but these entailed the manipulation of relationships between ruler and subject that do not exist in the new ones.

A modern-style democratic state needs sources of active and informed criticism—organized interest groups, a well informed press, universities where the pursuit of knowledge is seen as an affair of questioning received ideas. When a nation has all these, the demand for free discussion is widely enough diffused for attacks on it at any one point to be resented from the others; if it has not, the sources of inconvenient criticism can be silenced one by one.

This discussion brings one back to the fact that all members of a society are not equally ready to seize new opportunities, particularly when to do so entails as great a

---

[8] 'Political Development in the New States', in *Comparative Studies in Society and History*, Vol. II, pp. 265–92, 379–411.

departure from the mode of life they are used to as it does in many of the developing countries today. Some of them, indeed, are debarred from doing so, because the valued roles of the 'modern sector' cannot be attained without a considerable amount of school education. These people may well be distressed by the dislocation that is produced by the changes going on around them and feel that the old ways were better. But the anthropologists of today no longer consider that their main interest should be in a sympathetic attitude towards these discontents. Rather they try to trace out the process of change with an equal interest in the aspirations of those who welcome it.

SUGGESTIONS FOR READING

The earliest book by a British anthropologist to be focused on social change is M. Hunter, *Reaction to Conquest* (1936), on the Pondo of South Africa. A collection of essays by pupils of Malinowski, *Methods of Study of Culture Contact*, ed. L. P. Mair (1938), is valuable today perhaps more for the information it gives on what was going on in particular places than for the ideas offered on method; the long introductory essay by Malinowski is the first exposition of his own views on the subject. H. Kuper's study of the Swazi was published in two parts, one describing the traditional political system and the second, *The Uniform of Colour* (1947), discussing the fate of Swazi reduced to depend on the wages earned by unskilled labour; the title indicates that in the eyes of their white employers they form an undifferentiated mass. J. A. Barnes' material on the Ngoni of Zambia and Malawi is presented in the form of two studies of the evolution of different institutions, *Marriage in a Changing Society* (1951) and *Politics in a Changing Society* (1954). A comparable study from the same part of the world is A. I. Richards, *Bemba Marriage and Modern Economic Conditions* (1940). From another part of the world comes, more recently, a set of essays by educated women in South-East Asia on the way they view their changing status, with an interesting introduction by a woman anthropologist (B. E. Ward, ed., *Women in the New Asia*, 1963). M. Freedman, *Chinese Family and Marriage in Singapore* (1957), is an anthropologist's study from this area.

The work done by anthropologists among recent immigrants to cities is in its nature concerned with social change. In Africa the first anthropological studies were made in great industrial concentrations of the centre and south. A. L. Epstein, *Politics in an Urban African Community* (1958), discusses the movement of urban Africans away from reliance on tribal leadership to membership of associations representing the interests of all Africans vis-à-vis Europeans.

J. C. Mitchell, *The Kalela Dance* (1956), shows with data from the same region in what circumstances the solidarity of townsmen from the same home area outweighs their feeling of common interests as Africans. More recent studies are V. Pons, *Stanleyville* (1969), about the city on the Congo which is now called Kisangani, A. Cohen, *Custom and Politics in Urban Africa* (1969) and D. Parkin, *Neighbours and Nationals in an African City Ward* (1969). Cohen's book is about Hausa traders in Ibadan, Parkin's about the very mixed population of Kampala. There is interesting material in a collection of essays edited by P. H. Gulliver, *Tradition and Transition in East Africa* (1969).

A series of studies made in the South African city of East London show how strong conservative forces can be among men who spend the greater part of their working life in the urban environment. These are P. Mayer, *Townsmen or Tribesmen* (1961), R. Reader, *The Black Man's Portion* (1961), and B. Pauw, *The Third Generation* (1963).

Studies made by anthropologists revisiting areas where they have worked themselves and seeking to measure the sum total of change include R. W. Firth, *Social Change in Tikopia* (1959), M. Mead, *New Lives for Old* (1953), a sequel to her *Growing Up in New Guinea*, R. Redfield, *A Village that Chose Progress* (1945), and O. Lewis, *Life in a Mexican Village* (1951).

F. G. Bailey's work in India has been directed entirely to the nature of the changes in caste relationships and village structure that have been produced, first by the penetration of India by world commerce, and more recently by the introduction of representative government. His three books, *Caste and the Economic Frontier* (1959), *Tribe, Caste and Nation* (1960) and *Politics and Social Change* (1963) are all worth the attention of students. Another most interesting book on India is T. S. Epstein's *Economic and Social Change in South India* (1962), contrasting the process of economic development in two villages, one of which was included in an irrigation system while the other was left just outside it. This was followed by *South India: Yesterday, To-day and To-morrow* (1973), in which the same author evaluates events in the fifteen years after her first visit.

P. Stirling, *Turkish Village* (1964), describes the realities of village life in a country which the government has sought to modernize by revolution.

CHAPTER 16

Related Subjects II: Applied Anthropology

SOCIAL change and applied anthropology are two sides of a penny. Anthropologists first became interested in social change as a problem that needed to be solved; in Britain very few of them have thought of it as a subject for explanatory generalizations. The preceding chapter suggested that it is not really a phenomenon requiring this kind of explanation, and that the pursuit of advantage by the exercise of choice, which is open to the members of all societies, will lead to change when there are opportunities to pursue new kinds of advantage by entering into new relationships.

The attention of anthropologists was directed towards particular social changes in particular places because they were a matter of concern to people with work to do in these places. At the end of the First World War, as at the end of the Second, people with humanitarian ideals sought to make their voice heard in the creation of institutions such as the League of Nations. One of the objects of their concern was the condition of peoples subject to colonial rule. At that time there was no move to bring this rule to an end, such as has characterized the years since 1945; its continuance was taken for granted, but the idealists sought to ensure that it should be so conducted as to benefit the peoples subject to it. Such ideals were responsible for the assertion made in the Covenant of the League of Nations that the 'well-being and development' of 'peoples not yet able to stand by themselves' formed a 'sacred trust of civilization'.

A good many people thought 'development' meant primarily the inculcation of values vaguely associated with western civilization (without recognizing very clearly that values vary from one nation to another). But the feeling was also growing that all developments directed to this end had not been improvements, and that the peoples subject to colonial rule cherished their own traditions and resented having them treated with contempt; and also that the rules governing the everyday relationships of kinship and family could not be altered by a stroke of the pen or even by any number of prosecutions in courts of law. Much earlier in South Africa, where European rule had been longest in force, attempts to abolish bridewealth payments—described as 'the sin of buying wives'—had had to be given up. In 1927 the missionary Edwin Smith published his famous book *The Golden Stool*, in which he showed how monstrously a British governor had failed to understand the significance of that most precious emblem of the Ashanti nation, and applied the moral to a more general argument that colonial administrators should be prepared to treat with respect the traditions of the peoples subject to them. The general climate of opinion had moved away from the idea that the 'civilizing mission' of colonial rulers was to westernize their subjects at all costs, and in the direction of the preservation of what was indigenous—always 'purged of abuses'; what the abuses were, those who controlled policy of course were to judge. Missionaries began to allow their converts to pay bridewealth, educationists to value traditional art, music and dancing. In the field of politics this was the heyday of the theory that 'natural rulers' should be recognized, entrusted with administrative authority, and expected to use their influence on the side of improvement policies in such fields as public health, soil conservation, or the control of plant pests.

Gradual improvement through the adaptation of indigenous institutions was the order of the day. People who made this their aim naturally wanted to know what the social systems and cultures they were dealing with were like. Missionaries and government servants in training began to be given courses in anthropology—not very exhaustive ones. At the same time the new school of anthropologists who had been taught by Malinowski began to offer their services in the world of affairs, and Malinowski himself began writing about 'practical' or, as people might now prefer to call it, 'applied anthropology'.

A science is applied when you use its principles to manipulate something, and if the science is social anthropology the material manipulated must be society. This idea is abhorrent to some, but their protests could be answered by saying that all acts of public policy are essays in such manipulation.

Anthropologists, flushed with the enthusiasm that Malinowski's teaching gave them, offered, in a general way, to solve problems in which a knowledge of the nature of the simpler societies was of importance. But there was not the same community of aim between them and their potential employers that is characteristic of most applied science; nor, as it soon proved, was there as good a guarantee of results.

An architect or an engineer, given a job to do, makes the necessary calculations and gets on with it; his end is chosen for him by the body that engages him. The end which society imposes on a physician is the improvement of health and preservation of life. Neither has to argue, except within very narrow limits. The anthropologists' position was different. Most of them were involved in argument from the start, since they sought to tell the 'practical man'—administrator or missionary—what he *ought* to want before they would begin telling him how to get it.

Administrators and missionaries and technicians, however, being men with very specific aims and often profoundly dedicated to these aims, were not in general willing to be told. Each had a clear idea of the direction in which he wanted some small-scale society to move, and all he wanted from the anthropologists was to make his task easier by filling gaps in information of which he was aware. There is a story of an anthropologist—and not so long ago either—who offered to make inquiries about matters that might interest the District Commissioner and was asked, 'Where do they hide the cattle that they steal?'

Malinowski's advice to those in authority, as was mentioned in the previous chapter, was to refrain from interference as far as possible, and he was prepared to offer a justification for any usage that was forbidden as 'repugnant to humanity and natural justice'. This latter attitude I would still commend as preferable to the ready assumption that unfamiliar usages are necessarily inferior to those one knows; it is a counter to what used to be called ethnocentric judgements and what is now called racial arrogance, and it carries no implication that anyone wants to preserve people in zoos. But the advice to refrain from interference was simply a non-starter in the world of the 'practical man'.

Hence the practical value, or application, of anthropology between the wars was pretty well confined to giving information about customs which those in authority were already willing to recognize; in effect this meant mainly the law enforced by native courts, and the nature of claims to authority where it was official policy to recognize such authority. In solving 'problems', in the sense of dealing with situations that somebody finds unsatisfactory, anthropologists were much less successful, especially if they diagnosed the trouble in a manner that the 'practical man' would not accept. An example was the anthropologist's recommendation that, since most African peoples believe in witchcraft, and without this belief would not be able to explain to their satisfaction why people suffer undeserved misfortunes, colonial law should not make it an offence to accuse somebody of witchcraft. Anthropologists found that many Africans supposed witches were on the increase because the government would not allow them to be punished. But it is easy to see that the government's legal staff, entrusted with the duty of imposing a civilized code of penal law, were not likely to include witchcraft, which they themselves knew to be imaginary, in their list of crimes.

Some anthropologists in the thirties felt that they were not worth their salt unless they could at least offer solutions to problems of which administrators were aware—for example the over-stocking of grazing grounds with cattle which were valued for numbers rather than quality. Most of us found that giving a sympathetic explanation of the herdsmen's attitude towards their cattle was the best we could do. An amateur anthropologist, approaching the situation with the explicit statement that anthropology was no use unless it could solve problems, proposed that Africans in

Kenya who sold their cattle should be given—in addition to the price—a coin stamped with the figure of a cow, which they could then use in bridewealth transactions. The professional could only give reasons why the coins were not likely to be accepted as a replacement for the cattle, and this, we felt uncomfortably, laid him open to accusations of defeatism.

But, as we came to realize that we could not produce simple recipes, most of us found ourselves admitting that anthropologists had not discovered a philosopher's stone. Debate went on, however, not only about what anthropologists could offer to policy-makers, a question which was enough for the more modest, but also about the claims we were entitled to make, which in some cases were still quite far-reaching. At this stage the argument began to be heard that anthropologists should not offer advice to colonial rulers because this would help them to maintain their rule; it could, I think, have been answered by saying that, if one is able to indicate to any government ways in which its policy could be better directed in the interests of its subjects, one may and should do so. The argument, however, recalls the climate of opinion of a time when we thought that, as students of 'whole societies', we were entitled to pronounce on all aspects of policy affecting non-European populations. Malinowski's writings on 'successful culture contact' were of this kind. He criticized the policies of the South African government of his day in the same way as many liberal writers were doing, often without relying at all on his special knowledge as an anthropologist. But one cannot say, 'As an anthropologist I am in a position to tell you what justice is.' One can only sometimes say, 'As an anthropologist I am in a position to tell you what your policy has produced,' with the rider, express or implied, 'And can you square that with your idea of justice?' If the policy-makers say they can square it, or that circumstances force them to adopt a policy in which other considerations take precedence of the interests of Africans (as the anthropologists sees them), there is nothing about being an anthropologist that entitles him to insist that he is right. These questions are for citizens as citizens to decide. An anthropologist who feels strongly about them—as many do—can use his special knowledge to brief the organizers of protests. But it must never be forgotten that there are anthropologists whose professional studies have led them to support *apartheid*.

In the late thirties Malinowski's pupils began to suggest that anthropologists should ask to be consulted when important policies were under consideration. It was generally political decisions that were envisaged. The Royal Anthropological Institute established a committee on applied anthropology, which drew up a memorandum for submission to the Australian government on the question whether the joint Anglo-French administration of the New Hebrides should be continued, and actually sent a deputation to the Colonial Secretary to put arguments against the cession to South Africa of Swaziland, Basutoland, and Bechuanaland. Some members of the committee believed that a move might be made to avert war with Germany by offering to restore her former colonies, and were anxious to have anthropologists included in the conference that they assumed would be held for this purpose.

When the war came they hoped to be able to offer their services in reconstruction plans. In fact the increased funds that were made available for research immediately after the war were granted in principle for work expected to be of use to governments. Much of the research that was actually done was justified on the ground that *any* knowledge about the societies subject to their authority must be useful to them, but a few pieces of work were actually directed to specific problems of the existence of which the governments were aware. Thus Philip Mayer in Kenya suggested that agricultural extension work should be conducted through an approach to the traditional work-groups of people from a number of neighbouring villages which he found to be operating among the Gusii. He also suggested ways in which the continual increase in the cost of bridewealth—recognized as a problem by administrators and Africans alike—could be checked.[1] S. F. Nadel made a detailed study of the complicated land tenure system of the Eritrean plateau,

---

[1] P. Mayer, *Two Studies in Applied Anthropology in Kenya*, 1951.

then an ex-Italian colony under military administration, now a part of Ethiopia, and concluded with a few hints on modifications which might reduce injustices and conflicts.[2]

Suggestions were made at the end of the Second World War that colonial governments should employ anthropological departments as they did other technical staffs, and one of them—Tanganyika—actually at one time had three anthropologists on its payroll (called sociologists so as not to offend anyone who might not like to be thought primitive). A more practicable proposal, for which there had been earlier precedents in West Africa, was that there might be one Government Anthropologist in a territory, who would be a man of standing with recognized advisory functions. When, from 1945 onwards, the Colonial Office adopted an active policy of 'development and welfare', it became a usual practice to bring together in planning teams specialists from the different technical departments. Anthropologists thought they could usefully have been members of these teams. In practice it seems that only Nadel, while serving with the military government of Eritrea, was accorded a position of any standing in the counsels of government.

Nadel had strong views about the right and duty of anthropologists to give advice on policy. By their right he only meant that they should be present at high-level discussions, as he had apparently been himself; one could hardly ask, though Malinowski came near it, that the voice of the anthropologist should at all times be decisive. But when he wrote about duty he went further than any of his colleagues. He expounded his views on this subject in his inaugural lecture as Professor of Anthropology in the Australian National University at Canberra.[3] This belongs to the time when people had just begun to be aware of the terrible potentialities of atomic weapons, and some held that the scientists whose research was being applied to the making of these weapons could be held guilty if a nuclear explosion should make the world uninhabitable. They ought to insist, people said, and some scientists said so too, that radio-

[2] S. F. Nadel, 'Land Tenure in the Eritrean Plateau', *African*, 1946.
[3] *Anthropology and Modern Life*, 1953.

activity should be manipulated only for the good of mankind. A scientist, it was argued, who allowed his discoveries to be used to destroy humanity would share the guilt of the destruction.

In Nadel's lecture an analogy with this argument is implicit. Anthropologists, he said, provide those in authority with data about the people over whom they rule. If they leave the governments to use this knowledge as they please, it may be used to do harm. He never indicated how this could be done, and when one considers what governments can do without the benefit of any data on social structure, one cannot help thinking that the additional risk was not great. Nadel went on, however, to argue that anthropologists, in virtue of their knowledge, must claim a voice in the making of policy. They should not take a coward's refuge in the argument that their knowledge is incomplete. Like anyone else, they might make blunders, but theirs would be 'better blunders'.

This was the last time a British anthropologist offered his services as a general problem-solver, though some American anthropologists interested in Indian tribes continued to do so. We now propose for ourselves a humbler role.

One reason for this is that the situations in which our knowledge can be applied have radically changed in the last twenty years or so. The governments which might make use of it are no longer manned by our fellow-countrymen; they are independent. It is very likely that the educated leaders who now hold power in the new states have as little knowledge of the social systems of the peasant masses as most British administrative officers did, and it is by no means certain that, just because they are Africans, or Indians, or Malays, they will prove better equipped to guide the destinies of other Africans, or Indians, or Malays. But the system of values of the western nations, from among whom still the majority of social anthropologists come, is such that we must accord a greater legitimacy to the aims of leaders belonging to the same nations as their followers than we do to alien rulers. Their desire to press on with westernization at a faster rate than the colonial governments did is not met with the same arguments against the disruption of traditional society that used to be heard between the wars.

There are a number of reasons for this. One is that we do not regard the westernized élites of the new nations in the same light as foreigners arbitrarily imposing on their subjects laws and policies which they take for granted as the only right ones; men must be free, if they choose, to repudiate *their own* traditions. Another is that we have become more keenly aware of the need to introduce scientific techniques of production in those regions where the population is already pressing on the means of subsistence. Then it is certainly true that the desire for the material goods of the industrial world is felt everywhere, even if willingness to make the necessary social changes to obtain them is not. And finally, the questions that are posed to the anthropologist of today are much more specific, and are such that they can be answered without a crisis of conscience.

The new leaders are not asking whether or how to preserve traditional authority, or what is the 'natural' line of development for people whose traditions are those appropriate to a simple technology. They are aiming at technical improvement, and if they ask for advice from anthropologists it is advice which will help to secure this.

In point of fact the governments of the new states do not very often seek the advice of anthropologists, for a number of reasons. They associate anthropology with the study of the primitive, and they do not wish their peoples to be thought primitive. Also, they are apt to assume that they must know more about their own fellow-countrymen than a foreigner can—a fallacy that is also cherished by many members of western stratified societies.

So, if anthropologists are invited to have a say, it is usually in projects initiated by other bodies than the new governments—by the various specialized agencies of the United Nations, the American State Department's Agency for International Development, or by those American foundations which sponsor development projects in many parts of the world. Sometimes anthropologists are attached to the specialist teams that carry out these projects. Sometimes they are invited to share in the training of different types of specialist intending to work in peasant societies. Occasionally it has been practicable for an anthropologist to select as the subject of his fieldwork an area in which some type of planned development is going on.

A particularly interesting subject for study is provided by the very many land settlement schemes which have been inaugurated in the last twenty years. The aims of these schemes has been to enable peasants to increase their incomes by giving them holdings of an economic size, and teaching them how to manage these efficiently. In the nature of things the removal of people from their own land to the new holdings also necessitates the development of a new set of social relationships—ideally the creation of a new community. But this aspect of settlement schemes, the aspect in which a social anthropologist is most interested, has commonly been taken for granted by the planners. Studies of land reform projects from this point of view have been made in Japan and in southern Europe, but not much in the traditional fields of the anthropologist.

Some studies of land reform schemes, and of other development projects, have been hindsight appraisals, or post-mortems on failures, which are made in the hope of providing warning signals to future planners. Most of the few books that have been published on this subject consist of warning lessons drawn from schemes that have failed. It may seem rather a declension from the high hopes of Malinowski and his first pupils to admit that this is all the anthropologist can do, but it is more honest to admit it and then to make a new claim that the warnings are in fact indispensable; to neglect them really may ruin a scheme.

It is clear that, when planning aims at technical improvement, the anthropologist must respect the superiority of the technician in his own field. He cannot presume to say what is the best way to control mosquitoes or increase the yield of cotton. Nevertheless, he has something to say, and it is that knowing about the people you are working with—and knowing about them in the particular way that the anthropologist does—is just as important as knowing the habits of the swollen shoot virus of cocoa or the boll weevil cotton pest.

The anthropologist no longer offers a blue-print; he offers a map—a map on which the dangerous passages and obstacles to communication are marked in red. He is more competent to account for resistance to change than to give recipes for bringing it about, and he has entirely abandoned any claim to decide what the direction of change should be.

What the anthropologist offers in the name of the application of science is, then, no more, *and no less*, than the elementary principles of social analysis, along with certain simple facts about the 'clients' of development projects that are too easily overlooked. This may seem to be not very much, until it is remembered that many technicians are going round the world assuming that all they have to do is to give the same lecture on, say, soil conservation in Lesotho as in Tennessee, and others are instructing mothers how to feed their babies without a moment's thought about the relation between the cost of nutritious foods and the family income.

The projects on which anthropologists have mainly commented are of three kinds: public health campaigns, community development projects (in which attempts are made to enlist the voluntary co-operation of villagers in constructing local improvements such as dams, walls, access roads) and land settlement schemes (in which peasants are moved to holdings expected to give them an adequate income if properly farmed).

Perhaps the anthropologist's contribution to all these can be epitomized by saying he can explain why obvious improvements in technique are not accepted as soon as they are demonstrated; why people are not moved by arguments the validity of which is not in doubt. Impatient development workers blame this on the stupidity or the laziness of their 'clients'—assuming, in effect, that any man should be expected to respond to a rational exposition of reasons why he should change his mode of behaviour.

The comment of the anthropologist on such explanations would be to call attention to the nature of the pressures for conformity in any society. He would ask the technician to consider what relationships are likely to be affected by the changes that are being advocated, and what are the sanctions that support these relationships. He would not beg the technician to refrain from disturbing the existing scheme of things; rather he would urge him to remember that the range of people to be persuaded is wider than he may have supposed. Nutritionists in Africa frequently come up against the food restrictions that deny nutritious foods to the people who need them most. It is, for example, very common for eggs to be taboo to women. Sometimes one reads that women on some domestic science course have been persuaded to eat the tabooed foods, and this is taken as a triumph—but back at home they accept the restrictions just as before. Of course they do. It is not 'superstitious fear' that stops them eating eggs, it is knowing what their husbands would say if they knew.

This example illustrates a wider, but very obvious, principle—that any person is more susceptible to moral pressure from people he meets every day than to the exhortations of somebody who just passes through the village. Neighbours can make their neighbours feel uncomfortable much more easily than development workers can make anybody feel uncomfortable.

From this point we advance to the proposition that no betterment scheme can work without local support. It is fair to say that most technicians recognize this, but it is still an important question where to expect support, and it may not always be easy to know where to look for it. The old-fashioned 'indirect rule' principle, 'Get the chief on your side', is fine where there is a chief, but even there it has to be applied with caution. In these days of rapid change it may be that the chief is the rallying-point of the conservatives—the symbol of the traditions that they would like to see preserved. In that case it may be that he cannot afford to align himself actively on the side of change. Moreover, many chiefs now have only influence, not the coercive power that supported some of them under colonial rule. On the other hand, he can be actively hostile if his claim to be a leader of opinion is ignored.

Within a village or a small political unit there may be rival leaders of opinion—chief versus teacher, or chief versus local representative of a political party. Or there may be factions, that is to say the community may be split by some long-standing quarrel. What is important in such circumstances is to avoid becoming identified with one of the rivals, since this will inevitably alienate the other. No anthropologist can tell in advance what the particular configuration of rivalries will be; he can only warn the development team to look out for it.

An anthropologist advising a public health propaganda team in Indonesia noted that different kinds of community might look in different directions for leaders of opinion whose support would be worth having; it was not necessary to assume that if there was no identifiable holder of authority, there was no one at all. In a village in central Sumatra, there were a number of men whom the people regarded, and would themselves describe, as their appropriate leaders. These were the village head, the elders of descent groups, priests and other men learned in religion, and a less clearly defined class of men who were regarded as of superior intelligence. In a suburb of the capital no such recognized statuses existed. If, then, asked the anthropologist, there are no leaders of public opinion, how is public opinion formed? He would not entertain the assumption that there were no 'collective representations', no commonly held value-judgements and interpretations of events. On such an assumption he could not help the health propagandists, and they would indeed have nothing to rely on but their attempts to instruct and convince individuals. The anthropologist observed that bands of men would go round together in the evening visiting the homes of their friends, bringing with them the day's news and views and collecting more as they went. In such discussions, he perceived, was public opinion formed; and somehow those who sought to introduce new ideas must take advantage of this process.

Anthropologists with their knowledge of social structure can identify lines of communication along which ideas may spread. Thus in India, a villager has links with men of his caste outside his own village; he meets them at weddings, funerals and all kinds of ritual; so it is likely that news of community development projects will spread from the place where these are introduced to neighbouring villages of similar caste constitution, and the development agent can judge from the village where he is working the possible reactions in these others.

Another piece of general purpose advice, perhaps particularly significant for community development, is a warning against the assumption that people in simpler societies are 'communally minded', and therefore more willing to give labour for the public good than the community development agent (paid to do his job) would be. To make this assumption is really to assume that the peoples among whom money does not circulate freely are in some way intrinsically different from those of the western world. An anthropologist would find it much more illuminating to assume that, although their circumstances are different, their motives are essentially the same. Where there is no money to pay for services, people co-operate with their neighbours in the expectation that they will receive help in their turn; but as soon as payment is offered for labour, many people will seek to make the most of this opportunity, and many more will ask why, on some particular occasion, they should be expected to work without pay—particularly if the invitation comes from 'the government', which in their past experience has been the main source of payment. The community development worker may even be the most altruistic person in the set-up; but he will have to come down to earth and realize that X and Y are bound to be asking 'What's in this for me?'

A much quoted study from Peru of a campaign to induce women to boil water shows how and why the response to such a campaign varied with the social status of the woman approached. This is not the story of a foreign visiting expert, but of a resident health worker born in the area, though not in the village where she was working. In this village of about a thousand people, all of whom would seem to members of an affluent society to be desperately poor, several gradations of income level are recognized, and expectations of the health worker's role, and the manner in which she was received, varied in relation to them. It was understood that such people operate among 'the poor'—

because 'the poor' are ignorant and dirty. This was a reason why the better off should resent and reject her advice. But vis-à-vis the poor she had another difficulty. The image, by then established in many minds, of the health worker was of one whose snooping you put up with because she is a source of free medical treatment; but this health worker was not offering treatment, only exhortations to add to the daily chores by boiling water. A middle group, who had time to tidy up their houses and stop work to talk to her, were more willing to listen. Then there were people who had formed no image of the health worker and could not understand what she was there for; unfortunately our authority does not specify the 'truly spectacular guesses' made about her activities.

In more than one context anthropologists have had to give the rather damping advice that the outsider who offers instruction is not necessarily assumed to have superior knowledge. His audience may dismiss his counsels with the argument that they may be all right for him, but he belongs to a different kind of people. Or his motives may be suspected because he is associated with a suspect group; this was the case particularly with the government technicians at periods of tension between nationalists and colonial rulers. There is no recipe for dealing successfully with such a situation. A fact that may well be disappointing to the employees of a new independent government is that villagers sometimes look on its agents as 'they', with much the same attitude as they had towards their predecessors. In India, as Adrian Mayer observed, they asked suspiciously what the development agents were getting out of their job.[4] To overcome that kind of suspicion people have to be willing to stay long enough in one place to make friends and inspire trust. But this again may be impossible if the government has a vast plan intended to be carried out within a fixed time. Here applied anthropology would mean suggesting a different kind of programme—and this kind of advice is as little likely to be accepted as was the pre-war advice to leave people in peace.

In the field of public health anthropologists have been

[4] 'Development Projects in an Indian Village', *Pacific Affairs*, 1956.

able to elucidate ideas about health and sickness that run counter to the arguments which the medical experts are seeking to propagate. They are of course familiar with the ideas of sickness as a punishment, or a misfortune produced by some person's malevolence, that were discussed in connection with religion; and also with the food taboos imposed on social groups such as lineages, or on categories such as women or eldest sons. But they have also sometimes found that people have their own socially standardized ideas, unconnected with religious beliefs or observances, about the kinds of food that are beneficial or dangerous, particularly to children or sick people. These ideas may be completely wrong-headed, as when in Java women thought dried fish, the cheapest available animal protein, was bad for little children because it gave them a long list of complaints— all the most prevalent children's diseases. Even in hospitals fish was not provided, not because the doctors forbade it but because the hospital cooks were so sure it was bad. But parents have to have *some* way of feeling that they have done what they can to protect their children—and even if they are told that the way they have been taught is no use but actually harmful, they are not likely to give up in a few minutes the ground on which this confidence rests.

The Peruvian study already referred to brought to light a whole complex of ideas about 'hot' and 'cold' foods, which had a direct bearing on the water-boiling propaganda. The food lore of the people of Los Molinos divides all edible objects, and some others as well, into two classes, 'hot' and 'cold', a division which has little to do with temperature; these qualities are held to be intrinsic to the objects to which they are attributed. When people are sick they must avoid anything that is regarded either as very hot or very cold, but in particular cold things are dangerous to them. 'Raw' water is a cold thing, so sick people must drink 'cooked' water—that is water which has been boiled, not necessarily hot water. One effect of this is that most people, through association, detest boiled water and cannot drink it without something to flavour it. What is perhaps worse is that boiling water regularly is the mark of a chronic invalid.

Not only is this set of ideas, which can be most ingeniously defended, an obstacle to intellectual persuasion, it also provides a rule of conduct. People who boil water when they are well are deviants. Some do it not because the health worker has convinced them but because they know it is done by people of high status outside the village; these may lead their neighbours to think they are 'giving themselves airs'.

What can the anthropologist recommend here? Unfortunately he has no recipe; all he can do is to warn the health visitor what she is up against and beg her to be patient in her efforts to persuade. These, alas, are the limitations of applied anthropology as we see them today. We do not claim to know any persuasion-magic.

A good deal of the advice that anthropologists give is just common sense. Some of it does not depend at all on their specialist knowledge, but simply on their recognition that there is usually some sense in the point of view even of uneducated people, and that you can find what it is by staying among them long enough and by imaginatively putting yourself in their place.

The Peruvian study is illuminating here too. It shows what the little action of boiling the water meant, in practical terms, for the housewives of Los Molinos. Some buy both wood and water; others cannot afford to, and must forage for both. They do not keep a fire going all day, but light it to cook the three meals they eat. When they are cooking, all their pots may be in use; the hearth may be so built that it will not take an extra pot to boil water anyhow. They cannot boil water overnight because of another piece of food lore; if it has been 'cooked' and then allowed to 'sleep', it is dangerously cold. If it is to be boiled, this must be done after a meal, when the fire is still hot. The time when people want to drink it is, naturally, midday when the sun is hottest. So it would have to be boiled after breakfast. But most women have to go out after breakfast on the quest for firewood and water, and food for their chickens or goats. Only the women who can stay in after breakfast boil their water.

In Indonesia, again, Maurice Freedman made some

calculations about the relation between people's incomes
and the cost of the foods they were being urged to give their
children. Even people who own cows, he observed, sell all
their milk; otherwise they could not get back their outlay
on the cow, and the price of a pint of milk will buy more
than a day's supply for a family of the rice and dried fish
that they live on. In the same way Paul Stirling, an anthropologist who recently worked in a land settlement area in
southern Italy, noticed that the water provided for irrigation could not be adeqately used without precise timing,
which it was impossible to organize, and without a high
degree of technical skill which the new field owners did
not have.

Such observations, incidental to an anthropologist's main
work, could be made by anybody with the time and the
patience to stay and observe what went on in the intervals
between the visits of persons in authority. In the field of
land settlement economists, and one political scientist, have
done this. Elsewhere it has in practice been left to anthropologists.

Anthropologists often wish that those in authority, and
particularly those at the lower levels in the hierarchy, who
have most contact with the villagers, knew more about the
analysis of society, and sometimes offer to teach them. It is
rarely possible for them to give much time to learning, and
quite impossible to impart to them all the knowledge expected of a professional anthropologist. A recommendation
made to the authorities in Java was that health workers,
before embarking on their campaigns, should spend a little
time just living in a village, and so become aware of the
realities of life there. Sometimes it is possible to teach social
workers in training about the actual social structure of the
people they will be working among. This is in a sense like
giving them a map to help them find their way. More often
we can only offer warnings of typical difficulties.

SUGGESTIONS FOR READING

Full-scale books on this subject come from American sources, and
tend to look for difficulties caused by cultural inconveniences, such
as finding that people who have been persuaded to sow higher-

yielding grain do not like the taste of the flour, rather than for questions of social status and social pressures. But a large number of examples are to be found in E. H. Spicer (ed.), *Human Problems in Technological Change* (1952), B. D. Paul and W. B. Miller (eds.), *Health, Culture and Community* (1955) (which contains the Peruvian water-boiling story), and G. Foster, *Traditional Cultures and the Impact of Technological Change* (1962). A later book by Foster, *Applied Anthropology* (1969), takes into account the resistance to change of development agencies, as well as that of the peoples they work among. M. Freedman, *A Report on some Aspects of Food, Health and Society in Indonesia* (1955), is available only in mimeographed form, but its most important conclusions are published in the *South Pacific Quarterly Review*, April 1958. B. Benedict, *Preliminary Survey on the Needs of Youth in Nyasaland* (1963), applies the expert knowledge of the anthropologist to another theme.

Those interested in a historical approach to the subject should read 'Practical Anthropology' in *Africa*, 1929, in which Malinowski threw down the gauntlet, the reply by P. E. Mitchell, then a provincial commissioner in Tanganyika, 'The Anthropologist and the Practical Man', and Malinowski's rejoinder 'The Rationalization of Anthropology and Administration' (both in *Africa*, 1930). S. F. Nadel, *Anthropology and Modern Life* (1953), represents the highest claims made by an anthropologist since Malinowski. L. P. Mair, 'Applied Anthropology and Development Policies', in *Studies in Applied Anthropology* (1957), is in part a comment on this.

CHAPTER 17 # Related Subjects III: Race Relations

THE nature of the relations among populations held to belong to different 'races'—that is, distinguished, or supposed to be distinguishable, by physical characteristics—is a matter of grave concern to all thinking people. They ask whether it is really true that these physical differences go with differences in mental and moral characteristics, and whether there is something about them that makes it peculiarly difficult for people of different 'races' to live amicably together. If social anthropologists are expected to answer these questions, the reason is simply that the populations among which they have done most of their work have brown or black skins. The questions are asked by people who would like to see more amicable relationships between populations of different skin colour than exist in many countries today. In Britain such people are concerned about the disadvantages at which immigrants from Commonwealth countries find themselves, and about the violence that has sometimes broken out between them and their neighbours. In America they are concerned with policies aiming at the 'integration' of Negro and white populations and the resistance offered to such policies.

These are practical questions, not asked simply for the sake of knowledge. This would be no reaon why anthropologists should not try to answer them, but in fact the range of questions that is asked belongs to a number of different disciplines, and only a small part of them call for his special knowledge. Is it true that humanity is divided into races? Is it true that some are naturally superior to others? Is it true that there is a natural feeling of repugnance between people of different race? If not, why does one so often come up against such a feeling?

The nature of the relation between physical inheritance and mental or moral qualities belongs squarely in the field of physical anthropology. But when one turns to the actual situations of racial conflict that present us with problems today, there is not in fact anything about them that is peculiar to the confrontation of people with different physical characteristics. They are all manifestations of group exclusiveness on the one hand and reactions of the excluded on the other. Some situations of 'race conflict' have more in common with the problems of any immigrants in a new environment, some with those of social mobility in stratified societies. As such they belong to the broader field of the sociologist. The question why social antagonisms should be expressed in hostility towards groups symbolized by physical characteristics is one for social psychologists.

Social anthropologists, as was explained at the beginning of this book, are not nowadays expected to master the field of physical anthropology, but many students of the subject are probably interested in that corner of it which bears on current controversies about racial characteristics. This chapter will give a brief account of this topic, but will not attempt to pursue the social aspects of situations involving 'race relations'.

The popular notion of 'race', important though it is as a social fact, has very little relation to knowledge established by scientific inquiry. A point on which a student might pause for a moment is the reflection that popular categorizations are based entirely on characteristics that can be seen when people are fully dressed, namely skin colour and the appearance of face and head. Why should it be so readily assumed that these are the most significant of the great number of physical characters that interest biologists? And why, if different mental and moral qualities are ascribed to different 'races', should it be assumed that the operations of the mind and brain are somehow linked to the colour of the skin? Is this even plausible when you come to ask how the connection could work? Are such judgements any more rational than judging a person by whether he rides a scooter or a motor cycle? In point of fact, when physical anthropologists are measuring the characters of different popula-

tions they are largely concerned with data that are not
accessible at all to casual observation, such as the distribution of certain substances in the blood, or respiration rate
or blood pressure.

It should be noted too that when physical anthropologists
make their measurements, they do not expect to sort people
out—even for one character at a time—into clearly separable divisions. Pygmies are short, as we all know; and many
of us have heard of the immensely tall herdsmen of the
Ruwenzori mountains, the Tusi aristocrats who a few years
ago were driven out by a peasant revolution. The popular
stereotype shows us a little pygmy beside a tall Tusi, and
measurements confirm that the *average* height of pygmies
is much less than that of Tusi; nevertheless you could find *a*
tall pygmy who was taller than *a* short Tusi. In other words,
the averages for any particular character differ for different
populations, but there is always an area of overlap. The
more characters that are measured, the harder it must be to
find any combination in all of which populations can be
placed in order on the same scale.

But since social anthropologists are concerned with behaviour, the question about which we need to be clear is
that of the correlation—if there is any—between physical
and mental characteristics. In popular categorizations,
people ascribe all kinds of moral defects to 'races' other than
their own (as they commonly do also to peoples of different
language and culture, even if they do not regard them as
belonging to different races). Closer examination does not
show such correlations. Some studies of crime made among
immigrant groups in America failed to find significant differences among them, or between them and longer-
established Americans; in particular it was noted that
among the newer immigrants crime decreased with the
generations, as the descendants of immigrants were brought
up in the standards of American society. One study made in
Chicago showed that the city could be zoned into belts extending outwards from the centre, in which the crime rate
steadily decreased as one went further out. This relationship remained the same over a number of years, while the
population of the different zones was changing all the time.

In other words, it was always the new immigrants who took the inferior jobs and had to live in the 'criminal' slum quarters. Their children did better and moved gradually outwards. But if criminal tendencies were 'in their blood', the crime rate should have moved with them.[1]

The point was made in earlier chapters that it is actually quite inaccurate to talk of 'blood' kin as if a person's biological inheritance was conveyed in his blood. It comes in fact from the parental genes, in the male sperm and female ovum, which combine at the moment of his conception. At that moment a person receives his hereditary outfit, and everything in his physical constitution must come from this; thus he could not grow up with eyes of a colour for which he did not have the appropriate genes, nor attain to greater stature than his genes allow, though many circumstances might prevent him from reaching his potential height. But one cannot argue directly, either forwards or backwards, from the genes to the person we see in front of us, since the genes modify one another's effects, and environment begins to influence the person's development even while he is still in the womb. As soon as he is born, cultural influences get to work on him.

Nor is it possible to argue from what two parents are like to what their child may be expected to be like. Reasons which might be considered sufficient have just been given, but to them must be added the fact that the child inherits only half the genes of either parent, and it is a matter of chance which he will get from either. Hence it is vain to imagine that there is a special configuration of genes for army colonels or university dons—if you happen to admire either of these types—and encourage your daughter to marry one or other so that her children may be correspondingly admirable. The fact that every individual's hereditary make-up is unique is yet another argument against ascribing qualities to, or explaining them by, 'racial' origins.

Geneticists would agree that there are no genes for moral qualities; what individuals show here is a matter of the values of the society they grow up in and the success with which these values are imparted to them, and indeed the

[1] O. Klineberg, *Race Differences*, 1935, pp. 235–6.

social influences that they experience all through their lives. But intelligence—which is a matter of the functioning of the brain and the nervous system—*is* inherited; it is generally agreed that there is a correlation between the intelligence of a child and that of its parents. But what is innate is intelligence in the most undifferentiated sense of the word—the prospect of being a quick learner of whatever skill best engages the child's interest (which will be largely a matter of chance), not of being 'mathematical' or 'literary' or 'musical'. When one is considering the large populations that are generally thought of as 'races', there is within each as wide a range in the field of intelligence as there is in that of stature, so that there is little meaning in trying to grade such populations according to their intelligence. Moreover, whereas there is no difficulty about measuring stature, no one has yet succeeded in devising a test of intelligence that is not somehow linked with cultural experience and so biased in favour of particular cultures. Intelligence tests give some indication whether a child will do well in a particular educational system; they tell us little about whether a Peruvian or a Chinese child would cope better with an environment that was entirely strange to them both.

A *strictly* endogamous population could be said to have a 'genetic pool', a limited number of genes from which all its members must draw their physical characteristics, so that, to take the simplest example, none of them could ever have blue eyes. But in fact strict endogamy of this kind is only maintained among physically isolated populations, and there have not been many of these in historical times. Since the epoch of the great voyages of discovery—that is, in the last 400 years—there has been so much intermingling of genes that it would be vain now to look, outside a few small islands, for a population with an identifiable common inheritance. In these circumstances mere *claims* to practise, or to have practised, strict endogamy cannot be taken as evidence of 'racial' purity; for even groups that refuse to recognize legal marriage between their members and persons whom they regard as racially different have never been able to control sex relations of the disapproved kind. What they do is to refuse to recognize the offspring of such relations as belonging to their group.

It will be clear that this is not a subject in regard to which anthropologists have developed a body of theory related to other aspects of their studies. It can be pursued by reading in any number of different directions; but it is not a subject that is isolable for investigation in the context of a particular discipline.

SUGGESTIONS FOR READING

American sociologists, inspired by the situation of large numbers of new immigrants in their country, were the first to concentrate on the study of race relations. It is an interesting fact, obviously connected with historical events, that before the Second World War the term 'race prejudice' primarily suggested anti-Semitism, whereas today it would be more likely to suggest attitudes towards darkskinned persons.

O. Klineberg, *Race Differences* (1935), discusses the distribution of physical traits among the populations generally thought of as 'races', and the correlation, or lack of correlation, between these and intelligence and between them and moral qualities. A valuable short essay is P. E. Vernon, 'Race and Intelligence', in P. Mason (ed.), *Man, Race and Darwin* (1960).

J. S. Huxley and A. C. Haddon, *We Europeans*, also published in 1935, covers somewhat similar ground in the discussion of the social significance of biological heredity, and goes on to show the impossibility of identifying a 'Nordic' race. D. G. MacRae, 'Race and Sociology', in his *Ideology and Society* (1961), discusses some early theories of race.

One of the first tasks undertaken by UNESCO was to popularize information on the actual state of knowledge concerning the social significance of biological qualities. This activity was inspired in part by revulsion against the enormities of the Hitler regime, and in part by the growing insistence of dark-skinned peoples on equality of treatment. A number of pamphlets of unequal value were produced. The most useful are G. M. Morant, *The Significance of Racial Differences*, and L. C. Dunn, *Race and Biology* (1952); both are succinct statements of the facts as physical anthropologists see them.

British students will probably be most interested in literature dealing with the difficulties faced by post-war immigrants to Britain from Commonwealth countries. K. L. Little's *Negroes in Britain* (1947) is a history of the changing attitudes of the people of Britain towards Negroes, with some account of the attitude towards the British of the Negro population in the Cardiff docks. M. P. Banton, *The Coloured Quarter* (1955), gives the results of a study made in the East End of London; the same author's *White and Coloured*

(1959) and *Race Relations* (1967) discuss problems of prejudice and discrimination in general terms. R. Glass, *Newcomers* (1960), is about West Indians in London. M. Freedman (ed), *A Minority in Britain* (1955), is a study of the Jewish community. Leon Poliakov, *The Aryan Myth* (1974), gives the history of attitudes towards the Jewish communities among them of the different European nations.

The best-known work on Negro–White relations in America is G. Myrdal's *An American Dilemma* (1944). Also to be recommended are J. Dollard, *Cast and Class in a Southern Town* (1937), and O. C. Cox, *Caste, Class and Race* (1948).

There is also a considerable literature on South Africa. Books worth looking at are I. D. MacCrone, *Race Attitudes* (1937), and S. Patterson, *Colour and Culture in South Africa* (1953), and *The Last Trek* (1957). The second of these deals with the Cape Coloured community, the last with the Afrikaners.

Index

Aborigines, 27, 50, 64, 110, 162, 212, 215, 217
Abuja, 129–30
Administration, 113, 130, 134; modern, 286–7
Adultery, 55, 93, 94, 119
Affines, affinity, 21, 71, 88, 96, 98–100, 156, 174, 184, 203–4
Age, basis of organization, 64–6, 117–22
Age-grades, 65, 118, 127
Age-regiments, 126
Age-sets, 66, 118–21, 151
Agnates, agnation, 23, 71, 73, 74, 94, 98, 116, 122, 240
Akan, 73
Allan, C., 159
Alternation, 64–6
Alur, 239, 259
Ancestors, 59, 77–9, 92, 101, 107, 125, 168, 173, 186, 213, 219, 221, 223, 225, 234, 239, 244, 248, 253
Anderson, E., 260
Anglo-Saxons, 71, 82
Animism, 213
Ankole, 131
Anuak, 46
Arabs, 24, 168, 220, 233
Armstrong, W. E., 200, 208
Arusha, 65–6, 121–2, 148, 151–2
Ashanti, 16, 72, 79, 96, 126, 158, 169, 286
Associations, 66–8, 74, 118–20, 168–9, 250
Australia, 15, 27, 64, 72, 110, 162, 182, 212, 215–16, 217–18, 219, 228, 290
Avoidance, 79, 98, 217–19, 232, 237

Bachofen, 21
Bailey, F. G., 14, 172, 264, 284
Balance, 272–4
Balandier, G., 253, 260
Banton, M. P., 309
Bantu, 61, 73, 128, 158
Barber, B., 68

Baric, L., 208
Barnes, H. E., 47 n.
Barnes, J. A., 283
Barter, 180, 190–3
Barth, F., 134 n., 136, 188, 193, 204
Basseri, 204
Bastian, 19, 20
Beattie, J. H. M., 7, 31, 44, 100 n., 107, 128, 222 n., 229, 233, 254, 259, 274
Bemba, 54, 97, 138
Benedict, B., 207, 303
Bergdama, 112
Biak, 251
Bilek, 75–6, 81
Bisipara, 172
Bloch, Marc, 138
Bloch, Maurice, 160 n.
Boas, F., 9, 25, 28, 49, 185
Bohannan, L., 81; P. J., 144–6, 153, 159, 164, 193, 197
Bott, E., 82
Bridewealth, 92, 93, 94, 95, 166, 188, 190, 193, 197, 199, 275, 286, 289, 290
Brothers, 16, 78, 80, 102, 136
Buganda, 131, 133, 138, 154, 168
Bung'a, 154–5
Bunyoro, 127
Burma, 88, 199, 270
Burundi, 134
Bushmen, 110, 112, 115, 162–3, 164
Busoga, 138
Buxton, J., 187 n.

Canoes, 169–70, 172–5, 178, 179, 196, 201, 203
Capital, 164, 173, 200–5, 208
Cargo cults, 253
Caribbean, 276
Cash, 172, 253, 266–7, 276, 277
Category, defined, 15–16
Cattle, 3–4, 55, 61, 93, 94, 98, 116, 126, 148, 162, 165–6, 187, 193, 197, 198, 210, 275
Cewa, 97

Ceylon, 165
Charter, mythical, 125, 255, 257, 259
Cheyenne, 145
Chicago, 306
Chiefs, 121, chapter 8 *passim*, 154,
  155, 167, 169, 173–6, 186, 187, 192,
  196, 202, 211, 235, 236–7, 238, 239,
  245, 270–1, 274, 280; subordinate,
  125–8, 133
Children, 83, 90, 91, 92, 93, 94, 101–2,
  232
Childe, Gordon, 162–3
China, Chinese, 11, 67–8, 72, 181,
  191, 202, 263, 265, 267
Church, 223
Circumcision, 117
Clans, 48, 77, 79, 149, 173, 176, 191–2,
  237
Class, 63–4, 276
Clientship, 134
Codrington, 214
Cognates, cognation, 23, 71, 86
Cohen, A., 284
Cohn, N., 252, 253
Colson, E., 82
Commoners, 125, 132, 174–5
Comparative method, 47 ff.
Compensation, 116–17, 118, 121, 143,
  145–7, 148, 152, 198, 199
Concubinage, 94
Congo, 197, 253, 260
Coulanges, F. de, 220–2
Courts, 126, 141–3, 149, 150, 249, 250
Cousins, cross, 24, 88–9; parallel, 87
Couvade, 48
Cox, O. C., 310
Craftsmen, *see* Specialists
Credit, 181, 199 ff., 205 ff.
Crime, 146–7
Culture, 8, 9, 10, 20, 24, 25, 49, 86,
  185, 226, 258, 268–9, 279, 289, 307

Dahomey, 94
Dalton, G., 178, 193, 195, 208
Darwin, C., 19, 38, 41–2
Death, 80, 224, 233, 257
De Brosses, 18
Debts, 122, 199, 205–7
Descent, 15–16, 29, 54, 64, 65, chapter
  5 *passim*, 94, 97, 111, 135–7, 249,
  276; double unilineal, 73–4; groups,
  74–8, 80, 90, 121, 148, 153, 184,
  185, 186, 196, 197, 203, 216, 217,
  219, 242, 248, 255, 297; local, 75,
  80, 88; unilineal, 71, 74–5, 80, 86,
  102–3, 217

Detribalization, 13, 278
Diffusion, 19–20, 49
Dinka, 61, 104, 114, 222, 249–50, 260
Disputes, 115, 120, 121–2, 124, 126–7,
  135–6, 139–40, 143, 146, 148–9,
  150–2, 192, 238
Divination, diviners, 94, 198, 241–4,
  246, 249, 275
Djuka, 152
Dollard, J., 310
Dorobo, 157
Douglas, M., 178, 193, 197 n.
Driberg, J. H., 149
Drucker, P., 193
Dunn, L. C., 309
Durkheim, E., 5, 9, 12, 14, 26–8, 30,
  34–6, 78, 147, 180, 211–12, 215–16,
  220–9, 230, 232–3, 234, 235, 237–8,
  240 n., 254, 264
Dyaks, 207

Ecology, 162
Economics, defined, 160, 179
Economy, commercial, 179; sub-
  sistence, 161, 163, 170, 196, 197
Eggan, F., 51
Einzig, P., 208
Eisenstadt, S., 68
Elders, 66, 118, 119, 121, 148–9, 151–
  2, 192, 242, 248, 279, 297
Endogamy, 22, 90, 308
Epstein, A. L., 159, 283; T. S., 193–4,
  284
Equilibrium, 149, 269–70, 272–4
Eritrea, 291–2
Ethnography, 9
Ethology, 6
Ethnology, 8, 50, 52
Evans-Pritchard, E. E., 14, 21, 31,
  43–4, 46, 52, 78, 81, 93, 94, 111,
  112, 114 n., 116, 122, 138, 139, 140,
  182, 211 n., 215, 232, 233, 240, 241,
  245–6, 259, 260, 272
Evolution, 21 ff., 40–1, 45, 49
Exchange, commercial, 179–80; gift,
  175, 180–91, 203
Exogamy, 22, 24, 37, 48, 64, 84, 86,
  87, 88, 95, 111, 217–18.

Fallers, L. A., 64, 138
Family, 92, 94–8, 101–2, 204, 221,
  275–6, 286; extended, 78, 105, 177,
  275; ghost, 95; joint, 78, 277;
  nuclear, 85, 94, 275
Fathers, 93, 96, 97, 101, 103, 105;
  proxy, 93–4

Fetishism, 215
Feud, 24, 116–17, 149, 199
Feudal system, 133–4
Fieldwork, 28–30, 39, 52, 106, 161, 185
Filiation, 74, 75; complementary, 73, 102
Firth, R. W., 31, 44, 47, 68, 76, 82, 158, 160, 170, 172–4, 176, 177, 178, 190 n., 193, 196, 201–3, 208
Forde, D., 16, 68, 81, 107, 119, 123, 177, 260
Forge, A., 82
Fortes, M., 16, 24, 31, 39, 43–4, 74, 75, 76–7, 79, 81, 86, 96, 107, 111, 112, 114 n., 122, 138, 219, 235, 236–8, 239, 268, 272
Foster, G., 303
For, J. R., 81, 85 n.
Foxtribe, 106
Frazer, J. G., 25, 30, 48–9, 211, 212, 213–14, 217, 230
Freedman, M., 68, 81, 283, 301, 303
Freeman, J. D., 76, 81, 171–2
Freud, S., 85, 217–18
Frobenius, 20
Fulani, 165
Function, 19, 32–40, 45, 111, 112, 185, 263–4
Funerals, 80, 199, 205, 206

Ganda, 79, 127, 128, 149, 154, 155, 215, 239
Gellner, E., 39
Genealogy, 59, 71, 78–9, 85, 86, 105, 137
Genitor, 93, 95
Ghana, 72, 73, 77, 79, 81, 90, 103, 107, 191, 199, 228, 235, 277
Ghost Dance, 252–3
Glass, R., 310
Gluckman, M., 51, 143–5, 150–1, 154, 177, 235–6, 259, 270–3, 279
Goldenweiser, A., 47
Goodenough, W., 82
Goody, J. R., 81, 82, 102–3, 107, 108, 227–9, 231, 260
Gough, E. K., 95 n.
Gould, J., 81
Government, 109–14, 139; centralized, 125–30, 147, 274; colonial, 285, 286, 288, 291
Groups, corporate, 15, 54, 71–2, 74–7, 79, 155–6, 185
Guilds, 168–9, 177
Gullick, J. M., 138

Gulliver, P. H., 65, 68, 121, 123, 145, 148, 151–2, 159, 188 n., 193, 284
Gusii, 171, 290

Haddon, A. C., 29, 310
Hadza, 115, 142–5
Haida, 50, 185
Hapu, 76
Harris, M., 16, 31
Herodotus, 17, 21–2
Herskovits, M. J., 177
Hierarchy, 58–60
Hindus, 11, 62–3
History, 39, 40–1, 43–7, 264–6
Hobbes, 18
Hoebel, E. A., 143, 145–6, 159
Hogbin, I., 159
Holleman, J. F., 158
Homans, G., 102, 107
Homicide, 60, 71, 72, 116, 147, 148, 184
Hong Kong, 207
Hopi, 51
Horton, R. F., 227 n., 230, 257, 261
Howell, P. P., 158
Hubert, J., 82
Hunter, M. (Wilson), 283
Huntingford, G. W. B., 123
Husbands, 48, 92, 93, 96, 97, 99, 154, 296; woman, 94
Huxley, J. S., 310

Iban, 75–6, 81, 91, 172
Ibo, 14, 66, 124, 158, 165
Ifugao, 71
Incest, 48, 84–7, 89, 90, 147, 259
India, Indian, 14, 21, 62–3, 95, 134–7, 178, 202, 206, 265, 277, 284, 297, 299
Indians, American, 18, 21, 22, 50, 64, 72, 104, 106, 110, 185–7, 216–17, 251, 252–3, 292
Indonesia, 297, 303
Industrialization, 265–6
Inheritance, 29, 73–4, 76, 93, 102, 192; biological, 3, 305–6, 307–8
Initiation, 56–8, 65, 83, 117–18, 198, 234–5
Institutions, 10, 37, 127, 140, 141, 182, 185, 212, 221, 262–4, 268, 274, 286
Interest, 199–201, 205
Investment, 203–5, 206–7
Iroquois, 21, 104
Irrigation, 165

Japan, 8, 294
Jarvie, I. C., 52
Java, 300
Joking relationship, 100
Jones, G. I., 123
Jukun, 138
Junod, H., 236
Justice, 127, 129, 144, 240, 289

Kachins, 88, 255, 258, 270–1
Kamba, 157
Kardiner, A., 30
Kede, 138
Kenya, 4, 64, 83, 133, 148, 157, 165, 171, 289, 290
Kgatla, 59
Kikuyu, 157, 165, 235
Killing, *see* Homicide
Kin, kinship, kinsmen, 8, 16, 21, 24, 66, chapter 5 *passim*, 84, 86, 91, 92, 94–7, 99, 101, 103, 104–6, 116, 120, 122, 125, 130, 132, 136, 147, 150, 152, 168, 171, 173–6, 181, 188, 196, 198, 205, 234, 244, 275–6, 286; terminology, 21, 70, 104–6; Omaha, 106
Kindred, 71
Kingmakers, 131
Kings, 129, 131, 132, 134, 154, 155, 237, 239–40, 256, 274; divine, 239
Kipsigis, 83
Klineberg, O., 310
Köbben, A. J., 152
Kolb, W., 81
Konkomba, 191–2
Kula, 180, 182–3, 185–7, 190–1, 200
!Kung, 162
Kuper, H., 237 n., 259, 283
Kwakiutl, 185–6

Labour, 165–8, 170–7, 201–2, 298; wage, 179, 267, 275, 277–8, 298
Lafitau, 18
Lambert, H. E., 68, 123
Lancaster, L. (Barić), 82
Land, 134–7, 152–8, 164, 172, 269, 277, 291; pledging, 156–7, 200, 205–6; settlement schemes, 294, 295, 302; tenancy, 156
Law, chapter 9 *passim*
Laws, scientific, 40–4
Laws (social rules), 128, 139, 140, 141 ff., 286, 288
Leach, E. R., 15, 36, 75, 80, 81, 88, 107, 177, 225–9, 230, 255, 258, 259, 260, 261, 269–72

Leaders, 115, 117, 119, 120, 132, 135–7, 188, 249, 280, 297
Lee, R., 162–3, 178
Lele, 197–8, 199
Lenshina, Alice, 254
Lévi-Strauss, C., 25, 28, 38, 44, 51, 52, 86, 107, 187, 219–20, 230, 258–9, 261
Lewis, O., 284
Lienhardt, R. G., 31, 122, 222, 249, 260
Lineages, 21, 54, 59, 72–3, 77–80, 86–7, 88, 92, 93, 95–6, 98–9, 101–3, 105–6, 116, 119, 121–2, 125, 132, 133, 135, 136–7, 149, 153, 155–7, 183–4, 219, 237–8, 239, 242, 248, 275–7, 300; fission, 78, 248–9; segmentary, 78, 79, 221
Little, K. L., 309
Llewellyn, K. N., 159
LoDagaa, 228
LoWiili, 103
Lozi (Barotse), 150–1, 154–5, 159
Lugbara, 242, 244, 248–9
Luhya, 148
Lumpa, 254

MacCrone, I. D., 310
McLennan, J. F., 22, 24
MacRae, D. G., 7, 19 n., 31, 310
Magic, 25, 169, 183, 197, 212–14, 220, 223–7, 229–30, 232, 238, 245, 255
Maine, H. S., 22–3, 78, 110, 146, 158
Malawi, 171
Malays, 177, 189, 203
Malaysia, 277
Malinowski, B., 6, 9, 28, 29, 30, 31, 34–7, 39, 45, 49, 52, 86, 102, 104, 105, 106, 111, 125 n., 141, 158, 159, 170, 175, 176, 178, 180, 182, 185, 193, 224–5, 230, 236 n., 254–7, 260, 262–4, 268, 279, 286, 287, 289, 290, 303
Mana, 215, 216
Mandari, 187
Maori, 76
Maquet, J. J., 134, 260
Marett, R. R., 214
Markets, 129, 191–3
Marriage, 21, 22, 24, 48, 72, chapter 6 *passim*, 115, 142, 144–5, 167, 176, 184, 187, 189, 197, 198, 234, 276–7; cross-cousin, 24, 87–9; ghost, 93–4; payment, 199 (*see also* Bridewealth); preferential, 87; prescribed, 87–9;

prohibitions, 86–7, 308; woman, 94, 95
Marx, Marxism, 41, 63, 273, 274
Mason, P., 310
Matriarchy, 22
Matriliny, matrilineal societies, 23–4, 47–8, 72, 73–4, 79, 80, 83, 89, 92, 95–7, 101, 102, 103–4
Mauritius, 207–8
Mauss, M., 28, 180, 186, 193
Mayer, A. C., 299
Mayer, P., 284, 290
Mead, M., 284
Meek, C. K., 138, 158, 159
Melanesia, 29, 138, 185, 214, 216
Men's houses, 136, 188, 189
Merton, R., 37
Middleton, J. F. M., 123, 159, 248 n., 260
Miller, W. B., 303
Mitchell, J. C., 68, 284; P. E., 303
Models, 272
Moieties, 64, 65
Monboddo, 19 n.
Money, 67–8, 160, 161, 177, 179, 181, 186, 187–9, 193, 195–9, 208, 298
Monogamy, 21, 22 n., 91, 176
Montaigne, 18
Montesquieu, 18–19
Morant, G. M., 310
Morgan, Lewis H., 21, 23, 31, 70, 81, 104, 109–10
Morris, H. S., 81
Morton-Williams, P., 68
Mother's brother, 88, 96–7, 100–4
Murder, *see* Homicide
Murdock, G. P., 85
Myrdal, G., 310
Myth, 77, 125, 135, 237, 244, 252, 254–9

Nadel, S. F., 12, 46, 68, 81, 138, 169, 177, 211 n., 250, 260, 291, 292, 303
Nats, 255, 258
Nayars, 95, 107
Ndembu, 228, 242, 249
Needham, R., 88 n., 107
Nephews, 100–1
New Britain, 193–4, 199
New Guinea, 29, 104, 168, 184, 195, 200, 252, 263
Ngoni, 276, 283
Nilotes, 215, 222
Nkole, 149
Norms, 26, 146
Nuer, 14, 57, 59, 61, 78, 81, 87, 93–4,

116–17, 122, 140, 143, 148, 215, 232
Nupe, 46, 138, 169, 177, 250
Nyakyusa, 228, 235, 247
Nyikang, 239, 256
Nyoro, 99, 100, 107

Oberg, K., 131 n.
Officers, officials, 112, 124, 125, 129, 132, 188, 199, 236, 280
Ole, 248
Oracles, 242
Orissa, 205, 206

Pakhtuns, 135, 137
Parsons, T., 228, 274
Pater, 93, 95
Pathans, 134, 138
Patriarchy, 22, 24
Patriliny, patrilineal societies, 22, 23, 47–8, 72–3, 74, 77, 79, 80, 83, 89, 92–5, 97, 99–103, 276
Patterson, S., 310
Paul, B. D., 303
Pauw, B., 284
Peristiany, J. G., 68
Peru, 298, 300
Plumb, J. H., 265–6, 267
Pocock, D. F., 31
Pokot, 57
Polanyi, K., 198
Political community, 110, 112–13, 116–17, 124
Political Systems, 111–13, 280; acephalous, 116–22, 191; *see also* States
Politics, 108–14, 130 ff., 141, 188, 279–80, 286
Pollution, 62–3, 80, 147, 172, 228
Polyandry, 91, 95
Polygamy, 22 n., 91
Polygyny, 91, 95, 176
Polynesia, 100, 177–8
Pondo, 283
Pons, V., 284
Population, 162, 163
Pospisil, L., 144, 178, 200, 208
Potlatch, 185–7, 190, 203, 206
Powell, H. A., 52
Preble, E., 30
Prestations, 92
Prime ministers, 128, 131
Princes, 130–1
Purum, 88

'Race', 304–9
Radcliffe-Brown, A. R., 6–7, 9, 10,

28, 31, 36, 37, 38, 39, 50, 53, 65, 78,
  81, 101, 105, 107, 108, 139–45, 147,
  158–9, 218–19, 228, 264
Rank, 58–60, 72, 173, 185–90, 227
Ratzel, 19–20
Reader, R., 284
Reciprocity, 28, 73, 141, 184, 274
Redfield, R., 284
Reification, 10
Religion, 23, 25, 27–8, 175, 203,
  chapters 13, 14 *passim*, 281
Residence rules, 80, 97
Richards, A. I., 68, 177, 283
Rites de passage, 233–7
Ritual, rituals, 25, 37, 48–9, 55, 57–8,
  64, 72, 74, 77, 78, 79, 95, 116–17,
  118, 124, 127, 169, 170, 172, 203,
  212, 216–18, 219, 220–30, 251,
  255–6
Rivers, W. H. R., 29, 69, 75, 81, 104,
  106
Robertson Smith, 24–5, 27, 220
Roles, 11–12, 54, 106, 112, 121, 127,
  150, 188, 223, 236, 239, 242, 280
Romans, 22–3, 221
Roscoe, J., 131
Rossel Island, 200, 208
Rousseau, 18
Rwanda, 62, 134, 260
Rulers, 125–8, 130, 132, 133, 143,
  147, 149, 168, 272–4, 282

Sacred, the, 223–4, 226, 228, 255–6
Salisbury, R. F., 180, 184, 193, 196,
  201–2, 208
Samoa, 58
Sanctions, 140, 184, 236, 279, 281,
  295
Sarawak, 207, 209
Sarwa, 61
Schapera, I., 51, 53, 110, 112, 122,
  128 n., 138
Schmidt, Pater, 215
Schneider, D., 102, 107
Scott, R. C., 177
Seligman, C. G., 29
Serfs, 60–2
Sex, 83–6, 89–90, 92, 276, 308
Sheddick, V. G. J., 159
Shilluk, 132, 239, 256, 259
Shils, E. A., 282
Shrines, 120, 192, 215, 219, 239
Siane, 184, 196, 202
Silcock, T. H., 68
Sin, 84, 147
Slaves, 60–1

Smith, Adam, 19, 166, 180
Smith, E. W., 286
Smith, M. G., 129, 130, 138
Social anthropology, defined, 1, 2,
  5–8
Social control, 11, 139, 142, 247
Society, 1, 2, 6, 8, 9, 10, 27, 33–5, 38,
  110–11, 116, 224, 236, 237, 287;
  industrial, 8, 63, 265; peasant, 13,
  294; primitive, 2, 12–13; stratified,
  63, 276, 293, 305
Sociology, sociologists, 1, 6–8, 26–8,
  40–1, 63, 281, 291
Sommerfelt, A., 114 n.
Sorcerers, sorcery, 193, 206, 245, 249
Southall, A. W., 259
Southwold, M., 133 n., 138
Specialists, economic, 168–70, 174,
  196
Spencer, H., 26, 32–4, 36, 38, 40–1,
  47, 273
Spicer, E. H., 303
Spirit mediums, 241–2
Spirits, 23, 119–20, 127, 147, 156, 173,
  212–13, 214–15, 227, 243–4, 248
Spokesmen, 121–2
States, 110–11, 124–5, 147; new, 280,
  282
Status, 10–11, 23, 49, 59, 61, 64, 69,
  92, 117–18, 127, 190, 206, 226, 228,
  232, 233–6, 239, 276, 297, 298, 300
Stirling, P., 302
Stratification, 60–2
Structure, 8, 10, 28, 36, 74, 77, 86, 88,
  106, 185, 218, 220, 223, 237 ff., 297,
  302
Succession, 29, 78, 93, 131–2
Sumatra, 297
Surinam, 152
Surplus, 167, 180
Survivals, 24, 29, 38–9, 52, 262
Swat, 134–7, 188
Swazi, 236, 239, 283

Taboo, 237, 296, 300
Tait, D., 81, 123, 191 n.
Tallensi, 77, 81, 89, 126, 219, 237, 259
Tambu, 199
Tanzania, 65, 115, 121, 123, 146, 291
Territory, 110–11, 115, 135
Theft, 119, 120, 147, 192, 245
Thurnwald, R., 201
Tien, J. K., 209
Tikopia, 47, 101, 173–5, 178, 196–7,
  238, 256, 259
Tiv, 144, 146, 164, 197

Tlingit, 185
Tolai, 195
Tonga, 80, 168
Torres Straits, 29
Totemism, 50, 79, 215–20, 228, 230, 237, 255
Toulmin, S., 42 n.
Trade, 168, 178, 180, 190, 191, 205
Tribes, tribal, 13–15, 22, 90, 116–17, 140, 279, 281
Tribute, 124, 126, 134, 154, 167, 176, 274
Trobriand Islands, 30, 52, 96, 169–70, 175–6, 180, 185, 190, 203, 224, 245
Tsimshian, 185
Tsonga, 236
Tswana, 14, 59, 61, 126, 128, 129, 137, 143
Tupi-Guarani, 251
Turkana, 4, 64–5, 148, 187–8
Turnbull, C., 195–6
Turner, V. W., 228, 243, 259, 260
Tusi, 134, 306
Tylor, E. B., 9, 23–4, 30, 47–8, 211–13, 223, 230

Uberoi, J. P. S., 113 n., 138, 193
Umor, 119 ff.

Van Gennep, 28, 48–50, 233–5, 259

Vengeance, 116, 136, 143, 147, 148
Vernon, P. E., 310

Wagner, G., 149 n., 177, 188 n.
War, 116, 124, 126, 127, 263
Ward, B. E., 207 n., 209, 283
Water, 164, 165
Weber, M., 28, 133, 134, 138
Westermarck, 85
Widows, 93, 269–70
Wilson, G. and M., 228, 259, 269–70, 274
Winter, E., 260
Witchcraft, 147, 245–51, 253; accusations, 248–50, 269, 288
Witches, 84, 147, 244–51, 269
Women, 54–6, 92–4, 217, 242, 296, 300
Worsley, P., 260

Xhosa, 98, 279

Yakö, 74, 118–20, 215, 221
Yamey, B. S., 193, 208
Yao, 97, 249
Yoruba, 67, 68, 94, 132
Yurok, 145

Zande, 44, 245–6
Zaria, 138
Zulu, 94, 130, 138, 271, 273